tear here

The Six Steps Involved in Most Lawsuits

1. **Pleadings.** The case begins by filing documents necessary to identify the parties (the person suing and the person being sued), explain what the claim is about, and ask the court to do something—usually to give you money.

2. **Service.** You have to formally notify someone that he or she is being sued. Service is normally obtained by preparing a summons and then having it and a copy of the complaint personally delivered to the defendant.

3. **Discovery.** Both sides have to gather facts and information to prepare for trial. Discovery can involve examining documents, records, and other pieces of physical evidence as well as taking the depositions (statements) of witnesses or the parties themselves.

4. **Pretrial motions.** If the parties need the court to make procedural decisions or other rulings as the case moves along toward trial, they do so by filing the appropriate motions with the court.

5. **Trial.** The court hears the evidence offered by both sides and decides issues of both fact and law during this process.

6. **Enforcing the judgment**. If you win a judgment at trial, you still have to collect the money. You can enforce a judgment by putting a lien on property, garnishing wages, or obtaining a court order for the turnover of bank accounts or other property.

The Top Seven Things To Remember When You Prepare Your Own Legal Documents

1. If you feel that you're in over your head, don't try to do it yourself just to save money. Bad agreements or incorrect documents can become expensive if they turn into a lawsuit down the road, and lawyers usually don't charge that much for routine documents or simple transactions.

2. Make sure that you understand all the legal issues involved. If you know what to look for in an agreement, you're better able to judge the quality of a form, book, or software program.

3. Don't assume that one form can be used for every situation. It's not a good idea, for example, to use a standard apartment lease form if you lease a house, because the house lease has to cover such issues as property taxes, maintenance of the structure and the yard, and other things that don't apply if you rent an apartment.

4. If you run into legalese in a form you're using, don't just skip over it. Make sure that you find out what it means before you make it part of a final document.

5. When in doubt, always use plain English in agreements.

6. Make sure that you find out whether you have to include anything special because of your state's laws. Check with a local bar association to see whether the agreement or document you've prepared satisfies your state's requirements.

7. Try to avoid preprinted forms and form kits (such as the ones available in office-supply stores) that come with few or no instructions about how or when to use the forms.

alpha books

The Complete Idiot's Guide Auto-Accident Information Checklist
(Fill in Completely in Case of an Accident)

Date: _____ Time of accident: _____

Where did the accident occur? _____

Describe the road conditions: _____

Describe the weather conditions: _____

Describe the lighting conditions: _____

Other conditions to note: _____

How many vehicles were involved? _____

Was anyone injured? _____

Was property (other than the cars involved) damaged? _____

Other driver

Driver's name: _____

Address: _____

City/State/ZIP: _____

Telephone: (hm) _____ (wk) _____

Driver's license number: _____ State: _____

Does address on license match address driver gave?   Yes/No

If not, other address: _____

Does driver own vehicle? _____ If not, vehicle owner's name and address: _____

_____

Insurance company: _____

Telephone number: _____

Agent's name: _____

Policy number: _____

Other vehicle

Make: _____ Model: _____

Year: _____ VIN: _____

License plate number: _____ State: _____

Color: _____ Place of impact: _____

Were police called? Yes/No   Officer's badge number: _____

Officer's name: _____

Police/sheriff's department: _____

Report number: _____ Were tickets issued? Yes/No

Witnesses

Name: _____

Address: _____

Telephone: (hm) _____ (wk) _____

Name: _____

Address: _____

Telephone: (hm) _____ (wk) _____

The COMPLETE IDIOT'S GUIDE TO

Protecting Yourself from Everyday Legal Hassles

by Brent Terry

alpha books

A Division of Macmillan General Reference
A Simon & Schuster Macmillan Company
1633 Broadway, 8th Floor, New York, NY 10019-6785

This book is dedicated to my wonderful wife, Pamela, and to my mom, dad, and grandfather—thank you all for your unfailing love and support.

A special thanks to my dear friend and mentor, John Morreale, who taught me a little about the law and a whole lot about life.

International Standard Book Number: 1-56761-602-X

Library of Congress Catalog Card Number: 94-073517

98 97 96 95   8 7 6 5 4 3 2 1

Interpretation of the printing code: The rightmost double-digit number is the year of the book's first printing; the rightmost single-digit number is the number of the book's printing. For example, a printing code of 95-1 shows that this copy of the book was printed during the first printing of the book in 1995.

Printed in the United States of America.

Publisher
Theresa H. Murtha

Associate Publisher
Lisa A. Bucki

Acquisitions Manager
Tom Godfrey

Production Editor
Rebecca Whitney

Imprint Manager
Kelly Dobbs

Cover Designer
Scott Cook

Designer
Kim Scott

Illustrator
Judd Winick

Manufacturing Coordinator
Paul Gilchrist

Production Manager
Kelly Dobbs

Production Team Supervisor
Laurie Casey

Indexer
Brad Herriman

Production Team
*Angela Calvert, Kim Cofer, Jennifer Eberhardt, Erika Millen,
Gina Rexrode, Karen Walsh*

Contents at a Glance

Contents

Foreword

A lawyer who represents herself is said to have "a fool for a client." Does it follow that a non-lawyer should never take legal action *pro se*, or without an attorney? Although this nation now boasts hundreds of thousands of licensed attorneys who are in need of sustaining a livelihood, not every legal move requires a lawyer. There are certainly times, however, when professional legal advice is indispensable.

As a judge, I see litigants without attorneys come into the courtroom every day to argue cases—both civil and criminal. These people are often successful if they use common sense and are truly seeking justice. The American rule of law is really nothing more than a code of conduct and procedure to peacefully resolve or avoid disputes. The complexity of modern life is mirrored in our modern law. Armed with a little education, however, you can often crack the code and complete the puzzle with little or no legal assistance.

Most people require a lawyer at a stressful, uncomfortable time of life—after a criminal arrest, when a loved one has died, or at the end of a marriage. Times like these are not the best in which to educate yourself about how to retain an attorney who can provide quality professional services at reasonable fees. Hiring a lawyer is not a task for the timid. You can find good representation only by asking the right questions and nailing down a fair and workable contract for professional services.

The Complete Idiot's Guide to Protecting Yourself from Everyday Legal Hassles is a nuts-and-bolts primer for anyone considering handling a legal problem without consulting a lawyer. This book also clearly identifies when and how to retain an attorney when it is absolutely necessary.

Brent Terry, an experienced practicing attorney, brings basic legal concepts to the layperson, with a specific common-sense approach to solving everyday legal problems. He starts at the beginning by defining where our laws come from and outlining our state and national court systems. Painting a realistic picture of the litigation process through these court systems, Brent then explains the alternative dispute-resolution methods that are becoming increasingly more available: arbitration and mediation. He succinctly directs you in how and when to obtain an attorney's advice—offering a "Top Ten" list of things to avoid doing when you're working with your attorney. Brent also includes sample legal forms and a glossary of legal terms.

This *Complete Idiot's Guide* exposes the dangers of litigation, where inevitably one side wins and the other side loses. The gamble of taking a dispute to court means that the parties are willing, in most cases, to abide by the decision of an impartial judge or jury. Unfortunately, a defendant (the person being sued) has no choice but to litigate. In defending a criminal or civil charge, it is essential to know the available options, the legal system, and the best way to prepare and present the case. When the stakes are high, good legal representation is usually essential when push comes to shove before a jury in the courtroom.

Less than five percent of cases filed in the court system actually go to trial because most people settle matters through negotiation. Brent provides the basic tools necessary for you to resolve common legal disputes short of trial. In divorce, the parties can choose mediation so that Mom and Dad can decide on custody and visitation with the kids rather than allow a judge to make this vital decision in their lives. Before the bank files a lawsuit for collection on an old loan, you may be able to negotiate a reasonable settlement to avoid the costs and uncertainty of a trial. Depending on the amount of money and animosity involved, an attorney often makes the difference in finalizing a settlement that both parties can live with. This book provides simple strategies to resolve common legal issues with or without representation.

Brent keeps legalese at a minimum and clearly defines legal terms in sidebars. Only the most basic terms are used so that you can interpret the context and meaning of legal proceedings and documents. Tricky or more deceiving legalities are highlighted as Legal Pitfalls so that you can beware and take the necessary precautions. This book is organized in a casual yet concise format—providing information without intimidation. It covers, with clarity and useful illustrations, substantive issues in areas of family, consumer, employment, contract, traffic, immigration, and estate law. Although the law in this book is not oversimplified, it is humanized and defined in plain English.

Brent has achieved a difficult task: He has effectively brought law to the layperson. The legal profession need not fear, however, because he acknowledges the vital role an attorney should play in overcoming life's legal hurdles. This book gives you a solid and basic legal education, identifying when you should have a healthy deference to experts for complex legal problems. Thomas Jefferson, one of this nation's most beloved legal philosophers, would approve of Brent's efforts. Three centuries ago, Mr. Jefferson noted:

> "I know of no safe depository of the ultimate powers of the society but the people themselves, and if we think them not enlightened enough to exercise their control with wholesome discretion, the remedy is not to take it from them but to inform their discretion by education."

In his own humble way, Mr. Terry has drafted a "Declaration of Independence" from the legal quagmire everyday people must navigate.

Enjoy!

Judge Hollis L. Webster
Circuit Court of the 18th Judicial Circuit
DuPage County, Illinois

Introduction

About a year ago my car needed some repair work, and I had to take it back to the dealer for servicing. The guys in the service department were really great to deal with—they told me what was wrong with my car, which repairs were needed, how long it would take, and how much it all would cost. Everyone was friendly, polite, and efficient—in fact, it was probably some of the best service I'd received in a long time (except that I still felt like an idiot).

It wasn't anything the service people did, of course. I just don't know anything about cars. I can change the oil and check the tires and maybe even jump-start the battery on a good day. Beyond that, though, forget it. So when the service manager began talking about the inner workings of my car's front-wheel drive, I was completely lost. He could've been explaining it in Japanese, for all the good it was doing me.

Shortly after I got my car back, I realized that many people feel the same way when they're talking to a lawyer or dealing with legal documents. Technical information about a car can be bad, but there's nothing like a good dose of legalese to make you really feel like an idiot. But you're not an idiot—you simply don't speak the language, just as I don't speak "car repair."

That's where this book comes in handy. It helps you learn the language of the law and guides you through common legal issues that may come up in your life. It helps you decide when you can handle a problem or transaction on your own and when you need to get a lawyer involved. And if you do need to hire an attorney, this book can help you work with and communicate more effectively with the person you choose so that you can get the most from your legal dollar.

This book is divided into six parts, and each part relates to a different area of your life in which legal issues may come up:

Part 1, "You, Lawyers, and the Law," explains what lawyers do and how they charge for their services, and it outlines the basic steps involved in litigation. One of the chapters in this part discusses alternative dispute resolution, a new and rapidly growing area of the law.

Part 2, "All in the Family," takes an in-depth look at family-law issues, such as prenuptial agreements, marriage, adoption, and divorce.

In Part 3, "Dollars and Common Sense," you learn how the law affects your wallet. This part deals with the issues of getting credit, debt collection, and bankruptcy and provides information about your workplace rights and retirement benefits. This part even has a chapter about handling problems with the IRS.

In Part 4, "A Roof over Your Head," you learn about some of the legal issues involved in leasing property and in buying and selling a home. You also find out about liability issues that may arise and how to use homeowner's insurance to effectively protect yourself from this and other kinds of risks.

Part 5, "Your Life and Legacy," looks at legal issues that commonly arise as we get older. Health-care issues, basic estate-planning techniques, and the probate process are all explained.

The last part of the book, "Everyday Legal Issues," discusses all kinds of legal issues that touch your life on a daily basis—from cars to contracts and from consumer protection to the Constitution.

Because I'm a lawyer, it goes without saying that I can't write a book like this one and not include some kind of disclaimer, so here it goes: This book cannot substitute for the advice of an attorney. It's just that simple. This book explains general legal principles, but you must recognize its limitations. Always remember that state laws and procedures can vary greatly and that even the specific facts of your situation can greatly affect which rules apply to you. Whenever you have any questions or doubts, err on the side of caution and get professional advice.

Extras

As you flip through the pages of this book, notice that clever icons appear frequently throughout the chapters. (Go ahead and flip. I'll wait.) The boxes in which these icons appear hold valuable information to help you navigate especially tricky or confusing areas of the topic being discussed in the text. Here's what each icon means:

Legalese
To learn the lingo of law, check out the definitions offered in these boxes.

Legal Pitfalls
These boxes contain warnings about potentially serious problems and about common legal mistakes people make. Additionally, these boxes alert you to situations that generally shouldn't be handled without the help of an attorney.

Tip
Tips provide helpful information about ways to save money, manage your personal affairs more efficiently, and reduce the number of legal hassles in your life.

It's the Law!
Check out these boxes to learn extra background information about topics in the text. The boxes point out things you should consider when you make legal decisions.

Acknowledgments

On a personal note, I want to thank the people who helped me put this book together, especially the folks at Macmillan. Special thanks goes out to Theresa Murtha, for giving me the chance to work on this project and for encouraging me along the way.

I also want to thank Rebecca Whitney, production editor; and Di Ricker and Fred Franklin, technical reviewers, for their suggestions and guidance. I especially want to thank my old pal Lisa Bucki, associate publisher, for her help throughout this project. See, Lisa? I told you that it would get done. And by the way, I hope that the ulcer I gave you heals quickly.

Finally, thank you to my longtime friend and client Scott Ahlsmith (who also happens to be the author of *The Complete Idiot's Guide to the Perfect Vacation*), for getting me involved with the *Idiot's Guides* in the first place. Almost ten years ago, he and I did our first small-business seminar together, and now we've both written books for this series. So, Scott, what do you want to do next?

Special Thanks to the Technical Reviewers

The Complete Idiot's Guide to Protecting Yourself from Everyday Legal Hassles was reviewed by experts in the field who not only checked the technical accuracy of what you'll learn here but also provided insight and guidance to help us ensure that this book gives you everything you need to know to avoid legal pitfalls and better manage your legal affairs. Special thanks are extended to the following two people:

Frederick R. Franklin is a retired attorney and longtime Director of Legal Education for the American Bar Association. Mr. Franklin also served as a federal prosecutor and taught at the Indiana University School of Law.

Di Mari Ricker, a former practicing attorney, is a legal-affairs writer in Los Angeles. She is the author of several consumer books about the law and the legal system.

Part 1
You, Lawyers, and the Law

Before this book discusses any specific topics, such as divorce or estate planning, you have to learn how our legal system works in general. This part of the book tells you how to navigate the maze that is our court system. It looks at the different types of courts, how lawsuits move through the system, and the roles that judges and lawyers play. One chapter in this part discusses alternatives to rushing down to the courthouse when you have a dispute with someone.

For you do-it-yourselfers out there (I sound like Bob Vila), this part even has a chapter that discusses how to handle common legal problems without using a lawyer.

So sit back and get ready to begin your tour of the American legal system.

WINICKD

Chapter 1

For Everyone Who Slept Through High-School Civics...

In This Chapter

➤ Where our laws come from

➤ Why jurisdiction is the first issue whenever a lawsuit is filed

➤ How cases move through state and federal court systems

The law is everywhere. It touches every part of your life, even though you probably don't think about it in those terms on a daily basis. Stop and think about it. When you drive to work in the morning, you are subject to a number of laws governing how you drive. While you are working, your employer is subject to different federal and state regulations about how to treat you and other employees. The money you earn every day is subject to IRS rules and regulations. When you stop at the store on the way home to buy a new stereo, your purchase is governed by contract law and probably the Uniform Commercial Code and various consumer-protection laws, too. That steak you have for dinner is subject to U.S. Department of Agriculture standards. And if you're a divorced parent, your state's divorce statute governs whether tonight is one of the evenings when your child-visitation schedule says that you can visit your children.

The law really is everywhere, and this chapter introduces you to the legal system and what you need to know about it.

Where Does All This Stuff Come From?

Laws help control and organize society. Even in a free country like ours, we can't have absolute freedom or else there would be chaos. The law provides the structure, the guidelines, and the rules for society as a whole, and it can also be used to bring about social change. What makes our country unique is the ability we have as citizens to influence what laws govern us. Our country has several sources of law:

➤ The constitutions of the United States and individual states.

➤ State and federal statutes and city and county ordinances (laws).

➤ Administrative regulations and rulings.

➤ Common law, or case law.

A constitution is a broad document that defines the general rights and responsibilities of both citizens and government. Despite what you might see in movies and on TV, cases over constitutional issues don't come up all that often. Chapter 29 looks at some situations in which the Constitution may have a direct impact on your life.

Statutes make up a large part of our law. Congress gets its authority to make laws directly from the United States Constitution (specifically, Article I, Section 8, in case you want to go look it up), which is the supreme law of our country. Similarly, state legislatures get their authority to make laws from their state constitutions. These laws are created by Congress and our state legislatures. Examples of statutes include the Equal Employment Opportunity Act, the Michigan Motor Vehicle Code, and the Truth In Lending Act.

Administrative law comes from various government agencies, boards, departments, and officials. Congress delegates some of its broad law-making power to these governmental units and agencies, giving them the authority to make laws in certain, specific areas. For example, the Environmental Protection Agency can regulate the way you dispose of toxic waste, but it can't go beyond the narrow limits placed on it. So the EPA can't say, "Hey, we're on a roll—let's make a law about commercial banking." Administrative laws are usually regulatory (they set various standards and control how something is done); they deal mainly with issues of public safety, health, and welfare. They cover an enormous variety of topics: everything from election rules to licensing requirements for new pilots and from the processing of Medicare claims to the processing of milk.

Common law, or case law, comes from our courts and really represents our entire legal heritage. Even though the courts do not technically "make law," the interpretations and rulings handed down by appellate and supreme courts establish precedents that other courts are likely to follow.

Jurisdiction, or How To Tell Whether You're in the Right Courthouse

As you probably already know, our judicial system is divided into two separate court systems—state courts and federal courts. State and federal courts both decide disputes, but they generally decide different types of disputes. State courts usually decide cases involving state law— things such as probate cases, divorces, and personal-injury cases. Federal courts usually decide cases based on federal law and cases involving parties from different states. This ability of state and federal courts to decide disputes (called *jurisdiction*) sometimes overlaps, and certain cases can be brought before either a state court or a federal court. (Jurisdiction is discussed more fully in Chapter 4.)

Before you read much further, I should make one more distinction: the distinction between civil cases and criminal cases. In a criminal case, the government (either state or federal) brings a legal action against an individual, charging that person with a crime. A *crime* is an illegal act punishable by fine, a prison sentence, or, in severe cases, even death. The government is referred to simply as "the People" because it is representing the interests of all of us as a society, and the individual who has been accused is called the *defendant*. Criminal cases can be brought only by the government, and it has a different set of rules and procedures than civil cases do.

A civil case, on the other hand, generally involves a dispute between private individuals, although the government can occasionally be a party in the case. The goal of a civil case is different too, usually involving money—money to pay me for your breach of contract or money to pay the hospital bills after you run over me with your car. A court can do other things in a civil case, such as issue an *injunction* (a court order to stop doing something), but civil courts cannot impose the same kind of penalties a criminal court can.

This book deals primarily with civil, not criminal, law; Chapter 4 goes into the nuts and bolts of how our courts operate and what you can expect if you're involved in a lawsuit.

State and federal courts are set up in the same basic way. Each system consists of three levels:

➤ Trial court.

➤ Appellate court.

➤ Court of final appeal.

At both the state and federal levels, a trial court has *original jurisdiction*, which is a fancy way of saying that it's the first court to hear a case. These courts decide cases based on evidence and legal arguments. If you believe that the trial court made an incorrect ruling, you or your attorney may be able to appeal the decision.

(By the way, throughout this book, I use the terms "attorney" and "lawyer" interchangeably.)

No evidence is heard at an appellate court. This court's only function is to review what took place at trial and decide whether the case was handled properly. If the appellate court finds no significant errors, the decision of the trial court is affirmed. If significant errors exist, the decision is reversed or modified by the appellate court. If necessary, the case is remanded (sent back) to the trial-court level for additional hearings or a retrial on one or several issues.

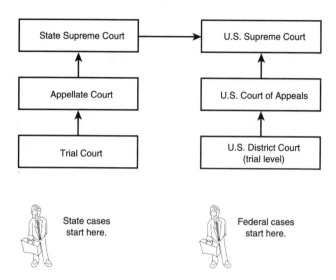

How state and federal cases move through the legal system.

A Short Tour of the Federal Courts

On the federal level, trial courts are called *district courts*. They have the authority to hear many kinds of cases, and every state has at least one district, though some of the larger states have more. New York, for example, has four district courts, and Illinois has three.

The federal appellate-level court is called the *U.S. Court of Appeals*. The United States is divided into 12 judicial circuits, and each circuit has a court of appeals that hears cases from the districts within that circuit. The 11th U.S. Circuit Court of Appeals, for example, hears appeals from cases in the district courts of Florida, Georgia, and Alabama. U.S. Courts of Appeals sometimes also review the administrative orders of government agencies.

The federal court of final appeal is the United States Supreme Court. The court is made up of nine justices (lawyers just call them "the Supremes"), who hear appeals from the U.S. Courts of Appeals, in addition to cases appealed from the state supreme courts. Each Supreme is first nominated by the President, and his or her nomination is sent to the Senate. The Senate then holds confirmation hearings to determine whether the nominee is qualified for the job.

The Supreme Court obviously cannot hear every case that comes up on appeal, so the justices try to choose cases that have real importance to everyone, not just to the parties involved in the case. To choose cases, the justices periodically review the list of pending appeals and vote on whether to hear the cases. If four or more justices decide that a case should be heard, the Court issues a *writ of certiorari*, asking the court that last heard the case for the court records.

Legalese
A **writ of certiorari** from the U.S. Supreme Court requires a lower court to produce the records of a case so that an appeal can be heard.

If a writ of certiorari is denied, it doesn't mean that the Supreme Court endorses or approves of the outcome of the case, but it does mean that the current ruling in the case will stand.

After the Supremes decide to hear a case, the attorneys for each side prepare written arguments called *briefs* (no, not underwear) and also make oral arguments to the court concerning the case. After the case has been argued, the Supremes rule on it and the case is decided by the majority vote of the justices. One of the justices who voted with the majority then writes an *opinion,* which is a formal document stating what the court ruled and, maybe more important, why. If a justice doesn't agree with the majority opinion, he or she can write a *dissent,* an opinion saying why the majority got it all wrong. And there's one more option: A justice may like the results produced by the majority's decision but still think that the majority's reasoning was wrong. This kind of "you got the right answer for the wrong reason" type of opinion is called a *concurring* opinion.

The federal court system is unique because, in addition to the standard trial and appellate levels, it has (at the risk of sounding like Mister Rogers) "special" federal courts. The following courts hear only specific types of cases:

➤ Bankruptcy Court (bankruptcies—surprise!)

➤ Tax Court (disputes over federal taxes).

➤ U.S. Claims Court (disputes and claims against the United States).

What's in a (Court's) Name?

State courts are set up in the same way as federal courts: A case begins at a trial court, and the decision can be appealed through an intermediate appellate court and ultimately to the state supreme court. State trial courts go by different names depending on what part of the country you're in; sometimes they're called district courts, county courts, or circuit courts, unless of course you're in New York, where they call the trial court the "Supreme Court." (Okay, they got it backward—but hey, it's New York.)

To make the system run more efficiently, state trial courts are broken up into divisions based on the type of cases they hear. Probate courts, family-law courts, and traffic courts all are examples of this kind of division. (You'll learn more about probate, family law, and traffic courts later in this book.)

Who Gets To Decide What

A basic principle of our legal system is the concept of jurisdiction. Jurisdiction can get pretty complicated. A federal court, for example, can hear only certain issues. Bankruptcy cases and copyright cases are two good examples—both can be heard only by a federal court because they involve federal laws. When the law says that only a federal court can hear a particular kind of case, the federal court has *exclusive jurisdiction*.

State courts have jurisdiction over any kind of case not expressly reserved by law for the federal courts. These cases include, of course, the bulk of the lawsuits filed. They can include personal-injury suits, contract cases, most criminal cases, and more.

Legalese
Jurisdiction refers to the authority of a court to hear a specific kind of case.

Other types of cases can be heard by either a federal court or a state court. The courts are said to have *concurrent jurisdiction*, which means that either one of them can hear the case. One common kind of case in this category is a *diversity suit*. (You don't have a diversity suit just because your pants don't match your jacket.) When the parties to a lawsuit are from different states and the case involves $50,000 or more, the suit can be brought in either state court or federal district court. It's called a diversity suit because the parties are residents of different states.

Suppose that I live in Illinois and you live in Oregon and that you're driving through Chicago on vacation. While we're on the expressway,

Legalese
Diversity suits are civil cases that involve parties from different states; if the case involves $50,000 or more, a federal court can hear the case.

you cut me off and I hit the median, demolishing my car and injuring me. If my claim is for $50,000 or more, I can file suit against you in a circuit court in Illinois or in federal district court. But if I'm suing you for only $10,000, I have to bring the case to state court.

State and federal courts can also have concurrent jurisdiction if a case is based on a federal question (federal issue).

I Know This Book Isn't About Criminal Law, But...

Federal and state law don't just overlap in civil cases— they can overlap in criminal cases too. Murder is normally a state crime, for example, but under certain circumstances (if the killing was racially motivated, for example), it can also be considered a federal crime—a violation of the victim's civil rights. The defendant can be tried on both the state and the federal charges because the charges against him are completely separate and distinct offenses, even though they came from the same act.

In case this isn't getting murky enough, some overlap can also exist between civil and criminal law. If I get really mad at you one day and vandalize your new car, you can file a complaint with the police, who will then arrest me for criminal damage to property. If convicted, I will be fined (the money goes to the state) and maybe even jailed. Additionally, though, you can sue me in civil court for the damage I caused. If you win your civil suit, I will be ordered to pay you for the cost of the repairs.

The Least You Need To Know

➤ Laws come from our Constitution, state and federal statutes, administrative orders, and common law.

➤ Whether a court has jurisdiction over a case depends on several factors, including the nature of the dispute, the amount of money involved, where the parties reside, and where the dispute arose.

➤ Whether you're talking about state or federal courts, the trial court decides the case based on the evidence, and an appellate court reviews a trial court's findings for errors.

Chapter 2

Is There a Lawyer in the House?

In This Chapter

➤ Deciding whether you need a lawyer and finding one if you do

➤ Handling a small-claims suit without a lawyer

➤ Using form kits, software, and "how-to" books

➤ Understanding different fee structures and knowing what to look for in fee agreements

When do you need a lawyer? As a lawyer, I want to answer that question with *"Always! Absolutely every time you have a question even remotely legal in nature!"* Unfortunately though, for the more than 820,000 attorneys in this country that's not the right answer for many situations.

There are times when you can handle your own legal affairs, usually in situations involving simple transactions or documents. Buying or selling personal property, negotiating simple leases, buying a car, and other simple transactions usually do not require you to make a trip to your lawyer's office. On the other hand, you have to use common sense. The more complicated a transaction becomes, the more likely that legal problems can arise. Leasing a one-bedroom apartment in a 125-unit complex is different from drafting a lease agreement with an option to purchase on a single-family home. Be honest with yourself; if you don't feel comfortable with the paperwork in front of you, get a lawyer to look at it. The fee will be worth your peace of mind.

Not all the legal issues you run into will involve contracts or other business matters—some legal problems hit closer to home. For example, someone might discriminate against you during a job interview, you might be injured by a defective product, or your car might get totaled by a drunk driver. You should take these kinds of cases—especially the ones involving injuries to you or serious damage to your property—to an attorney experienced in the field of your concern.

Legalese
Litigation is just another word for a lawsuit. People usually bring a lawsuit for one of two reasons: to enforce some right that they have or to ask the court to remedy a wrong that's been done to them.

With the exception of small-claims suits, you should always hire an attorney if you're involved in litigation of any kind. You can represent yourself, but it's not wise to do so, especially if the other side is represented by counsel. If you insist on representing yourself, you'll be held to the same rules and standards as your opponent's attorney, a person who has spent years studying to do this job and who probably has several years' worth of practical experience in just this type of matter. It's true that you generally have the right to represent yourself, but to do so in these circumstances is just plain foolish.

You probably will be able to handle some legal situations without consulting an attorney. Some examples of when you might feel comfortable "winging it" are shown in this list:

➤ Traffic court.

➤ Small-claims court.

➤ Preparing a simple will by using estate-planning software or other materials.

➤ Negotiating a simple apartment lease.

The important thing, of course, is to know when you need professional advice. The preceding examples are simple enough, but what if one of the following happens:

➤ You're ticketed for speeding… and driving under the influence.

➤ You file suit in small-claims court against the guy you sold your car to and he files a claim against you for breach of warranty.

➤ You buy an estate-planning book but find that its sample wills don't cover your situation.

➤ Your landlord wants to add an "option to purchase" rider to your lease agreement.

Where Do I Find a Good Attorney?

I know that many of you out there are dying to add a punch line to that question. But joking aside, finding an attorney can be a difficult decision if you've never worked with one.

Remember that you usually see an attorney because you already have a problem. Hiring an attorney who's "wrong" for you may make matters even worse.

Notice that I didn't say "wrong for your case"—I said "wrong for *you*." An attorney can be perfectly qualified for a certain piece of work, and she may do an excellent job of handling it. But if the two of you have trouble communicating, if there's no rapport or trust, you won't feel satisfied when the matter's closed, no matter what the results were in dollars and cents.

Let's Define "Good"

Attorneys are much like doctors. Some have general practices and deal with a variety of issues, and some concentrate on specific areas of the law and do not accept cases outside that area. Just as doctors specializing in stomach problems don't accept patients who need open-heart surgery, many personal-injury lawyers don't do divorces.

The first step in choosing a "good" attorney, then, is finding one who has experience in problems like yours. In most states, lawyers (with some exceptions) are not allowed to use the term "specializing in" when they advertise, but look for words like "practice limited to" or "concentrating in."

To find out whether your state recognizes any "specialization" or "certification" in a specific legal field, contact your state bar association or your state's Department of Professional Regulation.

Tip
When you call to schedule an initial interview with an attorney, ask whether you'll be charged for the consultation. Many firms do not charge for the initial meeting; don't pay for it unless you have to.

You should talk to at least two or three attorneys before hiring one, and when you meet with each attorney for the first time, ask about her experience in the area of your concern. For example, find out how long the lawyer has been in practice and what percentage of his cases have been in your area of concern.

When you meet an attorney for the first time, don't let your judgment be swayed by how his office looks or the suit he's wearing. Just because an attorney has nice furniture and a Brooks Brothers suit and drives a Porsche doesn't automatically mean that he's good at what he does. Even if the office looks like the Taj Mahal, make sure that you remember to ask all the important questions about the lawyer's experience and qualifications.

Where Do I Look?

Begin by asking your friends and family members for referrals. If you like what you hear about someone who's been recommended, schedule an initial interview with that attorney. During the interview, don't focus solely on the attorney's experience, but also look at him like you would anyone else you're meeting for the first time. Do you think that you'll be able to communicate well with this person? Does this person seem like someone you can be open and candid with? You may be working with him for a long time, so make sure that your personalities will allow you to work well together. If the chemistry doesn't seem right, keep looking.

If you still need referrals, avoid picking a name from the telephone book. Try calling your local bar association instead. Almost all of them have a referral system and can provide you with the names of attorneys in your area who handle the type of case you have.

Be advised, though: A bar association referral isn't a guarantee that you'll get a great lawyer. You should still interview the attorney thoroughly, just as you would do under any other circumstances.

> **Legalese**
> A **bar association** is an organization made up of members of the legal profession, including lawyers, judges, law professors, and others. These organizations provide continuing education programs, social events, and many other services to their members. They also encourage their members to do pro bono (free) legal work for the poor and the elderly and often conduct seminars for the general public.
>
> WHAT!?

This Old Lawsuit (or Can't I Do It Myself?)

There isn't an attorney in practice who hasn't had a client be shocked, or even downright angry, about a fee quote. Usually it's because the client sees the work as "simple" or "routine," and he doesn't feel that the work justifies the fee. Often these people decide to do the work themselves, and sometimes that's not such a bad idea.

Look at it this way: If you have a painting to hang in your living room, are you going to call a professional carpenter? Of course not. You just hang it yourself. Maybe it won't be exactly centered on the wall, and maybe you'll have a few extra nail holes in the wall, but it will be hung, and you'll have saved the cost of hiring a carpenter. A simple small-claims suit or the drafting of a simple will may well be something you can handle on your own. The trick is to know when your do-it-yourself work has gotten out of hand. Let's look at some common do-it-yourself areas and see where you might have problems.

Aren't You That Judge on TV? (Small-Claims Court)

Every circuit or district court has a small-claims division that handles, well, claims that are small. "Small" normally means less than $2,500, but the exact dollar limit can vary slightly in different states. These

15

suits involve disputes only about money, so if you're looking for the court to do anything else for you other than award you a money judgment (such as making your neighbor tear down a fence), you have to consult a lawyer about how and where to file.

Legalese
A **jury trial** is conducted before a group (usually consisting of 6 or 12 members) of average men and women who hear a case and decide the dispute.

If any of the terms in this section sounds foreign to you or if you don't have any idea about how the court system works, you may want to look at Chapter 4 to get a better idea about the mechanics of a lawsuit.

Cases in small-claims courts move through the system more quickly because the cases themselves are less complex than cases in other divisions and because the procedural rules in small claims are relaxed. (If you doubt me, check out an episode of "The People's Court" sometime.) There are usually no jury trials in small-claims court, and there are few if any pretrial proceedings. Small-claims courts not only are set up so that a person can navigate them without hiring an attorney, but the dollar amounts involved in these cases also often make it hard to justify the additional expense of doing so. If you're being sued for $750, can you justify paying an attorney $750 to represent you?

How do you file a small-claims suit? The basic steps are listed next, but you definitely have to check with the clerk of the court in your area before starting the process, because procedures and rules do vary widely.

➤ **Obtain and fill out a complaint form.** Almost all court-clerk offices have complaint forms for your use. In the complaint, you have to include the names and addresses of the parties, a brief factual statement about your dispute, and a statement of what you want the court to do (or order the other party to do).

➤ **File your complaint with the court clerk.** You always have to pay a filing fee, usually somewhere between $25 and $75. After the complaint is filed, the clerk also assigns you your first court date and tells you where the case will be heard (where you have to go on your court date).

➤ **Obtain service on the person you're suing.** When a person is "served," it simply means that she has been officially notified of your lawsuit and how she may respond to it. Again, the rules on service vary from state to state, so you have to check with your court clerk's office or a local bar-association office for information. Whatever your local rules are, follow them exactly, or else the court will not have jurisdiction over the other party and won't be able to hear your case. Make sure that you read the rules on service carefully! For example, the way you serve an individual differs from how you serve a corporation.

➤ **Go to court on your assigned date, and be prepared.** Small-claims cases move quickly. It's not unusual for a case to go to trial the first time it's in court. Make sure that you are ready to present your case on your court date and that you bring with you any witnesses, documents (such as receipts, written estimates, canceled checks, and the like), or other evidence you may have.

In addition to having to go to trial on your court date, two other things can occur. First, you might arrive at court only to be told by the judge that the other party was not served. In this case, the judge may continue the case in order to give you more time to obtain service. Second, you may have served the defendant but find that he isn't in court. In this case, the judge may just decide, in order to save time, to rule in your favor without hearing arguments. If the other party doesn't show up, he is essentially conceding to you.

OOOOOH...

Tip
Whatever you do, make sure that you appear on each assigned court date. If you don't, the judge can dismiss your suit, and you'll have to start all over.

Using Preprinted Legal Forms and Software

If you want to do some of your legal work yourself, plenty of preprinted form kits, software programs, and how-to books are on the market. Almost every bookstore has a section on the law, and, depending on the size of the store, you can find any number of "How To" titles that contain sample forms and directions about how to use them. Several computer software packages are also available to guide you through the preparation of standard legal forms. Common how-to topics covered in these books and software packages include incorporating a small business, writing your own will, selling or buying a home, and filing for bankruptcy. Obviously, the cheaper software packages cover fewer topics and have fewer forms from which to choose, but depending on your needs, that may not be a problem.

For simple or "one time" transactions, you probably can find the preprinted legal forms you need at any of the larger office-supply stores in your area. For example, these stores routinely stock bills of sale (if you're selling personal property, such as your car), leases, promissory notes (if you're borrowing or lending money), and simple sales contracts. Additionally, many office-supply stores carry bankruptcy kits that contain all the forms you need to file either a Chapter 7 or Chapter 13 bankruptcy. (See Chapter 15 for more information about bankruptcy.)

If you're still not completely comfortable preparing your own documents, consider using a preprinted form and then taking it to an attorney for a professional review. The attorney will charge you less money, but you'll still have the comfort of knowing that the document is in good shape.

Whether you're talking about form books, software, or form kits, keep in mind some basic guidelines when you use these kinds of legal aids:

➤ **Don't prepare your own legal documents only because it seems cheaper.** If you're not comfortable working with forms or a software package, go to a lawyer. Don't try to do it yourself if you feel like you're in over your head. Bad agreements or incorrect documents can become very expensive if they turn into a lawsuit down the road. And lawyers usually don't charge that much for preparing routine documents or handling simple transactions.

➤ **Be certain that you understand the legal issues involved in your situation.** If you know what to look for in an agreement, you can better judge how good a form, book, or software program is. If you've never read a lease agreement, for example, you may not know what terms are commonly included. This could make it difficult for you to judge whether a preprinted lease form is right for your situation. In this kind of situation, consider working with a lawyer the first time, to learn about the issues.

➤ **Don't assume that one form can be used for every situation.** If you buy software that comes with eight different will forms, for example, make sure that you understand when each one is supposed to be used before you pick one. (That is, read the help information the software offers for each of the forms, or get a book that gives you the details about different kinds of legal situations.)

➤ **If you run into legalese in a form you're using, don't just skip over it.** Make sure that you find out what it means before you make it part of the final document. For example, you might run into the phrases "per stirpes" (five grandchildren divide one share, for example) and "per capita" (each grandchild gets one share) in a will form or estate-planning software. These terms have definite legal meanings, and your choice between them could have a big effect on the way your estate gets divided. (Again, get a book or some help from an attorney to answer these types of questions.)

➤ **When in doubt, always use plain English in agreements.** That way, a dispute over the meaning of the document is less likely, and the other party to the agreement will have a hard time saying that he didn't understand what he agreed to do.

➤ **Make sure that you find out whether you have to do anything special because of your state's laws.** For example, states have different rules for signing and witnessing wills. Check with a local bar association to see whether the agreement or document you've prepared satisfies your state's requirements.

➤ **A final note about those office-supply-store forms:** Unlike how-to books and software packages, preprinted forms and form kits you find in office-supply stores come with few, if any, instructions for how or when to use the forms. For example, one popular bankruptcy form kit comes with every form you could ever need in order to file a Chapter 7 but without a single instruction about what to do with it all. You might look at this as a stimulating mental challenge, but I don't recommend using preprinted forms or form kits if you're not prepared to do any additional research that's necessary.

If you want to get a feel for the different types of legal forms that are available, see Appendix B.

A Lawyer's Time and Advice...

Abraham Lincoln is usually credited with the observation that a lawyer's stock in trade is his time and advice. As a lawyer himself, Abe should have known. The point Abe was making was that lawyers need to bill for their time and advice and that these things are commodities just like anything else is. But few things can cause such hard feelings between clients and their lawyers as fees. Lawyers often complain about slow-paying clients, and clients often complain about being overcharged.

Different lawyers use different billing methods, just like different lawyers charge different amounts for the same or similar services. This section looks at some of the typical ways in which lawyers bill their clients, but keep in mind that billing practices (just like prices) vary from area to area.

Flat Fees

You should keep one thing in mind wherever you live: Get the fee agreement in writing. This step prevents any later disagreements between you and your lawyer about how you much you should be charged. This chapter talks more about fee agreements later.

A *flat fee* is the simplest kind of fee structure. You agree to pay one amount, and your attorney agrees in return to provide a specific service. This type of fee is normally used for work that involves a single transaction, a single court appearance, or the preparation of documents. For example, incorporating a business, drafting a will or trust agreement, handling a real estate closing, and a simple Chapter 7 bankruptcy are often flat-fee cases.

Flat-fee arrangements rarely lead to fee disputes, but they can. Suppose that you go to your lawyer's office and ask him to handle the sale of your home. Sure, on the surface, it's a classic flat-fee situation. Your attorney prepares the documents, clears title problems, and handles the closing; you pay him $500. Also assume that you forget to tell your attorney that you live near the Love Canal and that you occasionally have this little problem with toxic waste bubbling up in your backyard. You can be sure that the attorney will expect to be paid more than $500 for handling the transaction after dealing with the title company, lender, and both state and federal EPA to get your deal closed.

The moral of the story is that you and your lawyer should be clear about what is and is not covered in a flat fee and when the lawyer would require a switch from the flat fee to billing by the hour. Remember that every so often even the most routine situations turn into something really bizarre. If you don't believe me, ask your lawyer. I guarantee that she has a million "war stories."

Contingent Fees

In the best of all circumstances, clients can always be charged contingent fees. Under a *contingent fee* agreement, you don't pay the lawyer until he achieves a certain result. Suppose that a friend borrowed $5,000 from you but now refuses to repay the loan. An attorney might be willing to accept your case for "30 percent of whatever is recovered." If the attorney collects only $2,000 of the total amount you're owed, you pay the attorney a fee of $600. If he collects it all, you pay $1,500, and if he collects nothing, you don't owe anything.

It's important for you to realize that you still have to advance money to your lawyer under a contingent-fee agreement. The contingent fee doesn't cover out-of-pocket expenses (such as filing fees or other court costs), and you have to pay these items up front.

Lawyers commonly charge contingent fees in certain types of litigation, such as personal injury, debt collection, and workers' compensation cases. You should be aware that state law often prohibits contingent-fee arrangements in certain kinds of cases, but your attorney can advise you about your state's specific restrictions.

> OOOOOH...
>
> **Tip**
> In contingent-fee situations, expect to advance some money to your attorney as a deposit toward the out-of-pocket expenses and court costs you'll incur. Many attorneys also charge a modest flat fee that's payable at the beginning of the case to cover themselves from doing a great deal of work and then finding out that the client has lost interest in pursuing the case. The flat fee may or may not be deducted from the total contingent fee you owe at the end of the case.

Hourly Billing

The third major type of fee arrangement is *hourly billing.* As the term implies, your attorney bills you at an agreed-on rate for all the time she spends working on your matter. You can choose an hourly billing arrangement for almost any type of legal work.

Hourly billing can be a great source of headaches for attorneys and their clients. Part of the problem is that many clients don't realize that the "meter is running" whenever they're talking to their attorney or when the attorney is working on their file. If you call your lawyer to see what's happening with your case, for example, expect to be billed for the time you and your lawyer spend on the phone.

Another source of disputes is that almost all attorneys calculate time by a fraction of the hour, usually one-tenth, or six minutes, but it can be as high as one-quarter of an hour (15 minutes.) If you call your lawyer and talk for 30 minutes, you'll be billed for 0.5 hours. Multiply this figure by your lawyer's billing rate ($125 per hour, for example), and your call costs you $62.50.

Many lawyers use "minimum time" rules; for example, no telephone call gets billed for less than 0.3 hours, and no letter gets billed for less than 0.4 hours. Be clear about this point from the beginning so that you aren't shocked when you receive your first monthly billing invoice.

Ask your attorney the following questions if you're going to be billed by the hour:

> ➤ **What kind of retainer will I need?** You have to pay the retainer, or deposit, toward the attorney's fees, before any work begins.

> ➤ **What do you estimate that the total fees will be?** This question is often difficult to answer, but your attorney should be able to give you a rough estimate of what he thinks the total fees might be. Remember that this is only an estimate and not the maximum you'll be charged.

> ➤ **How will I be billed?** Most attorneys send out invoices once each month. The invoice shows what work was performed, how much time was spent on the work, whether any amounts were advanced on your behalf, and whether any payments were received since the last invoice. Finally, the invoice shows how much you owe and when your payment is due.

```
                         ALLAN ATTORNEY
                         123 Glen Avenue
                       Anytown, IL  60000


August 1, 1995


Ms. Cathy Thomas
1876 S. Oak Drive
Wheaton, IL  60187




                    S T A T E M E N T



For legal services provided regarding divorce proceedings in
    Case #: 94 D 3045

Flat fee per agreement ..................... $ 1,500.00

Court costs/Expenses

        Filing fee (petition) ........... $ 198.00
        Transcript ..................... $  32.40
        Federal Express ................ $  28.00


Total ....................................... $ 1,958.40

Retainer Received (12–05–94) ................ $   750.00



         BALANCE NOW DUE ................... $ 1,208.40




Our file #DM–1393
```

An example of a bill from an attorney.

You Mean, This Won't Be Pro Bono Work? (Fee Agreements)

One way to prevent billing problems is to make sure that you have a written fee agreement with your lawyer. If your attorney doesn't offer you one after accepting your case, ask for one. A fee agreement is simply a written agreement that sets some ground rules about how you'll be billed and how you're expected to pay. The fee agreement is a contract (see Chapter 27 for more information about contracts), but it may or may not look like other contracts you're used to seeing. Some attorneys simply send you a letter to confirm a fee agreement, but you should remember that this kind of letter (sometimes called engagement letter) is still a contract. It is usually short, but it should contain at least the following information:

➤ The lawyer's billing rate per hour, if it's an hourly fee arrangement.

➤ How often you will receive a billing invoice.

➤ When payments are due.

➤ Whether a retainer is required and how it will be used.

➤ What specific services will be provided to the client.

➤ What additional costs you can expect to pay (filing fees and transcripts, for example).

➤ What will happen if you don't pay a bill when it's due.

If you don't understand something or if you disagree with part of the agreement, bring it up to your attorney right away. Lawyers generally frown on clients who run up a $3,500 bill and then mention that they were unclear on something in the fee agreement. Both you and your attorney should sign the fee agreement.

Dealing with Fee Disputes and Other Problems

Suppose that you find a bill from your attorney in your mail one day, and as you walk back from the mailbox you're mentally calculating that it will probably cost about $800 for some estate-planning work you had done. When you open the envelope, you're stunned to see an invoice for $3,500. What now? Pay it without complaint? Throw it in the trash? Reread Chapter 14 to learn about debt collection? The answer, of course, is "none of the above."

As a client, you're entitled to voice your disagreement with what you've been charged. Start by calling your lawyer and asking him to explain why the bill is so high. There may be a valid reason for the amount charged; for example, the case could have turned out to be much more complex than either of you originally anticipated. If you're not satisfied with the explanation you receive, ask for a reasonable reduction in the bill. If your attorney will not reduce the bill, contact your local bar association office. Most of them have a fee-arbitration service that handles problems like this, and it is by far the quickest way to a resolution.

Whatever you do, don't just ignore the bill because you disagree with the amount charged. If your case is still pending, your attorney may ask the court's permission to withdraw from representing you because of your refusal to pay. After the case concludes, your attorney can even sue you to collect the amount you owe. As in so many situations, good communication can often be the key to settling your fee dispute before it gets out of hand.

Legal Pitfalls

Under the rules of professional conduct for attorneys, an attorney's fees must be "reasonable." If an attorney racks up more time working on your case than he originally estimated he would, though, you're still liable for his total bill as long as he has a reasonable basis for the new charges. If your bill looks like it's increasing faster than you anticipated, your attorney may talk to you about it and revise his earlier fee estimate. But if he does, he's doing it only out of a sense of good business practice, not because he has any professional obligation to do so.

The Least You Need To Know

➤ Talk to two or three attorneys before deciding to hire one. Make sure that the attorney has experience in the area of your concern and that you think you can work with her throughout your case.

➤ After you've hired an attorney, get a fee agreement that explains what she will charge. Also try to get an estimate of what the attorney expects to bill you in total.

➤ You may be able to handle simple legal transactions and document preparation with the help of preprinted forms, books, and software, but be careful not to get in over your head. Get advice when you need it.

➤ With the possible exception of small-claims cases, don't try to handle litigation without an attorney.

➤ If you have a dispute over fees you've been charged, ask your lawyer for an explanation of the charges or a reduction of the fees. If you can't resolve the problem by discussing it with the attorney, contact your local bar association for arbitration of the fee dispute.

Chapter 3

Can We Talk? (Communicating with Your Lawyer)

In This Chapter

➤ What attorney-client privilege is and why it's so important for you

➤ When privilege doesn't apply

➤ What happens if an attorney wants to withdraw from a case or if you want to fire him

"From your confessor, lawyer and physician,
Hide not your case on no condition."

—Sir John Harington, 1596

An attorney makes a living through communication. A client depends on the skill with which the lawyer communicates, whether it's through the spoken word or through writing. Good communication between you and your lawyer is just as important as the communication between your lawyer and the court. Yet poor communication accounts for a large portion of the complaints that clients have about their lawyers, and vice versa. This chapter clarifies the basics of communicating with your lawyer to get the most from your relationship.

It's a Privilege To Meet You

Attorneys routinely help people through difficult times. A client may be charged with a crime, involved in a bitter divorce, or going through some other kind of crisis. You may be emotionally hurt, depressed, or even embarrassed by your current problems when you first meet with a lawyer. If you ever find yourself in this kind of situation, it's important to remember that whatever you tell your lawyer, it's considered a privileged communication.

Caution: The privilege exists only when the attorney-client relationship has been established. Are you telling your story to your lawyer, or are you confessing to someone who happens to be a lawyer? For example, if you're at a party, casually discussing your problems with someone who just happens to be an attorney, you're not covered by attorney-client privilege because no professional relationship exists between you.

Legalese
A privileged communication means that any information you disclose to your lawyer is confidential and cannot be disclosed to anyone else.

The attorney-client privilege is legally significant. Except in rare circumstances, even a court cannot order an attorney to reveal information that's considered privileged. The law recognizes this kind of privilege to help make people more comfortable when they talk to attorneys. An attorney can be effective only if she knows all the facts, even if some of the facts are painful or embarrassing for you. Because your discussions are protected by attorney-client privilege, you can—and should—be completely candid with your attorney.

Your conversations with your attorney are confidential, but don't assume that your court records are. Most court proceedings (trials and other hearings) and court files are open to the public.

Usually, anyone can sit in the courtroom while your trial is going on, and anyone can look through your court file and obtain information about you from the pleadings or the final judgment of the court. The only court files not accessible to the public are those that the court orders "sealed," or closed to everyone except the parties themselves. The files that are most commonly sealed in this way involve minors.

When You've Got It and When You Don't

Generally speaking, the attorney-client privilege applies to all communications between you and your lawyer. It also covers anyone else working at your attorney's law firm, including partners and associates, paralegals, secretaries, and all other members of the staff. This privilege is important because your attorney does not do all the work on your case—others are involved. The requirement of confidentiality continues even after your attorney's work is complete and your file is closed.

The attorney-client privilege is not absolute, though. In certain situations, your attorney can—and sometimes must—reveal information you provided to him. Attorney-client privilege doesn't apply in these situations:

➤ If you authorize your attorney to reveal certain information to someone else (for example, if you ask your attorney to negotiate with a creditor and tell your attorney to let the creditor know that you are considering bankruptcy).

➤ If you provide information to your attorney in front of other people.

➤ If you tell your attorney that you intend to commit a crime, especially if the crime involves the serious injury or death of someone.

Additionally, the privilege may not apply in these situations:

➤ If you sue your attorney for malpractice or file a disciplinary action against him.

➤ If your attorney has to sue you to collect fees.

Tip
There are also restrictions on how your lawyer communicates with another party to your case. If a person is represented by a lawyer, your lawyer can communicate only with the other lawyer, not directly with the person. In a divorce, for example, your attorney can call your husband's lawyer, but not your husband. If another person's lawyer contacts you directly, notify your lawyer right away.

What We've Got Here Is a Failure To Communicate

No, this section is not a tribute to the acting genius of Strother Martin. It's about what to do when you and your attorney seem to be having a hard time working together. Problems can occur between an attorney and a client for various reasons. Sometimes problems occur because the client isn't cooperating with the attorney; sometimes they occur because the client doesn't like the job the attorney is doing or the fees the lawyer is charging.

If you want to end your relationship with your lawyer and if your legal matter doesn't involve a case that's before the court, simply contact your attorney and inform her of your decision. You can do so verbally, but be sure to confirm your conversation in writing so that there can be no dispute about when you notified her.

Find out the current status of the work, and specifically tell your attorney that you don't want any additional work done on your file. Ask your attorney to give you the contents of your file and to return any original documents you may have given her to work with. You should also expect to receive a bill from her for the work already done on your file.

If the problems between you and your attorney are bad enough and your case involves a court, the attorney may ultimately ask the court for permission to withdraw from your case by filing a motion to withdraw. Your attorney can't just withdraw on a whim, but if she can show a valid reason for wanting out, the court usually grants her request. An attorney can usually withdraw if she is not getting paid, if you're asking her to do something illegal or unethical under the Rules of Professional Conduct, or if you're not cooperating in a way that can lead to the successful resolution of the case.

When a court is deciding whether to let an attorney out of a case, one major factor it considers is the current status of the case. A motion to withdraw is more likely to be granted if it's brought early on, before much happens with the case. The withdrawal is much less likely to be granted if the case is already set for trial.

```
        IN THE CIRCUIT COURT OF THE EIGHTEENTH JUDICIAL CIRCUIT
                        DUPAGE COUNTY, ILLINOIS


THOMAS J. SMITH,                    )
                                    )
                    Plaintiff,      )
vs.                                 )     Case No.  95 - 12345
                                    )
CATHY JONES,                        )
                                    )
                    Defendant.      )


                        MOTION TO WITHDRAW

NOW COMES the attorney for the Plaintiff, BRENT W. TERRY, pursuant
to Supreme Court Rule 13, moves this Court for leave to withdraw as
counsel for the Plaintiff, and in support of this motion, states as
follows:

1.  The last known address of THOMAS J. SMITH is 123 Main Street,
Smalltown, Illinois.

2.  Irreconcilable differences have arisen between Counsel and the
Client, and it is no longer in the best interests of the Client to
be represented by Counsel.

3.  Counsel does not believe he can continue to effectively
represent the Client in this cause.

4.  The cause is currently set for hearing on August 2nd, 1995.

WHEREFORE, BRENT W. TERRY, moves this Court for leave to withdraw
as counsel for the Plaintiff in this matter.



                        _____
                        BRENT W. TERRY
                        Attorney for Plaintiff
```

When you and your lawyer can't work together, the lawyer may file a motion to withdraw from your case.

On the other hand, you can generally change lawyers if you don't feel that you're getting the kind of service you deserve. But if you do "fire" your lawyer, it's important that you retain another one quickly, especially if you're involved in litigation of some kind. If you don't, serious problems can occur and jeopardize your entire case.

Be sure to get your entire file back from your first lawyer, to give to your new one. Keep in mind that some documents may be the product of the first lawyer's work and are not yours to receive unless you paid for them.

Legal Pitfalls

If a case has been set for trial, a court may refuse to let a lawyer withdraw from a case, even if the client agrees. This is especially true if the court feels that the client is just trying to delay the trial in the case.

The Top Ten Ways To Aggravate Your Lawyer, Waste Your Money, and Ruin Your Case

Because Top Ten lists seem to be everywhere, I couldn't resist including one of my own. The list is tongue in cheek, of course, but it also makes the important point that how well you communicate and work with your attorney directly affect the kind of job your attorney can do for you:

10. **Don't tell your lawyer everything.** People sometimes forget things, especially when they meet a lawyer for the first time, but make sure that you tell your lawyer everything about your situation. Call your lawyer back after your first meeting, or drop the lawyer a short follow-up letter if you need to, but don't put your lawyer in the position of finding out from somebody else an important fact about you or your case.

9. **Don't pay your attorney.** You don't work for free—don't expect your attorney to, either.

8. **Ask your attorney to do something illegal or unethical.** Not only will your attorney withdraw from your case, but also in certain circumstances you even risk losing the attorney-client privilege. Lying under oath is a classic example.

7. **Argue with your attorney about what the law is.** If you have a serious legal problem, chances are you've already received dozens of free, "expert" opinions about what the law is and how your case should be handled. These opinions usually come from such people as your barber, your co-workers, your pals on your bowling league, your sister-in-law, and the guy who sits next to you on the train every morning. Trust your lawyer's judgment. If you want a second opinion, fine—just get it from another lawyer, not from a self-appointed "expert."

6. **Call your attorney every day to chat about your case and see whether anything new has happened.** Communication between you and your attorney is important, but use common sense. There will be times during your case when nothing much seems to be happening, especially if you're involved in litigation. If you're concerned, talk to your lawyer about the typical kinds of delays you can expect in a case like yours.

5. **Call your attorney every day to chat about your case, and don't expect to be billed for it.** This one's even worse than number 6.

4. **Don't follow your attorney's advice.** You're paying for your attorney's professional advice. Technically, you have the right to ignore it, but doing so is just foolish.

3. **Don't pay your attorney.** (Did I already say that?)

2. **If you lose your lawsuit, accuse your attorney of malpractice or of selling out to the other side.** No one can ever be absolutely sure of how a lawsuit will turn out. It does not automatically follow that just because you lost (or you didn't win as much as you thought you should), your attorney did a bad job, and it certainly doesn't automatically mean that she committed malpractice.

1. **Finally, I offer a simple rhyme that every attorney has heard and, even worse, has probably lived:** "Who lied to me about his case, And said we'd have an easy race, And did it all with solemn face? It was my client." —Anonymous

Malpractice: It's Not Just for Doctors Anymore

Whether the term *malpractice* is applied to a doctor, lawyer, or accountant, it has the same general meaning. It usually stems from either of these circumstances:

➤ Professional misconduct.

➤ An unreasonable lack of skill or diligence.

If a case involves misconduct or an unreasonable lack of skill, and the client (or patient) is harmed by it, the professional can be held liable.

As I've said, just because you lost your case doesn't mean that your attorney has committed malpractice. If your attorney handled your case with the same degree of skill and care that any other reputable attorney would have used in that particular situation, it's unlikely that your attorney committed malpractice.

If you have a complaint about the service you received, try talking it out with your attorney before you do anything else. If that doesn't get you anywhere, you may want another attorney to review your case and give you an opinion about how it was handled. If there's evidence that your first attorney was seriously negligent in the way he handled your case, that he was completely unqualified to handle the matter, or that professional misconduct occurred, you may have a claim for malpractice.

Legalese
Professional **misconduct** occurs when an attorney does something that violates the Code of Professional Conduct.

As a final note, every state has a set of rules governing how attorneys can practice in that state. These rules of professional conduct and ethics codes put important restrictions on what attorneys can and can't do—for example, the issue of attorney-client privilege is always discussed within these codes.

If you believe that your attorney may have violated the rules of professional conduct, you may want to call your local bar association for information about how to make a complaint. You can also call your state's department of professional regulation or attorney general's office for more information. But keep in mind that a malpractice claim and a disciplinary action are not the same thing. If you file a disciplinary complaint and your attorney is found guilty of the charge, she may be disciplined by her state board. You, however, probably won't be awarded any money damages, as you would in a malpractice action.

The Least You Need To Know

➤ Attorney-client privilege makes all communications you have with your attorney confidential.

➤ Attorney-client privilege also applies to the people who work with or for your lawyer.

➤ An attorney can withdraw from your case, even if you don't want him to, if he has a valid reason and the court approves the withdrawal.

➤ You can usually fire your attorney if you're not satisfied with the services you've been receiving. If you do fire your attorney in the middle of a case, be prepared to bring in another attorney quickly so that you don't jeopardize your case.

Chapter 4

That's Not the Way They Do It on Television! (What's Really Involved in Litigation)

"He that goes to law holds a wolf by the ear."

—Robert Burton, c. 1621

Burton's observation contains a fair amount of truth. Litigation can be an expensive and time-consuming process. And no matter how good your attorney is, no matter how eloquent your witnesses are or how much evidence supports you, no matter how much you believe that you're right, the results of litigation can never be guaranteed.

This doesn't mean that you should never consider litigation as an option, but it does mean that you should be realistic about what's involved. This chapter explains what you'll be getting yourself into if you decide to take a matter all the way to court.

I'll Take This All the Way to the Supreme Court!

Litigation, the process of arguing the facts of your case and the applicable law before a court, can be expensive and time-consuming. You can resolve disputes in alternative ways, from negotiating a settlement on your own to arbitration and mediation, in which a neutral third party is used to help resolve the matter. (Alternative dispute resolution is discussed in Chapter 5.)

It's the Law!

If you do manage to resolve a dispute without resorting to litigation, you may want to put the settlement agreement in writing so that no additional misunderstandings or problems can develop. Your settlement agreement should clearly state the terms of your agreement ("I agree to pay John Smith $1,000 by March 1"), and it should include a statement that the dispute is now considered completely resolved by both people involved. This type of statement, sometimes called a *release* or *waiver of claims,* helps prevent either side from rejecting the settlement and reopening the dispute later. If you are asked to sign any type of settlement document, especially one that contains a waiver of your rights, you may want your attorney to review it for you before signing on the dotted line. (Chapter 27 has more information about contracts.)

The decision to litigate requires a serious commitment on your part. In addition to committing yourself to the time and expense involved, you also must commit yourself to helping your attorney do the best job he possibly can.

The litigation process really begins when you first consult an attorney. (You may want to review Chapter 2 for some suggestions about how to choose the right attorney for you.) If you do nothing else, at least be honest and open with your attorney. It's the only way she can effectively advise and represent you. As you learned in Chapter 3, whatever you tell your attorney is confidential, so don't hold back information.

When you consult with an attorney about litigation, make sure that you leave that person's office with answers to some basic questions:

➤ Do I have grounds to bring a lawsuit?

➤ Do you think that I have a good chance of proving my claim?

➤ If I win the lawsuit, would the results justify the costs to me in money and time?

➤ If I win, how likely is it that I'll ever collect the judgment?

➤ How long does it normally take for cases of this kind to be decided?

➤ Approximately how much will my legal fees be?

➤ Do I have any alternatives to litigation (negotiation, mediation, or arbitration, for example)?

Your attorney should discuss all these issues with you, but keep in mind that an attorney can tell you only what his experience has been. Every case and every client are different. Some cases take years, some take months; fees can be tens of thousands of dollars, or they can be a few hundred dollars. Your attorney can tell you how the case will probably progress and give you an idea of what it will cost, but you must realize that the information you're receiving is not written in stone. Your specific case may take more time or less, and the actual fees you're charged may be higher or lower.

What You Should Expect During Litigation

No matter what kind of case you have, all litigation moves through the same general process. The basic steps are outlined in this section, but procedures do vary among jurisdictions. Your attorney can give you a more detailed explanation of what will be involved in your specific case.

1. **Pleadings.** You begin a lawsuit by preparing a document that identifies the parties involved, explains what your claim is about,

37

Legalese
The **plaintiff** is the person bringing the lawsuit; the **defendant** is the person who has been sued.

Legal Pitfalls
As you learned in Chapter 1, it's important to know where to file your case, or, if you want to sound attorney-like, to know which court has jurisdiction. Remember that in certain cases, such as the diversity actions discussed in Chapter 1, you may be able to file suit in either your state court or federal district court. Your choice can have an effect on which procedural rules apply to your case and even on how quickly your case can get to trial. Your attorney will explain where your case can be filed and whether you have any options to choose from.

Legalese
A **summons** document officially notifies a person that he or she is being sued and describes how to appear before the court and answer the complaint.

and asks the court to do something—most often, to award you money. This document, usually called a *complaint,* is filed with the clerk of the court. In legal terms, the person filing suit is called the *plaintiff,* and the person being sued is called the *defendant.*

The party you're suing may file a similar document, usually called an *answer,* that addresses each issue raised in your complaint. Your complaint and the defendant's answer are collectively referred to as the *pleadings.* The pleadings form the framework for the lawsuit and tell the court what issues are involved in your case.

2. **Service.** No, not as in tennis. Service, or service of process, to be more precise, is simply a formal way of giving someone notice that you're suing him. Service is normally obtained by preparing a summons and then having it and a copy of your complaint delivered to the defendant.

Depending on the type of case and your local court rules, service of process can be done by personally delivering the summons and complaint or by using certified or registered mail. In special situations, a summons may not be used at all. If you don't know where the defendant lives or works, for example, you might be able to give notice of your pending lawsuit by publishing a formal notice in the newspaper (a process called *service by publication*). Your attorney will tell you what kind of service is required in your case.

If a person is served but doesn't answer the complaint or appear before the court, you might be entitled to a default judgment.

After a defendant is served, she must do something in response to your complaint—the ball is in her court. (Maybe it *is* similar to tennis, after all.)

Completing a summons form and delivering (serving) it notifies someone of your intention to sue.

UNITED STATES OF AMERICA
STATE OF ILLINOIS   COUNTY OF DU PAGE
IN THE CIRCUIT COURT OF THE EIGHTEENTH JUDICIAL CIRCUIT

Plaintiffs

Case Number

Vs.

Defendants

File Stamp Here

SUMMONS

To each Defendant:

You are summoned and required to file an answer to the complaint in this case, a copy of which is hereto attached, or otherwise file your appearance in the office of the Clerk of this court, 505 North County Farm Road, Wheaton, Illinois, within 30 days after service of this summons, not counting the day of service. IF YOU FAIL TO DO SO, A JUDGMENT BY DEFAULT MAY BE TAKEN AGAINST YOU FOR THE RELIEF ASKED IN THE COMPLAINT.

To the Officer:

This summons must be returned by the Officer or other person to whom it was given for service, with endorsement of service and fees, if any immediately after service. If service cannot be made, this summons shall be returned so endorsed.

This summons may not be served later than 30 days after its date.

WITNESS   **JOEL A. KAGANN**, Clerk of the Eighteenth
Judicial Circuit, and the seal thereof, at Wheaton
Illinois. Dated _____

_____
Plaintiff's Attorney   CLERK of the EIGHTEENTH JUDICIAL CIRCUIT

_____
DuPage Attorney Number

_____   NOTE: The filing of an appearance or answer with the Circuit
Street Address   Court Clerk requires a statutory filing fee, payable at
                                                                      the time of filing.
_____
Town

_____   Date Of Service_____ 19_____
Telephone Number   (To be inserted by officer on copy left with defendant or other Person.)

CIRCUIT COURT SUMMONS

The form used to verify that a summons was served.

SHERIFF'S RETURN

I certify that I served this summons on defendants as follows:
(Check appropriate box, and complete information below)

[ ] (a) (Individual defendants - personal):
By leaving a copy and a copy of the complaint with each individual defendant personally.

[ ] (b) (Individual defendants - abode):
By leaving a copy and a copy of the complaint at the usual place of abode of each individual defendant with a person of his family, of the age of 13 years or upwards, informing that person of the contents and also by sending a copy of the summons in a sealed envelope with postage fully prepaid, addressed to each individual defendant at his usual place of abode.

[ ] (c) (Corporation defendants):
By leaving a copy and a copy of the complaint with the registered agent, officer or agent of each defendant corporation.

[ ] (d) (Other service):

Name of Defendant _____   Name of Defendant _____
Name of Person   Name of Person
Summons given to _____   Summons given to _____

Sex____Race____Approx. Age_____   Sex____Race____Approx. Age_____

Place of Service _____   Place of Service _____

_____   _____

Date of Service_____Time_____   Date of Service_____Time_____

Date of Mailing _____   Date of Mailing_____

_____,Sheriff of_____County

By,_____,Deputy

3. **Discovery.** After the initial pleadings are complete, both sides have to prepare for trial. Part of this preparation involves gathering basic facts and information. This fact-gathering is generally referred to as *discovery*.

    Discovery can be done in different ways. It can involve the examination of documents, records, and other pieces of physical evidence. It can also involve taking depositions from witnesses or from the parties themselves. To call someone for a deposition and request specific information from that person, your lawyer must file a notice of deposition with the court.

Legalese
A **deposition** is a person's sworn testimony, taken outside of court but still under oath and documented by a court reporter.

Other tools that can be used in the discovery process include such things as *interrogatories* (a list of written questions about the issues in the case, to be answered under oath) and a request for production of documents (sometimes called a *subpoena duces tecum*), which requires a person to produce various documents for inspection and copying.

```
2181 - Served
2281 - Not Served
2381 - Served By Mail                                              (4-81) CCG-14
               IN THE CIRCUIT COURT OF COOK COUNTY, ILLINOIS


           v.                           NO. ...............................




                        SUBPOENA FOR DEPOSITION
To:




           YOU ARE COMMANDED to appear to give your deposition before a notary public at
......................................................Street, Room.......,.................., Illinois
on ..............................................,19...., at ....................m.
           YOU ARE COMMANDED ALSO to bring the following.




in your possession or control.
           YOUR FAILURE TO APPEAR IN RESPONSE TO THIS SUBPOENA WILL SUBJECT YOU TO
PUNISHMENT FOR CONTEMPT OF THIS COURT.
                              WITNESS, ...............................19....
Name
Attorney for        ..............................................
Address                          Clerk of Court
City
Telephone
Atty No.

      I served this subpoena by handing a copy to ...........................
.....................on .............................19..... I paid the witness
$.................................................. for witness and mileage fees.
                    ..............................................
Signed and sworn to before me ..........................................,19....
                    ..............................Notary public
           MORGAN M. FINLEY, CLERK OF THE CIRCUIT COURT OF COOK COUNTY
```

A subpoena calls someone to provide information for a case.

Your state and local courts have rules about what kind of discovery can be conducted, and there are penalties for not providing information that has been properly requested. Your attorney will explain what kind of discovery might be useful in your particular case.

4. **Motions.** Many issues can come up during the litigation process, and the parties may need the court to make procedural decisions and other rulings as the case moves along.

Legalese
A **motion** is the way a party asks the court to do something in a case.

Numerous kinds of motions can be made. Although some may deal with the actual legal issues involved in your case, most will probably deal with procedure. If your complaint isn't properly prepared, for example, the defendant can move (ask) that the court dismiss your lawsuit entirely. Or to use the preceding example, if the defendant doesn't answer your complaint or appear in court after being served, you can make a motion for a default judgment.

5. **Trial.** The litigation process all comes down to trial. At trial, the court hears the evidence offered by both sides and decides both issues of fact (whether your pit bull, Rover, bit the UPS person) and of law (if you're legally responsible for the resulting hospital bills).

Legalese
A **bench trial** is a trial conducted before a judge, without a jury.

It seems that whenever a trial is televised, it's always being conducted before a jury, but this isn't necessarily the case in real life. If the parties agree that they don't want a jury trial, they can ask that the case be heard by a judge instead.

Bench trials are also routinely used in certain types of cases (divorce cases are a common example). Your attorney will explain whether your case can be heard by a jury and help you decide whether a jury trial or a bench trial is a better option for you.

After the trial is over, you receive a *verdict* (a formal way of saying "decision"), and the court announces its findings in the case and, ultimately, who has to pay what to whom. At this point the dispute is over, unless one party or the other wants to try to appeal the trial court's decision to the appellate court. Remember that you may not be happy with the court's ruling, but that doesn't mean that you automatically have grounds for an appeal. Appeals are used when the trial court committed some type of serious error during the proceedings and that error directly affected the outcome of the case. (Chapter 1 has more information about the appellate-level courts.)

Helping Your Lawyer Help You

Litigation can be a pretty long and involved process, but there are things you can do to help your attorney do a better job for you:

➤ Keep your attorney informed about all the facts that might affect your case, even if they seem potentially damaging.

➤ If you're asked by your attorney or the court to do something, do it. Don't sabotage your own case by refusing to comply with a court order or by ignoring your attorney's advice.

➤ Be open to settlement negotiations even after your lawsuit has been filed. Only 5 to 10 percent of all lawsuits go all the way to a verdict. Remember that you know in advance what the terms of a settlement are but that you can never know for certain what a judge or jury will do.

And in Case You Thought You Were Done...

Suppose that you sue me for breach of contract and, for the sake of argument, you win the lawsuit. The court will enter a judgment in your favor, requiring me to pay you some amount ($5,000, for example). Do you think that's all there is to it? Think you'll go home from court $5,000 richer? Forget it.

A *judgment* is the official decision of the court. It usually contains decisions about the facts of the case and about the legal issues involved. It resolves the dispute. It determines the rights and obligations of the parties. It's clearly an important document, but there's just one problem: It's not the same as money. You can't take it to the currency exchange and cash it, and you can't take it to your bank and deposit it.

If I refuse to pay you the $5,000, or even if I just don't have the money to pay you, you have to do more to collect on your judgment. The normal way is to return to court and ask the court to help you get paid. These proceedings go by different names depending on where you live. In some areas, they're called *enforcement proceedings,* and in others, they're know as *supplementary,* or *postjudgment, proceedings.*

A judgment can be enforced in several basic ways. One way is to garnish a person's wages.

Legalese
A **wage garnishment** is a court order to an employer, requiring him to withhold a specified amount from an employee's wages and pay it to the employee's creditor instead.

Another way you can enforce your judgment is to have some of the person's property taken and sold to pay back the money. Or you can ask the court for an order requiring the person's bank to turn over her savings account to you.

Procedures for enforcing a judgment vary widely under state law and can be complicated. There are also statutory limits on what you can do; for example, certain laws limit the amount of wages you can garnish, and others prohibit you from seizing certain kinds of property. If you're interested in enforcing a judgment, contact an attorney in your area for information on how to go about it.

The Least You Need To Know

➤ Because of the commitment you have to make in time and money, and because the results can never be guaranteed, make sure that you consider all your options before deciding on litigation.

➤ Good communication and cooperation from you can help your attorney do a better job for you.

➤ If you get a judgment against someone, you may have to return to court to enforce your judgment if the person refuses to pay.

O.K., LET'S HEAR FROM THE PLAINTIFF!!

Chapter 5

Hey, Where's the Guy in the Black Robe? (Alternative Dispute Resolution)

In This Chapter

➤ What alternative dispute resolution is and how you might encounter it

➤ How arbitration and mediation work

➤ What you should consider if you're involved in a mediation or arbitration case

➤ How to find an arbitrator or mediator

In the past several years, lawyers, judges, and legislators have been looking for new alternatives to litigation and the traditional way disputes are resolved. In fact, *alternative dispute resolution* (or just *ADR*) is now one of the fastest-growing areas of the law. Its purpose is to reduce the cost of settling disputes and to speed up the process of getting a binding result. Hey, lawyers may be a traditional bunch, but we still know that change is good once in a while. After all, we ditched the powdered-wig thing, didn't we? And most of us don't even use Latin anymore, unless we're at a party and want to impress our dates.

The goal of all ADR is to get disputes resolved without resorting to long, expensive litigation. Whether you use mediation or arbitration (both of which are explained in the next few sections), the aim of ADR is to reach a binding solution to your dispute quickly and efficiently. In the end, this solution is normally in the form of a written agreement, or contract (see Chapter 27 for more information about contracts).

In arbitration, your contract is made before the process begins—both people agree to be bound by the arbitrator's decision. Suppose that you and your neighbor had a dispute over whether you should pay for some damage you did to his lawn mower, and at the end of arbitration, it was decided that you owed him $100 for the repairs. You must pay him the $100 because you have already agreed that you would be bound by the arbitrator's decision.

Legal Pitfalls

Before I get into a discussion of ADR, you should know that this area is relatively new and that every state has different arbitration and mediation procedures. In fact, you may even find differences in ADR rules between neighboring counties within the same state. Although this chapter describes basic procedures, be sure that you consult a local attorney or bar association to find out how your local rules will affect your specific situation.

In mediation, the contract is formed between you and the other person after the process is over. After your dispute is settled, your agreement is written down so that there's no dispute later about who agreed to what. After the agreement is written in its final form, it becomes a contract.

The natural question you might have is, "What happens if the other person won't honor the agreement reached through ADR?" If that happens, you still have to sue the other person in order to enforce the agreement. This situation may seem as though it defeats the purpose of ADR (you're trying to avoid litigation, remember?), but, fortunately, most disputes don't go this far. If they do, the courts generally rule in favor of the person trying to enforce the agreement.

Agreeing To Disagree Through Arbitration

In principle, *arbitration* is similar to going to court to settle a dispute. You and the other party present the facts of your case to the arbitrator or a panel of arbitrators, and the arbitrator (or arbitrators) ultimately makes a decision about the case.

There are two kinds of arbitration: voluntary and involuntary. Arbitration is voluntary when you and the other person involved both agree that you'll use an arbitrator to settle any disputes that might come up between you. You can make this agreement at any time. For example, you might want to include an arbitration clause when you're putting your contract together, just in case problems develop down the road. On the other hand, you both might agree to use arbitration after a problem has already developed, because it's usually a faster, cheaper, and more effective alternative than going to court.

Legalese
Arbitration is a process in which parties bring their dispute before a neutral third party (the arbitrator), agree in advance to be bound by the arbitrator's decision, and ask the arbitrator to decide their dispute.

Voluntary arbitration has traditionally been used in labor agreements, construction contracts, and brokerage agreements, and it's becoming more common in other areas as well. If you're involved in arbitration, you may be able to handle the process without using an attorney, but you should use common sense. If the heart of the problem is a technical point in the contract, if the facts of the case are very involved, or if a large amount of money is at stake, you should hire an attorney to represent you in the arbitration process. The arbitrator will make a decision that is binding on you and that directly affects your wallet. Take arbitration as seriously as you would if you were going to court for a trial—be prepared to present your position clearly and have all your documentation copied and well organized.

Legalese
Mediation is a process in which parties bring their dispute to a neutral third party to help them negotiate their own resolution.

Courts and Arbitration

Many courts now use a mandatory arbitration process for certain kinds of cases. This kind of arbitration is considered involuntary because it's court-ordered. So far, I've talked about arbitration as an alternative to litigation, so it probably seems odd that a court would assign a case to mandatory arbitration. But many courts have found that using arbitration as part of the normal litigation process provides people with a faster, more economical way to resolve their disputes.

Tip
Should you be represented by an attorney if your case is subject to mandatory arbitration? Yes. The arbitration process is subject to procedural rules that are similar to the rules governing trials. An attorney can help you present your case in the best possible light and make sure that all important evidence is presented to the arbitrators.

Legal Pitfalls
Make sure that you contact your attorney immediately if you want to reject an arbitration ruling. If your rejection doesn't comply with local rules, you may find yourself stuck with the ruling.

Although mandatory arbitration is used in many places, the courts order it only in specific types of cases. First, your dispute can only be about money. I know, your first impulse is to say, "Aren't they all?" Yes, usually, but cases involving evictions, foreclosures, and divorces cannot be assigned to arbitration. That's because even though money is one issue, it's not the only issue involved.

Second, all state and local court rules set a dollar range for the cases eligible for arbitration. Your case will probably get assigned to arbitration if the amount involved is between $2,500 and $50,000. These amounts vary substantially between jurisdictions, so make sure that you check with your local bar association or the office of the county court clerk.

Third, the court can order you to go through the arbitration process, but you have the option of rejecting the arbitrator's decision. Each county court has a system in which you can get your case tried by the court if you don't like the final ruling. After an arbitrator's decision has been made, you can reject the ruling within 30 days. If you properly reject the ruling, your case is reassigned to the court's trial call (the court's list of cases that are unresolved and need to be scheduled for trial).

Overall, you can see that arbitration is similar to litigating a dispute the old-fashioned way. Mediation, on the other hand, is a much different system.

Meet Your Mediator: A Real "Middleman"

Mediation is often used when a couple is in the early stages of a divorce, but it can be used in business or contract situations too. In mediation, you still have a neutral third party, as in arbitration. And as with arbitration, mediation is often a voluntary process, although some courts have adopted a mandatory mediation program for divorcing couples who cannot agree on issues of child custody or visitation.

Unlike arbitration, you don't "present your case" to a mediator. The mediator does not rule on the case. Instead, the mediator tries to get you and the other person communicating effectively so that the two of you can work out your own solution.

That last sentence may make you cringe. How can you expect people who are already at each other's throats to sit down together and come up with a solution to their problem? Mediators are trained in conflict resolution and are skilled in opening lines of communication between people. Just like attorneys, different mediators offer different styles, and they can use an assortment of techniques to keep people talking. In a divorce mediation, for example, the mediator may decide to meet with you and your spouse together throughout the entire process, which can last from two to eight sessions. Or the mediator may want to have a session or two with each of you separately (*caucusing*). In cases in which there's a great deal of conflict between the parties, the mediator may find it useful to put each of you in a separate room and then run messages back and forth between you (*shuttle mediation*).

After the parties have reached an agreement, the mediator writes up a summary of the agreed-on terms. In a divorce, the parties typically take this summary to their respective attorneys and have them review it because it will probably become part of their divorce decree (see Chapter 7 for more information about this use of mediation). In a voluntary non-divorce mediation, this kind of attorney review may not be necessary. It's important to note that, even though the methods are different, successful mediation and arbitration both produce a legally enforceable agreement that resolves the parties' dispute.

> **WHAT!?**
>
> **Legalese**
> **Caucusing** is a mediation technique in which the mediator meets with each party separately; **shuttle mediation** is a mediation technique in which the mediator physically separates the parties during the session and then runs messages between them.

Legal Pitfalls

If you do meet with a mediator privately, be aware that there is no mediator-client privilege and that whatever you discuss might be repeated in one form or another to the other person involved in the mediation. However, most mediators will have both of you agree in writing that neither of you will subpoena records from the mediator nor call the mediator as a witness if your dispute goes to trial. This agreement does make the session more private, but it's not the same as attorney-client privilege.

Tip

If you use a mediator who's also an attorney (and many of them are), she cannot and will not give legal advice during the mediation process. For a divorce mediation, you and your spouse should each hire an attorney even if the mediation succeeds. Before you sign any final agreement that is reached during mediation, it's important that you have your own attorney review the agreement.

In a divorce, the greatest advantage to mediation is that you and your spouse can really put together the best type of agreement for your specific situation. If you're disputing custody and visitation, for example, mediation may enable you to reach an agreement that satisfies your needs, your spouse's needs, and the needs of your children. Why? Because nobody knows you and your family as well as you do. Compare this to litigating the same issues and having your family's fate determined by a judge who doesn't know you, your spouse, or your children.

Additionally, because litigation is an adversarial proceeding that pits you directly against your spouse, there will be a winner and a loser in the end. After a successful mediation, it's not unusual for both parents to feel that they've "won." They've worked out the agreement that's best for them, they've probably learned some communication skills, and they've probably also saved some time and money.

Like any other technique, mediation is not always successful, and it's not the right solution for everyone. The following few simple guidelines can help you improve your odds of having a successful mediation:

➤ **Be committed.** Focus on the real issues, not on personalities or who's right.

➤ **Be prepared.** Bring with you to the sessions any documents you might need. In a divorce, these documents might include tax returns, appraisals, W-2s, or your children's school or medical records. In a contract dispute, it might mean bringing in such documents as paid receipts, a copy of the contract, invoices, job estimates, or inspection reports.

➤ **Be open with the mediator.** Don't just state a position and dig in your heels. Explain to the mediator why you've taken a certain position, and be open to the mediator's suggestions and proposals.

Who Are These People (and Where Did They Come From?)

Mediators and arbitrators come from all sorts of backgrounds. Many are lawyers, but some are therapists, retired judges, or social workers. If you're going through court-ordered mediation or arbitration, you won't have a choice about who hears your case, but you can take comfort in the fact that your mediator or arbitrator has met specific educational and practical standards set by the court.

If you're looking for an arbitrator or mediator for voluntary alternative dispute resolution, you can contact any of the following organizations for suggestions (you might also want to ask your local bar association whether it has a referral list for arbitrators and mediators):

➤ **SPIDR (Society of Professionals In Dispute Resolution):** 815 5th Street NW, Suite 530, Washington, DC 20005; (202)783-7277.

➤ **American Arbitration Association:** 140 West 51st Street, New York, NY 10020-1203; (212)484-4041.

➤ **Academy of Family Mediators:** 1500 South Highway 100, Suite 355, Golden Valley, MN 55416; (612)525-8670.

The Least You Need To Know

➤ Alternative dispute resolution gives you the chance to resolve a conflict more quickly and more economically than going to trial.

➤ Arbitrators hear your case much like a court would and make a binding decision. Mediators don't make rulings. They work with you and the other party to help you reach a mutually acceptable solution to your dispute.

➤ A court can order arbitration or mediation depending on the type of case you have and your local court rules.

➤ If your case is in arbitration or mediation, you should still get advice from an attorney about your case, the dispute resolution process, and how the outcome is likely to affect you. And, definitely, don't sign any agreement until you've reviewed it with your attorney.

Part 2
All in the Family

Now that you have an idea of how the mechanics of our legal system work, it's time to get a little more personal—and what could be more personal than family law? This part of the book looks at all sorts of legal issues relating to you and your family: the good (marriage and adoption), the bad (divorce and separation), and the ugly (custody battles).

Family law is a constantly growing and developing area, primarily because so many changes are taking place in society as a whole. Being a judge in divorce court years ago used to be simple: There were certain rules you could always count on. People came in married and left divorced, and during the process, Mom generally got the kids and some alimony, and Dad generally got visitation and the household bills. Today, divorce-court judges arguably work harder than other kinds of judges because the rules are changing. More and more men today want custody, or at least joint custody, of their children. In most marriages, both spouses work, so alimony isn't the automatic rule it used to be. In fact, some states don't even use the term anymore. And courts still struggle to determine the rights of people who live together without being married.

So let's get started with a look at family law. After all, charity may begin at home, but so does the law.

Chapter 6

"Be Prepared" Isn't Just for Scouts: Marriage and Prenuptial Agreements

In This Chapter

➤ Legal issues to consider if you're living with your partner

➤ How prenuptial agreements can protect your financial interests

➤ What you need to do when you're working out a prenuptial agreement

Back in Chapter 5, I gave lawyers a collective pat on the back for being progressive enough to see that litigation doesn't work well in every situation and that new forms of alternative dispute resolution often prove to be better options. Call me fickle, but we have now reached a field of law in which case law and statutes barely keep pace with society. The field of law I'm talking about (just in case you didn't read the Part title) is family law.

Family law presents great challenges to judges, lawyers, and legislators. After all, few homes in 1995 America resemble the television households of the Cleavers, the Nelsons, or for that matter even the Bunkers.

The law, and society as a whole, is grappling with all the issues that arise in single-parent households and in homes in which couples, both heterosexual and homosexual, live together. Let's start our look at family law by establishing the differences between couples who live together and couples who marry.

"I Do" Versus "Someday, Maybe, I Might"

Marriage—the word alone is enough to make some people swoon with romance and others gag in disgust. However you may personally feel about that noble old institution, the law is relatively clear and detailed when it comes to marriage. Marriage itself is a unique contract. You experience certain legal consequences in either making or breaking it. Saying "I do" involves more than your promise to love, honor, and cherish. It involves statutory legal duties of spousal and child support, property rights, and (heaven forbid I forget the IRS) tax consequences.

> **WHAT!?**
>
> **Legalese**
> A **contract** is an agreement between two or more parties that creates a legal obligation to do (or not to do) something. Prenuptial agreements are one type of contract, and throughout this chapter the words *contract* and *agreement* are used interchangeably. Chapter 26 has more information about contracts.

In comparison, the "law of living together" is barely defined. In fact, no domestic or family-law provisions address the issue of living together, or *cohabitation,* as it's more formally known. The law in this area continues to grow and change, and it seems likely that cohabitation will eventually be addressed by statute in some areas. In fact, a few states already recognize claims for palimony, but it isn't generally part of family law.

Palimony is not recognized as a valid legal claim in most of the country, and even in states in which the claim can be made, it is extremely difficult to prove.

> **WHAT!?**
>
> **Legalese**
> **Legal duties** are things you are required to do by law either because a statute requires you to or because you've agreed to do them under the terms of a contract.

Living together does not create any legal duties or rights regarding support or property, unless you and your partner have a specific agreement. If you do have this type of agreement and can prove what the agreement is and that it has been broken, you may be able to bring an action under contract law.

If you and your partner plan to live together, it's best to put something in writing about how your relationship will work. "Do-it-yourself" books on this subject contain sample forms, but be careful if you use them. If significant assets are involved (for example, you own a great deal of property or your own business) or you have to consider other special circumstances (such as providing for children from a previous marriage), you and your partner should see an attorney for help in drafting the agreement.

> **Legalese**
> **Palimony** is a legal action that claims a share of someone's property or the right to receive support payments based on the fact that the parties lived together as an unmarried couple and acted as though there was a contract between them, even though they never had a formal written agreement.

Living together raises many questions and issues, just as marriage does. For example, will you each keep the property you brought into the relationship? What if you buy something together, start a joint savings account, or make a joint investment? What if you cosign for your partner's car loan? Who pays the rent and other household expenses? What if one of you works full time while the other goes back to school? Is there any responsibility to support the other? How will property and debts be divided if you break up? Remember that no family-law statute covers your relationship. If you and your partner break up, you have only your agreement to rely on.

The Contract Before the Contract: Prenuptial Agreements

A *prenuptial agreement* is simply a contract between people who are planning to get married, and it can be as broad or as specific as the couple wants. At a minimum, it usually describes how to divide property and debts if you and your spouse divorce or when one of you dies. Don't try to draft this kind of agreement by yourself.

Legalese
A **prenuptial agreement** is a contract between two people who plan to marry. It defines each person's property rights and describes what will happen financially if they later divorce or if one person dies.

Get an attorney and ask your soon-to-be spouse to do the same, for two reasons: Both sides will receive unbiased advice about their respective rights and responsibilities, and you'll minimize the chances of a court's refusal to enforce the agreement at a later date.

Make sure that you both hire different attorneys to review the agreement. This step may result in some additional expense, but it guarantees that you both get unbiased advice and that no problems will be caused by a conflict of interest.

When You Might Want a Prenuptial Agreement

Many people think that you need a prenuptial agreement only if you're rich, and maybe that was the case years ago. But today there are practical reasons for wanting this kind of agreement. Consider the following common situations.

You were married once before, for eight years. When that marriage ended in divorce, it took two years' worth of litigation and thousands of dollars in attorney's fees to settle the property disputes. A "prenup" can prevent the same thing from happening if your second marriage ends in divorce.

You have children from a previous marriage, and even though you have read Chapter 23 of this book and updated your will, you're still concerned about potential inheritance problems if you die. A prenuptial agreement can help guarantee that your children, not your new spouse, will inherit your assets.

You're a partner in a small, independent marketing firm. You've been doing well financially and are about to marry someone who is working part-time while finishing an MBA program. You're concerned about how your property will be divided if you divorce in a few years, and you're especially worried about claims that could affect the business.

Remember that you determine what's included in your prenuptial agreement—make sure that you explain all your concerns to your attorney so that she can draft the agreement that's best for you.

What Goes in the Agreement

To create an enforceable prenuptial agreement, you and your partner have to provide a full disclosure to each other about your respective finances. You have to provide information (including documentation) about the things in this list:

➤ Real property (land and buildings) you own.

➤ Personal property, including antiques, jewelry, and family heirlooms.

➤ Bank accounts and their balances.

➤ Other investments, including IRAs, CDs, money market accounts, stocks, bonds, and other securities.

➤ Income.

➤ Liabilities, including mortgages, credit-card debts, bank loans, and judgments.

➤ Insurance policies.

To save time and aggravation, put all your paperwork together before you meet with your attorney. You'll also probably have to provide copies of any previous divorce decrees, your most current tax returns, and your will or trust.

You and your partner control how long the prenuptial agreement remains in effect. It can do so indefinitely, or you can say something directly in the agreement, such as, "This agreement will terminate on our fifth wedding anniversary." Or, of course, you both can simply agree to terminate the agreement at any time. This type of termination should be done in writing, and each of you should consult an attorney before signing it.

OOOOOH...

Tip
Full disclosure means more than just turning in the necessary paperwork. It also means that you must reveal anything you know about money you expect to receive. If you know that your Aunt Gertrude left a $3 million trust fund for you and your sister, for example, and you know that your share of the trust will be distributed to you three years from now, you must reveal that information to your partner.

Do Prenuptial Agreements Work?

Yes, courts are usually willing to enforce a "prenup." To make sure that yours is enforceable, ask yourself the same questions a court would ask:

➤ **Is the agreement fair?** In other words, was there a full and fair disclosure from both people? Did both of you provide accurate and detailed financial information?

➤ **Did you both enter the agreement freely and voluntarily?** Suppose that a groom shows up at the church with a prenup in hand and says, "Sign it, or the wedding's off." Even if the bride does sign it, it's clear that she didn't make the agreement freely and voluntarily. If one person was forced into signing a "prenup," either financially or emotionally, a court won't enforce the agreement. See Chapter 26 for more information about duress and other contract defenses.

➤ **Are the terms of the agreement reasonable?** The word *reasonable* is used broadly here. If the agreement is so one-sided that one person would be left without a dime after a divorce, a court may find the agreement "unconscionable" and refuse to enforce it. Remember that your property division doesn't have to be equal and that you or you partner can reduce or waive your rights to property or support. But taken to an extreme, a waiver of all your legal rights jeopardizes the entire agreement.

If you can answer "yes" to each of these questions, your prenuptial agreement is more likely to be valid and enforceable. Your attorney will advise you about any special requirements your state may have concerning how the agreement is signed, whether it must be witnessed or notarized, and whether it must be recorded.

Suppose that you do have an enforceable prenup: Now what? Assuming that you don't get divorced, you'll probably never look at it again until one of you dies. Then the prenup and your spouse's will must be reviewed and the appropriate property distributions made. If you do get divorced, the court looks to the prenup for guidance about such issues as spousal support and the division of your property. The next few chapters more fully describe divorce, support, and related property issues.

The Least You Need To Know

➤ If you and your partner live together without being married, you should have a written agreement covering your respective property rights and other financial issues.

➤ If you're getting married, you may want to consider using a prenuptial agreement to settle any questions about support and property if you get divorced or one of you dies.

➤ It's critical that you and your partner make a full and fair disclosure to each other when you prepare a prenuptial agreement.

➤ Each person should be represented by an attorney when a prenuptial agreement is being negotiated and prepared.

EXCUSE ME?

Having a Child Without Morning Sickness and Labor Pains

In This Chapter

➤ The different kinds of adoption

➤ What's involved in an adoption

➤ The effects of adoption on the natural parent

➤ Confidentiality in adoption proceedings

Adoption can be a wonderful and fulfilling decision. It can bring people who really want a child together with a child who desperately needs a loving family. But unless the process is handled properly and legal requirements are followed to the letter, the adoption process can become an absolute nightmare. If you don't believe me, just think of some of the newspaper stories you've seen in the past few years.

This chapter clarifies the process for you and explains what needs to happen so that you can make sure that any adoption in your family is handled legally.

The Different Ways You Can Adopt

Adoption is a legal process in which all the parental rights and responsibilities of a child's natural parents are ended and the rights and responsibilities toward the child are then given to the adoptive parents. If the process, which is governed completely by state law, is done properly, it's permanent.

This process is different from foster care, in which a child is temporarily removed from her parents and placed with a foster-care family.

While a child is in foster care, the natural parents still have certain legal rights regarding the child, even if those rights are restricted. In an adoption, the natural parents' rights are terminated completely.

There are four kinds of adoption proceedings:

➤ Direct, or independent, adoptions.

➤ Agency, or relinquishment, adoptions.

➤ Related adoptions.

➤ Adult adoptions.

A *direct adoption* is one in which a child's natural parents place the child with the adoptive parents and no adoption service or agency is involved. In an *agency adoption*, a state-licensed adoption agency places the child with her adoptive parents.

The third kind of adoption involves a situation in which one of the adoptive parents is already related to the child (when a stepchild is being adopted, for example). This kind of adoption is called a *related adoption*.

If the *adoptee* (the person being adopted) is an adult, the adoption is appropriately called an *adult adoption*. This chapter deals only with the adoption of children, but the process of adult adoption is similar. Adult adoptions aren't that common, though they can be used in a situation in which an adoptive parent wants to make an adopted adult his legal heir.

Legal Pitfalls
Each state has strict laws regulating adoption agencies and services. These laws prohibit the "selling" of babies and are aimed at preventing a black market for adoptions. Contact your state attorney general's office or your attor-ney if you have any doubts about the individual or agency you're dealing with during the process.

The Legal Side of Adoption

The adoption process is governed completely by state law, and as you might expect, the specific procedures involved vary from state to state. You have to contact an attorney experienced in family law to find out what your state's requirements are and to guide you through the process.

All adoptions involve the same basic steps. You begin by filing a petition with the court, indicating that you want to adopt a certain child. The court then orders an investigation and a report on both you and the child. The investigation and report are prepared by a person appointed by the court, usually someone from an appropriate state agency or an attorney. Notice of the adoption proceedings are given to the child's natural parents or guardian.

How a Court Terminates the Rights of a Natural Parent

The next step in the process involves the termination of the natural parents' rights concerning the child. This step is important because, from a legal standpoint, a child can have only one set of parents. To put it another way, only one set of parents can have custody and control of the child. So if the petitioners in an adoption are asking the court to grant them that authority, the court must at the same time terminate the authority of the natural parents.

The least complicated way to end parental rights is to do so by consent. Consent is often used in related adoptions. Suppose that Mary is eight years old and has been living in Michigan with her mother and stepfather for the past five years. Her father lives in New Mexico and doesn't take an active role in her life. It's possible that Mary's father would consent to an adoption by his ex-wife and her new husband.

It's the Law!

The termination of parental rights is an extremely serious action. If you give your consent to an adoption, your decision is usually considered irrevocable, and you permanently lose all the rights you have as a parent. On the other hand, your consent also ends any responsibility you have for the child, including any obligation to pay support. If you're faced with this decision, discuss your situation with an attorney and consider the matter carefully.

Agreeing to give up your parental rights is a major step. It's not like giving up custody, where you still retain basic rights to see and interact with your kids, even though you don't have decision-making authority over them (Chapter 11 explains custody in more detail). When your parental rights are terminated by an adoption, you lose all your rights concerning your kids—including your right to see or visit them, even on a limited basis.

On the other hand, it's also a big step for the adoptive parents. In the preceding example, Mary's mother and her stepfather may have serious concerns that Mary could end up living with her natural father if her mother dies. This situation can be prevented by having Mary's step-father adopt her. But what if Mary's natural father is wealthy, pays large amounts of child support, and plans to also pay for Mary's college education? If her stepfather doesn't have the same kind of income, he has to take that fact into account in making the decision to adopt Mary. If the natural father's parental rights are terminated by an adop-tion, the child support and college-tuition payments are terminated too. It sounds mercenary, but it's a factor that must be considered.

Parental rights can also be terminated without the consent of the parent, but it requires a court hearing in which the adoptive parents must prove that the natural parent should be considered legally unfit. If sufficient evidence is presented at the hearing, the court may termi-nate the rights of the natural parent by court order. State law defines when a parent can be considered "unfit." This allegation is very serious, and proving it is not always easy. Having to go through a hearing on issues like this one can obviously be traumatic for everyone involved.

Assuming that the natural parent's rights are successfully terminated, that the investigation report doesn't reveal any problems, and that any other statutory requirements have been met, the court holds a final hearing and issues an adoption decree. If the adoptive parents want, the decree can even order the appropriate county agency to issue a new birth certificate for the child and to seal the child's original records.

Balancing the Right to Privacy and the Right To Know

Adoption proceedings are confidential. Unlike most other kinds of lawsuits, the court files on adoption proceedings are not open to the general public. While the adoption is pending, case names are not identified on the daily court call and instead are referred to only by number. When the case is concluded, the court file is sealed. Every effort is made, in fact, to conceal the identity of the parties involved— that's why newspaper accounts of high-profile cases refer to the child only by a fake first name, such as "Baby Michael" or "Baby Lisa."

This is all fine and good, unless you were adopted at the age of 2 and now, at 30, you want to find out who your natural parents are.

Even if you were a party to the adoption, it's possible that the only way you can get access to the sealed adoption file is to get a court order. Each state has its own particular rules governing when adoption records can be opened and who can have access to them. You can contact your state's Bureau of Vital Statistics or the clerk of the court where the adoption decree was entered for general information about how to get access to your file, but you may have to consult an attorney in your area for help in getting through all the red tape.

Tip
The majority of states have some way for children and natural parents to learn each other's identity and to contact each other. Of course, even if you find out the other person's identity by using this type of system, it may be difficult to locate him if many years have passed.

States handle this issue in one of two ways. Under one system, adoption information can be released if both parties (the natural parent and the child) agree to the release of information. Neither party can access the information without the other's consent. Under the other process, one party can ask the court to try to locate the other person, and, if she is found, ask her to consent to a release of information about the adoption, her identity, and how to establish contact.

Because adoption law and the rules regarding release of adoption records are all statutory, specific procedures vary from state to state.

Contact the clerk of the court in your county for information about how to access these types of records, or consult your attorney.

The Least You Need To Know

➤ Adoptions can be handled directly between the natural parents and the adoptive parents, or a licensed state agency can be used to help place the child.

➤ During the adoption process, the rights of the natural parents are terminated, either with their consent or by order of the court.

➤ If a parent consents to the adoption of his child, the consent is usually irrevocable.

➤ Adoption records are usually confidential, but most states have some procedure for a child and her natural parents to learn each other's identity.

Chapter 8

Trouble in Paradise

In This Chapter

➤ How divorce is different from legal separation and annulment

➤ How to know the difference between fault and no-fault cases

➤ How the basic divorce process works

"Love, the quest; marriage, the conquest; divorce, the inquest."

—Helen Rowland

Helen Rowland wrote that line around 1903, and back then it was more than just a wry observation. Years ago, divorces were usually granted only on the basis of fault; he did this or she did that. Rules about custody, property distribution, and alimony were all different from what they are today. The entire divorce process in 1903 was generally much more adversarial, and in some ways more arbitrary, than it is now. "No-fault" divorces, divorce mediation, and other developments have made the process simpler and less confrontational.

But divorce can still be emotionally traumatic and financially devastating for a couple. Even when it's a "friendly" divorce, it can still leave scars, especially on children. This chapter explains the divorce process and provides guidance in making a divorce as smooth as possible under the circumstances.

Going Your Separate Ways

Legally speaking, a divorce involves totally dissolving a marriage. When a marriage is "dissolved," the court officially ends the marital relationship. Afterward, both parties are free to marry again and can generally begin new, separate lives.

After a divorce, the parties have few, if any, legal responsibilities toward each other; if any of these responsibilities do exist, they're limited and specifically spelled out in the final court order (known as the *divorce decree*). If you were to get a divorce, the court might, for example, order you to pay child support to your spouse or order you to sign over a car title to your spouse. You're still divorced (your marriage is over), but you may have to follow through on parts of the court order even after the legal proceedings are finished.

A divorce completely ends a valid marriage. This might seem to be an unnecessarily long definition, but it clarifies the differences between divorce, legal separation, and annulment.

The final court order in a legal separation generally addresses the same issues and produces the same results a divorce decree does. Property gets divided, support issues get decided, and child custody and visitation rules are established. But (and this is a huge "but") the couple is still legally married after a legal separation. This means, of course, that neither spouse can legally remarry.

There are only a few reasons to consider a legal separation rather than a divorce. A legal separation might be the answer if you and your spouse don't want to live together but don't want to divorce for religious reasons. Or if you're currently insured under your spouse's

> **WHAT!?**
>
> **Legalese**
> A **legal separation** is a process which results in a court order that defines the terms about how you and your spouse will live separately from each other, without actually ending your marriage.

health insurance and aren't able to qualify for your own policy, you might consider legal separation.

An annulment is also different from a divorce. Some states use the term "declaration of invalidity of marriage" rather than "annulment." Hey, it's the first rule of legalese: Why use one word when you can use five? The label "declaration of invalidity of marriage" is used to clarify the difference between a legal annulment and a religious annulment.

Only a handful of circumstances justify an annulment. If you live in Backwoods, Tennessee, for example, and you find yourself the groom in a real "shotgun wedding," your situation probably qualifies. A 12-gauge pointed at your back is evidence that you're not entering into the marriage voluntarily, and it is legally considered *duress*. You can get this type of marriage annulled.

I'd like to point out that people from Tennessee are widely known for their wonderful sense of humor. Before I begin getting mail, here are some reasons that a court will grant an annulment:

Legal Pitfalls
Don't make the mistake of assuming that you're legally separated just because you or your spouse move out of the house. A legal separation can be established only by a court order, and separating informally, without any agreement, can sometimes affect the outcome of a future divorce case.

Legalese
An **annulment** is a court order which states that a marriage was never legally valid because of certain circumstances that existed when it took place.

WHAT!?

➤ The marriage was entered into under duress (you were forced into it), threats, or fraud.

➤ One person was mentally incompetent at the time or entered into the marriage under the influence of drugs or alcohol.

➤ One person did not have the legal ability to marry (usually because a previous marriage had not been properly dissolved or because of bigamy).

Annulments are controlled by state statute, and you will have to check your state's requirements for obtaining one.

Like a legal separation and a divorce, part of the annulment proceedings address property rights, support, and issues relating to the children. Like legal separations, annulments are often done by people who don't want to divorce for religious reasons.

Legal Pitfalls
A caution similar to the one about legal separation should be made here. Various religions recognize annulments and have their own separate proceedings within the church, but a religious annulment has no legal effect. Legally speaking, an annulment can be done only through the courts.

To make that Legal Pitfall a little clearer, suppose that you're Catholic and want an annulment. On one hand, the church has its own procedure for petitioning the church to grant you an annulment. You don't need an attorney to help you with this process, and the procedures involved should be relatively simple. If the church does grant you the annulment, however, it is effective only within the church (for example, it may enable you to receive sacraments or take part in certain services). Legally, however, you're still married under state law because the church's annulment has no legal effect. To get a legal annulment, you have to go to court the same as you would for a divorce.

The process for obtaining a legal annulment is more complicated and is similar to that of obtaining a divorce, so you'll probably need the help of an attorney. After you've obtained a legal annulment, you're no longer married under state law. Wherever the term "annulment" appears in this section, it means a *legal* annulment.

The following list sums up the differences among divorce, legal separation, and annulment:

➤ A divorce totally dissolves a marriage.

➤ A legal separation makes provisions for the spouses to live apart from each other without dissolving their marriage.

➤ An annulment is a declaration that a marriage was never legally valid in the first place.

What You Can Expect During a Divorce

A divorce goes through almost the same legal process as any other kind of civil case, but there are some differences. First, courts usually consider the divorce case in two separate parts: the grounds for the divorce and the marital settlement.

Saying that you have grounds for divorce means simply that you have a legal basis to end the marriage. Your state has a statute that lists what grounds are legally sufficient in your state. Traditionally, grounds were directly related to the idea of fault. Constant drunkenness, adultery, desertion, and mental or physical cruelty were (and still remain) common statutory grounds for divorce. To get a divorce on these grounds, you have to tell the court that your spouse committed this kind of misconduct.

In the past 20 years or so, courts and state legislatures have begun looking beyond the traditional ideas of fault. After all, plenty of people may not have a legal basis to get a divorce, but they still don't want to stay married. Under the old divorce laws, these people had only two choices: Lie to the court about the grounds for the divorce, or stay married. This dilemma has essentially been solved with the creation of the "no-fault" divorce.

Three important factors are involved in establishing grounds for a no-fault divorce. Generally, you must show the court, through your sworn testimony, that the following conditions exist:

➤ You and your spouse no longer live together.

➤ Irreconcilable differences exist between you.

➤ The marriage has broken down to the point where there's no hope of saving it.

Every state has some form of no-fault, even if it calls it something else, but procedures vary from state to state. You have to talk to an attorney in your area to find out your state's specific requirements for a no-fault divorce.

What To Consider When You're Deciding on Grounds

Some people still have the notion that they can prevent their spouse from getting a divorce, but that isn't really correct. In a divorce action based solely on fault, you can conceivably get the case dismissed if you can prove that you didn't do whatever you were accused of doing. But in a no-fault case, it's almost impossible to stop the process—there's just no legal defense.

No-fault cases often move through the court system a little more quickly than fault cases because no elaborate proof of grounds is necessary. But some people choose no-fault because they're afraid of what will happen if they don't. They may worry about having to testify in court about personal or embarrassing things in order to prove fault. They may fear that their spouse will refuse to negotiate a fair property settlement if they get accused of fault. They may even fear physical or emotional retaliation by their spouse. These are all valid concerns, and an attorney experienced in divorce and family law can help you decide the best way to handle your case.

If you're filing for divorce, don't just assume that no-fault is the best way to go. In some states, your choice of grounds can affect the final property settlement and even the amount of support that you and your children are awarded. Talk to an attorney in your area about which grounds to use.

In certain states, for example, the party found to be at fault in a divorce may receive a smaller share of property in the final settlement than if the divorce had been a no-fault divorce.

Courts in these states can also take fault into consideration if you're asking the court to give you custody of your children (it favors the party that's not at fault). Remember, though, that in many states the issue of fault has no effect on the court's decisions regarding property, support, or child custody. For more information about property division, support, and child custody, see the next three chapters.

After You've Made the Decision

A divorce case begins when one spouse (the *petitioner*) files a petition asking the court to dissolve the marriage to the spouse (the *respondent*). A divorce petition serves the same purpose as a complaint (see Chapter 4); it identifies the parties, explains the grounds for the divorce, and asks the court to do certain things. The respondent is then served with notice of the divorce case and given a copy of the petition.

The parties to a divorce often conduct discovery (see Chapter 4) and begin working out the terms of a settlement. The settlement agreement you reach touches every part of your life. It addresses the division of property, support for you or your spouse, child custody and visitation rights, and child support. Because of the scope of the settlement agreement, it can take a substantial amount of time to iron out all the details.

It's extremely rare for the parties to disagree on absolutely everything, so the first step in reaching a settlement is determining what issues you can agree on. The process then moves on to a discussion of the disputed issues. If you and your spouse can't reach an agreement on a certain point, the issue ultimately is brought before the judge to decide. In some jurisdictions, the court may refer you to a mediator before accepting the matter for a hearing. The reasoning is simple: You and your spouse know each other and your children better than anyone else does. It's usually better, therefore, if you can work out an agreement yourselves rather than ask a judge (who doesn't know you from Adam) to make a ruling after a short hearing in court.

Tip
Service of process in a divorce case is often handled differently than in other kinds of cases. You may even be able, under certain conditions, to waive your right to be formally served. This can potentially save the petitioner a little money and the respondent some embarrassment. Ask your attorney about local court rules in this area.

OOOOOH...

Despite all the war stories you may have heard, negotiating a marital settlement agreement doesn't have to rank next to chewing broken glass as a painful experience. Here are some things you can do to make the process go more smoothly:

➤ If your attorney is negotiating the settlement, be sure that he knows what's important to you and what's not. Unless you're clear with your attorney about what you specifically want in the settlement (such as "visitation with my kids at least every Wednesday night and from Friday to Sunday every third weekend of the month"), you make his job more difficult, and the process ends up taking longer.

➤ Do what you can on your own. Let your attorney negotiate big issues (such as support, custody, and division of large assets), and try to handle the minor stuff yourself. You want your attorney to negotiate the way your spouse's retirement benefits get divided, for example, but you don't want to have to pay her to negotiate who gets the goldfish or the black-velvet painting of Elvis.

➤ Remember that you can be firm without being hostile. You (and your attorney) should be clear about your position during negotiations, but don't turn to personal attacks if things aren't going well. If you and your spouse can't negotiate without sniping at one another, don't do it at all. Instead, consider using a mediator (see Chapter 5) or communicate through your respective attorneys.

➤ Make sure that your position is being communicated correctly. Ask your attorney to send you copies of any correspondence concerning the settlement and check to see that the information being relayed back and forth between the lawyers is correct.

➤ Document your position as much as possible. If you think that you should receive $400 per month in alimony from your spouse, be prepared to support your claim. Documentation you might want to use includes a monthly budget, copies of your paycheck stubs, recent tax returns, and copies of various bills and receipts for household expenses. See Chapter 9 for more information about the use of budgets and other records during settlement negotiations.

The next two chapters go into greater detail about actual settlement terms.

Other Things To Consider Before You File

Going through a divorce is traumatic for everyone involved. It divides a family legally, emotionally, psychologically, and financially. In some cases, one spouse may be so hurt and angry that he or she lashes out at the other. If this happens, problems usually develop in one of two ways: One spouse physically abuses the other, or one spouse tries to empty bank accounts or take control of other marital property.

You can do several things to protect yourself from the threat of domestic violence:

➤ Call a local shelter or crisis line for information about services available in your area. These organizations are usually listed under Crisis Intervention Service in the Yellow Pages.

➤ Call the police. They obviously should be your first call in an emergency, but they can also direct you to shelters or crisis centers in your community.

➤ Talk to your attorney, your local police department, or your county's state attorney's office about getting an order of protection against your spouse. An *order of protection* is a court order that prohibits your spouse from contacting you. This order may require your spouse to temporarily stay out of the house, for example, or even prohibit him or her from making threatening telephone calls to you at home or work. The procedures involved in getting this type of order vary from county to county, but you have to appear in court at a hearing in which the judge decides whether to give you the order. The process is relatively simple, and the order is usually granted the same day.

To protect yourself from financial problems:

➤ Set up a separate checking account and apply for credit cards in your own name so that you will have money available if you need it in an emergency.

➤ Review and make copies of all financial records, including tax returns, bank-account statements, and credit-card bills. If you have access to your spouse's business records, you might include them also. This step helps protect you if your spouse tries to destroy any financial records, and it also alerts you to any unusual account activity.

Be careful in these situations, and, when in doubt, get advice from your attorney before taking any action. Not every spouse is violent, and not every spouse will try to cheat you financially. Recklessly accusing your spouse of taking money or property or obtaining an order of protection without reasonable grounds can only make a bad situation worse.

Will You Need a Lawyer?

The short answer: Probably. Unless you and your spouse earn about the same amount of money, don't own any significant property, and have no children, it's a good idea to hire an attorney to handle your divorce.

Tip
Even if your divorce is relatively peaceful, you and your spouse cannot hire one attorney to represent both of you because it would create a serious conflict-of-interest problem.

Some states have developed a special procedure for people who have simple cases and want to get divorced without hiring an attorney. The process is greatly simplified and much quicker than the normal divorce process, but not everyone can use it. To qualify, a couple may have to show that they don't own any real estate and don't have children and that they want to use no-fault grounds. Call your local bar association to see whether your state has this kind of simplified divorce process and to find out what the restrictions on it are.

The Least You Need To Know

➤ Divorce, legal separation, and annulment are all separate and distinct legal proceedings.

➤ Whether you obtain a divorce, separation, or annulment, the final court order addresses such issues as property rights, support, and child custody and visitation.

➤ In some states, your decision between fault and no-fault can have an effect on your property rights.

➤ Unless no children are involved and your case is very simple, you should hire an attorney to represent you in your divorce.

Chapter 9

What's Mine Is Mine, and What's Yours Is Open to Discussion

In This Chapter

➤ The differences between community-property states and equitable-distribution states

➤ The advantages of negotiating a settlement instead of going to trial

➤ How to prepare for settlement negotiations

Unless you skipped over Chapter 8 (and if you did, shame on you), you know that a court usually handles a divorce in two stages: One stage deals with the grounds, and the other deals with the marital settlement. Depending on your particular situation, the marital settlement agreement can be a long, detailed document, but it generally covers three main areas: the division of property and assets; support for a spouse and the children; and child custody and visitation. This chapter looks at the first area: the way the settlement divides your property.

Figuring Out Which Rules Apply To You

The way your property is divided depends largely on where you live. The following nine states are referred to as community property states:

➤ Arizona.

➤ California.

➤ Idaho.

➤ Louisiana.

➤ Nevada.

➤ New Mexico.

➤ Texas.

➤ Washington.

➤ Wisconsin.

The other 41 states are referred to as equitable distribution states or, occasionally, as common law states.

In *community-property* states, whatever you owned before your marriage is still considered to be yours. Whatever you acquire during your marriage, with a few exceptions, is considered to belong to both you and your spouse. When you divorce, the court attempts to split on a 50-50 basis everything you acquired during your marriage. (If you want a graphic explanation of how community-property states work, find a copy of Eddie Murphy's old stand-up bit on living in California, getting married, and "50 percent.")

I'd really (and I mean really) like to tell you that the rules in the equitable-distribution states are just as clear-cut, but I can't. The underlying theory of *equitable distribution* is simple: It says that when a court must divide property between divorcing people, it should consider a wide range of relevant factors and try to make a fair distribution. It all sounds wonderful—who wants to go on record as saying that they don't want to be fair?

But the practical side of equitable distribution can be a real problem. Which specific factors should be considered by the court? And because the court is considering a variety of factors, should it give more consideration to some than to others? And my favorite question:

What exactly, in dollars and cents, is "fair?" Because of these and other similar questions, the law in equitable-distribution states isn't, and never will be, completely uniform.

How the Court Decides What To Do

If you live in an equitable-distribution state, here are some of the factors a court can consider in making a property division:

➤ The age and educational background of you and your spouse.

➤ How long you were married.

➤ Your current income as well as your future earning capacity.

➤ Your current standard of living.

➤ Your spouse's income and earning capacity.

➤ What property you each brought into your marriage.

➤ The property you accumulated during your marriage in addition to its current value.

➤ The effect that property distribution will have on your ability to pay child support.

➤ Pension or other retirement benefits you're each eligible for through your employer.

➤ The debts and liabilities each of you is responsible for.

➤ The type and extent of fault providing the grounds for the divorce (as I said in Chapter 8, this factor is considered in only a few states).

This process obviously can get pretty complicated, even if you have only moderate assets. Cases that go to trial over these issues can even require expert witnesses, such as accountants and financial planners, to testify about the value of a piece of property or the potential earning capacity of a person or a business.

The court ultimately balances all the preceding factors and makes what it considers to be a "fair" distribution of property. For example, if both you and your spouse work, earn about the same amount of money, and have no children, the court will likely split your property at closing on a 50-50 basis. If you work but your spouse doesn't and your two kids end up living with your spouse after the divorce, it's a fair bet that you'll receive less than your spouse will when the court divides your property.

No one, including your attorney, can predict exactly what the court will do if it's left to decide property distribution, but you don't have to let the court decide—you can work out your own property distribution. Always remember that you have a great deal of control over your divorce and that (almost) everything is negotiable.

Begin by using the following checklists to figure out exactly what you and your spouse own (and owe). Ask your attorney for guidance about what kind of property divisions are usually approved in your area and what would be considered reasonable in your specific situation.

Pay special attention to assets that are difficult to divide (your house, for example). How will you handle "dividing" your house—is it more important that one of you continue to live in the home after the divorce, or would you rather sell it and divide the proceeds? If you want to keep the house, can you afford the mortgage payments and all the other costs that go along with it?

Tip

No matter where you live, a well-drafted prenuptial agreement can save you a great deal of grief if you ever get divorced and have to deal with these types of issues (see Chapter 6 for more information).

If you keep the house, what will your spouse get? Will you trade another large asset (such as pension benefits) for the house, or will you buy out your spouse's interest in the house by giving him a single lump-sum payment? Your attorney can offer suggestions about handling difficult issues such as these. Remember that the greater number of issues you work out on your own, the more quickly your case moves through the system.

Where To Begin

Whether you're talking to your spouse about a possible divorce, preparing to meet with your attorney, or thinking about divorce mediation, you should begin by sitting down with a piece of paper and a pencil. Begin by listing all your assets. Include everything, no matter how the property is currently owned or how it was acquired. Write down the value of each item if you know it. Here are some of the items you should list:

➤ Your home and any other real estate you own.

➤ Furnishings, electronics, appliances, and other personal property in your home.

➤ Cars, boats, and any other vehicles.

➤ Stocks, bonds, and other securities.

➤ Checking, savings, money market, and other bank accounts.

➤ Insurance policies that have a present cash value.

➤ Collectibles.

➤ Pension or other retirement benefits each of you has.

After this list is complete, don't put the pencil down. Start a new list of all your debts and liabilities. Write down account balances, monthly payment information, and account numbers. Include the following information:

➤ Your mortgage balance.

➤ Financing for your cars or other vehicles.

➤ Credit-card accounts.

➤ Personal or unsecured loans.

➤ Any taxes you may owe.

Don't stop now—you're on a roll. Next, you have to figure out your monthly budget. First figure out how much money you receive every month, and then figure out where it all goes. Be as detailed as possible, especially if spousal support or child support are issues in the divorce.

Sure, it's a pain to go through all this homework, but it's important that you do it. First, you can't negotiate a fair settlement if you and your spouse don't know this kind of information. Second, you probably will have to prepare an inventory

OOOOOH...

Tip
Don't worry if you get stumped trying to put a value on certain assets. Determining the value of retirement benefits, investments, and business interests can be complicated. Your attorney can help you with these more difficult items.

and budget at some point during your divorce anyway, so why pay your attorney or accountant to do this kind of work for you when you can do most of it yourself? Third, you accomplish much more during a meeting with your attorney or a mediation session if you organize ahead of time all the information you'll be working with.

This basic checklist can help you begin assembling information for your divorce lawyer.

Asset and Liability Checklist

Present Income and Benefits

Wages per week/month gross/net	_____
Commission/bonus	_____
Profit sharing	_____
Company stock	_____
Pension/retirement benefits	_____
Medical insurance	_____
Life insurance	_____

Property Acquired During the Marriage

Cash on hand	_____
Checking account	_____
Savings account	_____
Money market account	_____
Stocks	_____
Bonds	_____
Real estate (marital residence)	
Present value	_____
Mortgage(s)/liens	_____
Approximate equity	_____
Other real estate	_____
Business interests	_____
Automobiles	
Year	_____
Make/model	_____
Financed/leased	_____
Balance owed	_____
Other vehicles	_____
Other assets (collectibles, art, furnishings, etc.)	_____

Property Owned Before the Marriage

Items and spouse owning each	_____
When acquired	_____
How acquired	_____
Value	_____

Joint Debts and Obligations

Creditor	_____
Amount	_____
Creditor	_____
Amount	_____
Creditor	_____
Amount	_____

Personal Debts and Obligations

Source	_____
Amount	_____
Who's responsible	_____
Source	_____
Amount	_____
Who's responsible	_____

Putting It All Together

A more accurate heading here would be "Taking It All Apart." After you and your spouse have all your information put together, you can begin the negotiation process. You can negotiate informally between yourselves, through formal mediation sessions, or through your respective attorneys. Remember that the more you accomplish through negotiation, the less likely it is that you have to go to trial. You can then keep your legal fees down, and you and your spouse can maintain a greater degree of control over what happens during your divorce.

One word of caution is in order here. Although you do have a great deal of freedom in negotiating a settlement agreement, the court will still want to review the final agreement before approving it and making it part of the final judgment or decree. The court can refuse to approve any part of the agreement that is contrary to state law or that seems extremely unfair. Courts usually take an especially long look at the provisions of the agreement dealing with child support, custody, and visitation (see Chapter 10 for more information about these issues).

This Agreement Is More Than a Handshake

Your settlement agreement is made part of your divorce decree or other final court order when the divorce is over. If you or your spouse violate part of the agreement, you also violate a court order. The guilty party can then be found in contempt of court for her actions.

After your property has been divided on paper in the settlement agreement, you have to take care of various details to make the actual division. Property may have to be moved or sold, accounts may have to be closed, and titles may have to be signed. To avoid unnecessary hassles, try to make these arrangements as quickly as possible after the court approves the settlement. You'll probably find that some arrangements are bigger headaches than others.

OOOOOH...

Tip
Recent changes to the U.S. Bankruptcy Code provide you with greater protection from an ex-spouse who files bankruptcy to try to avoid his obligations under a divorce decree. The amendments, which took effect in October 1994, protect your rights to support as well as your rights under the property settlement. If you have concerns about this kind of situation, consult your attorney.

Suppose that under the settlement agreement you are supposed to receive one of the family cars, a 1994 Mustang, and that the car is financed through the Smallville Savings Bank for 36 months. At the time of your divorce, neither you nor your spouse will have the title to the car—the bank will. Your spouse won't be able to sign over the car title to you for two more years.

Most divorce decrees contain a provision for what happens if a deed or car title doesn't get signed or if an important document gets lost or destroyed. If your former spouse is planning to leave the area after the divorce or if you have other concerns about enforcing the terms of the agreement, discuss them with your attorney before your divorce is finalized.

The Least You Need To Know

➤ Courts in community-property states try to divide all of a couple's assets equally between them; equitable-distribution states base the division of property on a long list of factors and try to reach a fair solution.

➤ Negotiating a settlement with your spouse is preferable to going to trial because it keeps your legal fees down and gives you both more control over the process.

➤ Before any negotiations begin, you and your spouse should prepare a detailed monthly budget and a complete list of your assets, property, and debts.

➤ Refusing to comply with the terms of a property settlement after they're made part of the final court order can make you liable for contempt of court.

Chapter 10

No Visible Means of Support: Alimony and Child Support

In This Chapter

➤ How a court decides spousal-support issues

➤ The tax consequences of spousal and child support

➤ How child support is determined

➤ When the obligation of support ends

This part of the book has described how the divorce process works and discussed the different ways in which property can be divided. Another major concern for most divorcing couples is the issue of spousal and child support. For some families, this issue may be the most important because it has a direct impact on day-to-day life after the divorce.

As with the topics discussed in earlier chapters, state law on this issue differs, and you have to consult an attorney in your area for help with specific questions. This chapter, however, introduces you to the basics.

The Cost of Leaving

One fairly common major misconception about spousal support is that it's some kind of automatic right. Years ago maybe it was, because it was usually presumed that a wife would have to be supported all or most of her life. She was the homemaker; her husband was the breadwinner.

As society changed, however, and as more and more women entered the work force and the earning capacity of women began to equal that of men, the law also changed. Two obvious results of this change appear directly in the divorce statutes. One change in the laws is that they are now written in neutral terms, referring only to the "spouse" rather than to the "wife." The second major change is that many states have eliminated the term "alimony" and replaced it with "maintenance" or "spousal support."

Legal Pitfalls

As discussed earlier in this book, in a few states fault can still play a role when the court determines spousal support. These states make fault a significant factor in setting the support amount, just as they do in dividing property. The discussion in the rest of this chapter doesn't apply to these states.

These changes are more than just semantics, and many states have completely rewritten their support statutes. These states have new standards for when support should be awarded, new rules for determining the amount, and limits on how long the support obligation lasts.

How a Court Decides the Issue of Spousal Support

If the facts of a case indicate that a spouse needs some sort of monetary support, the court will award that spouse maintenance, usually on a short-term or limited basis. The support order normally runs just long enough for the spouse to get back on his or her feet and reestablish financial self-sufficiency.

This type of support, often referred to as *rehabilitative maintenance*, encourages a nonworking spouse to get back into the work force and become self-sufficient. One of its advantages is that it can be tailored to fit the facts of each specific case. When the court is deciding on the amount and duration of support, it can consider a variety of factors, including the spouse's age, health, education, earning capacity, work experience, and share of the property split. It's not unusual, for example, for a spouse who has been a full-time homemaker to need a greater amount of support for a longer time than a spouse who has been working part-time as a real estate broker during the marriage.

No rules are etched in stone for a court to look at when it decides how much spousal support to award. As you learned in this section, a court doesn't use a percentage or a formula to determine support; instead, it considers a variety of factors in making its decision. If spousal support (either paying it or receiving it) is an issue in your divorce, ask your attorney for guidance about how much you should ask for and how much you're likely to receive.

Be sure to provide your attorney with detailed financial information (budgets, pay stubs, and tax returns, for example) about both you and your spouse so that your attorney can properly evaluate your situation. Chapter 9 has more information about getting your records together for your attorney.

Tip
Even in states that don't recognize rehabilitative maintenance, an order of spousal support is still normally subject to certain limitations. A court usually will reconsider a support order, for example, if one or both parties have a substantial change of circumstances, such as remarriage. See Chapter 12 for more information about terminating and modifying support orders.

OOOOOH...

Ways in Which Spousal Support Can Be Paid

Many divorce settlements call for support payments to be made on a biweekly or monthly basis. This arrangement is fine as long as your spouse keeps up with the payments, but if she doesn't, you have to enforce the support order just as you would any other civil judgment. These enforcement proceedings can include putting a lien on real estate, garnishing wages, or getting a court order to turn over a bank account. See Chapter 4 for more information about enforcing a judgment.

Even if you're successful, enforcing a support order can be a real pain. To avoid enforcement problems, you may want to negotiate a lump-sum payment of support

Legal Pitfalls
Lest we forget the IRS in all of this, the tax code says that alimony (but *not* child-support) payments are income deductions for the payor and income for the recipient. That much sounds simple, but various additional rules apply regarding the form of payment, the timing of the payments, and what language must be included in your divorce decree. Talk to your attorney or accountant about the way support payments will affect your income-tax liability.

JAIL
CAUTION

from your spouse or require that your spouse post a bond or other collateral guaranteeing his scheduled payments. Your attorney can help you figure out the best way to protect your interests.

And While You Have Your Wallet Open...

Unlike spousal support, child support is a much more uniform area of the law. Each state, in fact, has statutory guidelines to be used in calculating the proper amount of support. These formulas are based on percentages of net income, although the exact percentages vary from state to state.

The percentages and formulas set out by statute carry a great deal of weight, but the court can still exercise a good deal of discretion in deciding child support. If there are important factors that would justify deviating from the standard guidelines, the court has the power to rule accordingly. If your child had a serious medical condition, for example, the court can award you a larger amount to help you pay the additional medical bills.

Because both parents have a legal obligation to support their child, the court can look at other factors in reaching a decision about child support. In addition to using the law's guidelines as a starting point, the court can consider the financial resources of the child, the standard of living the child would have enjoyed if the marriage had not been dissolved, and the financial resources of both parents.

Back to the subject of taxes, child support is not deductible by the payor and is not considered income to the recipient. But the issue of who gets to claim the child as a dependency exemption often comes up. The IRS says that the presumption is that the custodial parent gets the exemption, but you should know that under IRS definitions the "custodial parent" is simply the parent the child lived with for more than half the year. The IRS definition is obviously based only on the amount of time the child lives with you rather than on the time the child lives with your former spouse. This parent may or may not be the same one who is named the "custodial parent" under your divorce decree. Under IRS rules, if you're a custodial parent, you can use IRS Form 8332 to waive the exemption for one year, certain specified years, or all future years.

Form **8332**	**Release of Claim to Exemption**	OMB No. 1545-0915
(Rev. March 1993)	**for Child of Divorced or Separated Parents**	Expires 3-31-96
Department of the Treasury Internal Revenue Service	ATTACH to noncustodial parent's return each year exemption claimed.	Attachment Sequence No. **51**
Name(s) of parent claiming exemption		Social security number

Part I   Release of Claim to Exemption for Current Year

I agree not to claim an exemption for_____

Name(s) of child (or children)

for the tax year 19_____ .

_____ | |
Signature of parent releasing claim to exemption   Social security number   Date

If you choose not to claim an exemption for this child (or children) for future tax years, complete Part II.

Part II   Release of Claim to Exemption for Future Years *(If completed, see **Noncustodial Parent** below.)*

I agree not to claim an exemption for_____

Name(s) of child (or children)

for the tax year(s)_____ .

(Specify. See instructions.)

_____ | |
Signature of parent releasing claim to exemption   Social security number   Date

General Instructions

Paperwork Reduction Act Notice.—We ask for the information on this form to carry out the Internal Revenue laws of the United States. You are required to give us the information. We need it to ensure that you are complying with these laws and to allow us to figure and collect the right amount of tax.

The time needed to complete and file this form will vary depending on individual circumstances. The estimated average time is: **Recordkeeping,** 7 min.; **Learning about the law or the form,** 5 min.; **Preparing the form,** 7 min.; and **Copying, assembling, and sending the form to the IRS,** 14 min.

If you have comments concerning the accuracy of these time estimates or suggestions for making this form more simple, we would be happy to hear from you. You can write to both the IRS and the Office of Management and Budget at the addresses listed in the instructions for the return with which this form is filed.

Purpose of Form.—If you are a **custodial parent,** you may use this form to release your claim to your child's exemption. To do so, complete this form and give it to the **noncustodial parent** who will claim the child's exemption. Then, the noncustodial parent must attach this form or a similar statement to his or her tax return each year the exemption is claimed.

You are the **custodial parent** if you had custody of the child for most of the year. You are the **noncustodial parent** if you had custody for a shorter period of time or did not have custody at all.

Instead of using this form, you (the custodial parent) may use a similar

statement as long as it contains the same information required by this form.

Children of Divorced or Separated Parents.—Special rules apply to determine if the support test is met for children of parents who are divorced or legally separated under a decree of divorce or separate maintenance or separated under a written separation agreement. The rules also apply to children of parents who did not live together at any time during the last 6 months of the year, even if they do not have a separation agreement.

The general rule is that the custodial parent is treated as having provided over half of the child's support if:

1. The child received over half of his or her total support for the year from both of the parents, **AND**

2. The child was in the custody of one or both of his or her parents for more than half of the year.

Note: *Public assistance payments, such as Aid to Families with Dependent Children, are not support provided by the parents.*

If both 1 and 2 above apply, and the other four dependency tests in the instructions for Form 1040 or Form 1040A are also met, the custodial parent can claim the child's exemption.

Exception. The general rule does not apply if **any** of the following applies:

• The custodial parent agrees not to claim the child's exemption by signing this form or similar statement. The noncustodial parent **must** attach this form or similar statement to his or her tax return for the tax year. See **Custodial Parent** later.

• The child is treated as having received over half of his or her total support from a

person under a multiple support agreement **(Form 2120,** Multiple Support Declaration).

• A pre-1985 divorce decree or written separation agreement states that the noncustodial parent can claim the child as a dependent. But the noncustodial parent must provide at least $600 for the child's support during the year. The noncustodial parent must also check the box on line 6d of Form 1040 or Form 1040A. This rule does not apply if the decree or agreement was changed after 1984 to say that the noncustodial parent cannot claim the child as a dependent.

Additional Information.—For more details, get **Pub. 504,** Divorced or Separated Individuals.

Specific Instructions

Custodial Parent.—You may agree to release your claim to the child's exemption for the current tax year or for future years, or both.

• Complete **Part I** if you agree to release your claim to the child's exemption for the current tax year.

• Complete **Part II** if you agree to release your claim to the child's exemption for any or all future years. If you do, write the specific future year(s) or "all future years" in the space provided in Part II.

Noncustodial Parent.—Attach Form 8332 or a similar statement to your tax return for the tax year in which you claim the child's exemption. You may claim the exemption **only** if the other four dependency tests in the Form 1040 or Form 1040A instructions are met.

Note: *If the custodial parent completed Part II, you **must** attach a copy of this form to your tax return for each future year in which you claim the exemption.*

*U.S. Government Printing Office: 1994 — 387-095/00303   Cat. No. 13910F   Form **8332** (Rev. 3-93)*

If the parent with custody of the child signs and provides this form to the noncustodial parent, the noncustodial parent may claim the child (or children) as a dependent.

You can sometimes use the dependency exemption as a bargaining chip when you negotiate a divorce settlement, because it is often more valuable to one spouse than to the other. Before you negotiate this point, get some professional advice from your attorney or accountant.

Does It Ever End?

Statutorily, the obligation to pay child support ends when your child reaches the age of 18 unless special circumstances justify an extension of the obligation. Your divorce decree can also specify certain events that would terminate the obligation of support: for example, the child's permanent move from the custodial parent's house. Your attorney can tell you what's customary in your area.

This general rule that the duty of support ends at age 18 may be changing. Although it's not technically considered child support, recently enacted laws in some states may require divorced parents to make financial contributions toward the cost of their child's college education. Each of the states that have this type of "college expense" statute has slightly different rules about when the obligation to contribute exists and how the amount of contribution is calculated. Contact your attorney to see what the rules are in your state.

It is important to note that your obligation to pay child support does not end if you die, and it's common for payor spouses to buy a life insurance policy as security for their child-support obligations. If you don't have this type of policy, be aware that your child can make a claim against your estate for unpaid child support. A claim of this type against your estate can cause huge problems if you die after remarrying.

The Least You Need To Know

➤ You generally have no automatic right to long-term alimony, but you may be able to get an award of rehabilitative maintenance.

➤ Maintenance is used primarily to help a spouse return to the work force and become financially independent again.

➤ Spousal support raises income-tax liability questions, and child support can create a question about which spouse is entitled to take the dependency exemption.

➤ The obligation to pay child support usually ends when the child reaches age 18; however, your state may have laws concerning your obligation to contribute toward a college education.

NOW, YOU GET 3 ADDITIONAL WEEKS IN THE SUMMER IN EXCHANGE FOR CHRISTMAS.

Chapter 11

Solomon Had the Same Problem: Decisions About Child Custody and Visitation

In This Chapter

➤ What custody is and the different kinds of custody that can be granted in a divorce

➤ How a court determines custody when the parents can't agree

➤ How visitation affects both parents

➤ When you can move children to another state

➤ When the courts will change an existing custody or visitation order

For many people, the most difficult issues involved in going through a divorce center around the children. Even though the roles of husband and wife may end, both divorcing people are still parents. But because of the divorce, many changes will occur in both parents' relationships with their children. It's normal for both parents to worry about how much control they'll have over how the children are raised and how much time they'll be able to spend with them after the divorce is over.

What Is "Custody," Anyway?

Legally speaking, having *custody* of your children means having the right, and the responsibility, of making all decisions concerning them. It's a broad definition, and custody issues typically include the ones in this list:

➤ Which parent the children live with.

➤ Where the children live.

➤ The school the children attend.

➤ How the children are disciplined.

➤ Choice of religious faith.

➤ All health and medical matters.

➤ Anything else that has to do with the care or control of the children.

While you and your spouse are married, you both have legal custody of your children; or to put it more simply, either one of you can make any of these kinds of decisions. Both of you, or either of you alone, can decide whether Susie needs braces or can attend Johnny's parent-teacher conference at school.

Custody is an issue that must be decided if you're getting a divorce or legal separation. The different types of custody arrangements are described in this section, but as you read about them, keep in mind that custody (like just about everything in your divorce) is negotiable. Divorcing couples normally negotiate custody issues through their respective attorneys, but you may find that you and your spouse can work out some of these issues directly between yourselves. There's generally no problem with that method, but avoid signing any formal agreements and don't make any final decisions or commitments until you've had a chance to consult with your attorney. It will save you money, time, and emotional energy if you and your spouse can communicate well enough to negotiate parts of your divorce settlement. But only your attorney can advise you about potential legal problems the agreement might present, both at the time of the divorce and years down the road.

Additionally, lawyers and judges may refer to physical custody and legal custody of the children. Physical custody simply refers to where the children live most of the time, and legal custody refers to the decision-making authority just described. Many times, if you are awarded legal custody of your children, you are also awarded physical custody, but it doesn't always happen this way. In a joint-custody situation, both you and your spouse have legal custody (or decision-making authority), but usually only one of you has physical custody.

> **Legalese**
> **Physical custody** means that a child lives with you on a day-to-day basis and is normally in your care. **Legal custody** means that you (and your spouse or both) have the right to make decisions about anything affecting the child, including such things as choice of schools, medical care, and religious training.

Sole Custody Versus Joint Custody

When a parent is awarded sole custody as part of a divorce, the court is saying that the parent has full authority over the children's lives. All decisions, large or small, about raising the children are made by that parent alone. If you're a noncustodial parent, you most likely still have the right to access all your children's school, medical, and other records, and you get to spend time with the kids (unless you're completely unfit or dangerous to them). But you don't have decision-making power over them.

> **Legalese**
> A **noncustodial parent** is one who doesn't have custody of a child. It doesn't mean that the parent can't see the child or that the parent can't be involved in the child's life and have some input about certain decisions, but it does mean that the other parent (the custodial parent) has the final authority to make decisions concerning the child.

On the other hand, joint custody allows both parents to continue to be directly involved in the children's lives. Under a *joint-custody agreement* (sometimes also called a *joint-parenting agreement*), both parents have input in raising the kids, and they make decisions together. Courts and parents alike usually prefer joint custody over sole custody because it prevents one of the parents from feeling left out of the children's lives.

It's the Law!

Remember that joint custody is a decision about legal custody (decision making). Joint custody does not mean that you and your ex-spouse share an exactly equal amount of time with the children. The vast majority of the time, one parent has physical custody of the children, and the other receives scheduled visitation time, even in a joint-custody arrangement. No matter what the custody arrangement is, courts are usually sensitive to the fact that children need a permanent home, and, generally speaking, judges will not approve an agreement that calls for the children to bounce back and forth between Mom's house and Dad's house on a weekly or monthly basis.

For example, joint custody isn't granted in cases in which there's a history of abuse, neglect, or domestic violence. And some people just can't make joint custody work because they're unable to work together, even if it's for the sake of the children.

As I'm sure your parents will tell you, it's common enough for married people to disagree on how to raise their kids. It's even more common for divorced parents to disagree. A well-drafted joint-custody agreement should contain a paragraph or two about what happens if you and your spouse just can't reach an agreement on an issue. This kind of provision normally requires you to consult with some third party about the situation in order to resolve it without having to return to court. This "someone" can be almost anyone (for example, a mediator, attorney, psychologist, member of the clergy, or even a close mutual friend). If an agreement still can't be reached, you may then bring the matter back to court and have a formal hearing on the issue.

How the Courts Make Custody Decisions

If you and your spouse can't agree on the issue of custody by simply working through your attorneys, you ultimately end up at a hearing before a judge who will make the decision for you. The hearing is sort of a minitrial, and the court hears testimony from both you and your spouse, as well as from any other witnesses. You and your attorney might even want to hire an expert witness (a psychologist, for example) to testify on your behalf. After all is said and done, the decision rests in the judge's hands.

The court's main concern is finding an arrangement that's in the best interest of the children, not one that's best for the individual parents. What is the judge looking at to help her decide? What kind of facts influence the final decision? Here's a list of some important factors the court considers:

> **Legalese**
> An **expert witness** is a person who has specialized training, education, and experience in a certain field or on a certain topic. This background gives the expert witness knowledge beyond that of the average person, and it enables her to testify and give opinions in court.

> WHAT!?

➤ The age of the children.

➤ The parents' wishes.

➤ The children's wishes (heavily dependent on how old the children are).

➤ The children's adjustment to their home, school, and community.

➤ The mental and physical health of both the parents and the children.

➤ The willingness of each parent to encourage the children's close relationship with the other parent.

➤ The work schedules of the parents and how much time each has available to care for the kids.

➤ A parent's alcohol or drug use.

➤ Anything else a court considers relevant.

You may have hesitated at that last item—anything that's "relevant." It means that the court can consider any facts that it believes may have an effect on the children. It opens the door, of course, to all kinds of things, including a look at the parents' personal lives and their lifestyles. It can also open the door to long, expensive court hearings on the issue of custody, maybe even requiring expert witnesses, such as psychiatrists and psychologists.

Legal Pitfalls
If you plan to fight for custody in court, don't do it without a lawyer. Courts can vary substantially on what should and shouldn't be considered in making a custody determination, and a family-law attorney in your area can help you evaluate your case before you begin. Additionally, it's possible that you'll need the opinion of a psychologist or other expert to establish your case.

Before you begin custody litigation, think about the effect it will have on you and your children, the expense involved, and the fact that you will be asking a stranger to decide your family's fate. You may want to try mediation or some other type of negotiation before committing yourself to a courtroom battle. In some areas, in fact, the court may order you and your spouse to mediation before it will allow your case to proceed. (See Chapter 5 for more information about how the mediation process works.)

Living with the Decision

Suppose that your divorce case has just ended. You probably think that everything is settled just because you have a copy of the decree in your hand. But people and circumstances change, and you may find yourself rethinking custody and visitation issues as time goes on. Remember that you and your spouse will be dealing with these things for a long time to come, at least until your youngest child turns 18.

This section looks at the issues and problems that typically come up after a divorce and describes things you can do to handle them more effectively.

It's a Nice Place To Visit

One parent, even in a joint-custody situation, will probably still have visitation. Visitation schedules should be fairly specific so that you, your spouse, and the children have some certainty in your lives. On the other hand, don't make the schedule so rigid that it doesn't allow for all the little problems that come up in everyday life—an extra soccer practice, a late business meeting, or a flat tire on the way home, for example.

Although it should be a fairly straightforward thing, many parents have serious misconceptions about visitation. Here are the three most common misconceptions you should be aware of and avoid indulging in:

➤ **"He (she) didn't pay child support last month, so I don't have to let him (her) see the kids until he (she) pays up."** Child support and visitation are completely separate terms in your divorce decree, and each obligation is independent of the other. You can't withhold visitation because of a late child-support check. Refusing to let visitation take place is legally a violation of the court's order, just as the failure to pay support is. If your former spouse brings the case back to court, you can be found in contempt.

➤ **"Let's use the standard visitation schedule."** Visitation is a completely negotiable issue between the parties, and you can develop whatever schedule fits your family's needs. There is no "standard schedule," and you shouldn't assume that the visitation schedule your neighbor uses is the same one you should use. People often do use a schedule of every other weekend, one evening during each week, alternating major holidays, and an extended period (two to six weeks) during the children's summer vacation, but this schedule is not etched in stone. You should look at it as a starting point and really think about what schedule would work best in your family's specific situation.

➤ **"My ex-spouse is always out on dates and never spends any time with the kids. I'll go back to court and force him (her) to use the visitation time."** As painful as it may be to accept, you can't force someone to use visitation time. Even more frustrating to most people is that you can't deny all visitation to a parent who has chosen to use it only occasionally in the past.

Moving the Kids to Another State

In today's job market, it's not uncommon for a person to be suddenly transferred out of state. Other people decide to move out of state for personal reasons. If you're the former spouse of one of these people and he or she has physical custody of your children, you're obviously going to have many concerns about how the move will affect your access to the kids. A parent with physical custody can move out of state with the children in one of two ways:

➤ Both parties can agree in writing to the move.

➤ The moving parent can petition the court for permission to move.

Tip
If there's any chance that you might be leaving the state in which you live, talk to your attorney about it while your divorce is still pending. That way, the attorney can make provisions for out-of-state moves directly in the settlement agreement. If you do end up moving later, everyone will know what the rules are, and you may be able to avoid a return trip to court.

However it's done, an out-of-state move involves many decisions. For example, how will the noncustodial parent exercise visitation? Who pays the airfare, lodging, and other expenses of cross-country visitation? Are there other ways for the parent who's left behind to keep an active role in the children's lives? These questions are difficult to answer, and often they require creative solutions.

Can you ask the court to block your spouse's move? In a word, no. Your spouse is free to move wherever she wishes and for whatever reason. You can, however, ask the court to stop the removal of your children. I'm not talking about letting your "ex" move from the state— just leaving your kids behind. If the court refuses to allow the kids to move, the court will probably also order a change in the custody and visitation arrangements so that the kids end up staying with the parent who's remaining in the state.

If a court is asked to decide this issue, it will probably look at the following factors:

➤ What are the chances that the move will improve the quality of life for both the moving parent and the children? For example, is your spouse moving to take advantage of a great job opportunity with better pay and benefits?

➤ Why does the parent want to move? Is it just to get away and start over? Is it a job requirement? Or is it just to prevent you from seeing your kids frequently?

➤ Why are you fighting the move? Are you really afraid that you'll lose all contact with your kids, or is it just out of spite or concern that the child-support payments will go up or down?

➤ What's the current visitation schedule, and how have you both followed it in the past? Do you take advantage of every opportunity to see the kids, or have you exercised visitation only when it was convenient for you?

➤ Can a reasonable visitation schedule be set up if the move takes place? For example, can you trade frequent, short visitations for fewer but longer ones? Will longer visits over the summer and holiday breaks make up for lost weekend visits?

More than any of these factors, though, the court always focuses on what's in the best interest of the children.

As a final note, removing children from the state really affects visitation. Custody, on the other hand, might not be affected at all. If you have joint custody, you still have the right to participate in decisions affecting your children, even if they live in another state. Your former spouse will still need to keep you up to date on such things as school, religious training, and medical and dental problems, and you will continue to help decide what happens in these areas.

Legal Pitfalls
Sometimes people change the way they're handling custody and visitation issues without going through the courts—they just ignore the terms of their divorce decree and do what they want informally. Everybody has to bend the rules occasionally, and it's not wrong to try to accommodate each person's schedule. But if you find that you're bending the rules all the time, get your divorce decree modified. Otherwise, you may end up back in court if a dispute develops, arguing about what should be given priority—the written divorce decree or the pattern you've established by your actions.

Changing an Existing Custody Order

Life would be much easier if you could just call the psychic hotline and find out how the decisions made during your divorce will affect you and your children down the road. Unfortunately, you can't. Find out, I mean. (You can still call if you have an extra $18.50 per minute.)

The point is that it's not uncommon for people to find out ten, five, or even one year after their divorce that something in the original agreement doesn't seem to work as well as it should. Can you change the custody or visitation terms of your divorce decree in situations like this? Generally you can, but, like many other things discussed in this book, the courts in each state differ on the question of which facts are enough to justify the change.

You and your spouse will probably be able to change the original order with little difficulty if you both agree on the change to be made, but, depending on your state's laws, you have to talk to an attorney if one of you disagrees. For example, some states do not allow a change in custody for two years after the divorce unless the children are in serious danger, either physically, emotionally, mentally, or morally. After the first two years have passed, these courts may allow a change if there has been a significant change in circumstances and it's in the best interest of the children to modify the existing order.

The Least You Need To Know

➤ Having legal custody means having the right to make all the decisions about your children's lives. Having physical custody means that your children live most of the time with you.

➤ Joint custody means that decisions about your children are made by both parents. It doesn't mean that the children will spend equal amounts of time with you and your ex-spouse.

➤ Visitation rights are separate from all the other terms of your divorce. You can't refuse to allow visitation because your spouse hasn't paid support, and, conversely, your spouse can't refuse to pay support because you withheld visitation.

➤ Courts will allow children to be removed from the state under certain circumstances. Your attorney can advise you on your state's laws.

➤ Courts will allow modification of custody and visitation orders, but states vary on when modification is allowed. Again, consult an attorney to find out whether you have grounds to change an existing order.

Chapter 12

It Ain't Over 'til It's Over: After Your Divorce

> **In This Chapter**
>
> ➤ How to handle a former spouse who's not following the terms of your divorce decree
>
> ➤ Using government agencies to help you collect overdue child support
>
> ➤ When a court may agree to modify an existing divorce decree

Your divorce case is over, and you're holding a copy of the final divorce decree. The emotional and financial upheavals are over at last. You can finally move on, get a fresh start, and start a new life—assuming that you don't have any children, that the property division is complete, that there's no obligation to pay spousal support, and that you and your spouse don't have to file any final joint tax returns.

You and your former spouse may still have to deal with one another on a limited basis after the divorce, just to clean up all the paperwork and other loose ends. But if you have children, you can count on dealing with each other periodically, at least until your youngest child reaches age 18. This contact can, of course, be as amicable as you want to make it. You probably can handle most situations after your divorce, but there is always the chance that you'll end up back in court if something serious happens.

Divorced couples return to court usually for one of two reasons:

➤ One party accuses the other of not obeying the divorce decree.

➤ A significant change has occurred in your life or in your ex-spouse's life, and now one of you wants the decree modified.

This chapter looks at both of these situations.

Handling the Difficult "Ex"

A person can violate the terms of a divorce decree in many ways. A husband may stubbornly refuse to sign over a car title; a wife may unreasonably refuse to cooperate with scheduled visitations. The list of potential problems is endless. How can you best protect yourself?

If your divorce has not been finalized, begin by expressing your concerns to your attorney. Tell her where you expect problems, and ask to structure the settlement agreement accordingly. See whether you can build in to the agreement some penalties for noncompliance; for example, your agreement could specify that if it becomes necessary for one spouse to return to court to enforce the decree, that person can recover from the other spouse any additional court costs and attorney's fees. Or, as you learned in Chapter 10, you may be able to structure the agreement so that it requires your former spouse to post a bond or some other type of collateral in order to guarantee compliance.

It's also a good idea to try to comply with as many settlement terms as possible before your divorce case is over. You can usually perform simple tasks (such as arranging for lump-sum payments, closing charge-card accounts, paying off joint debts, changing bank accounts, and signing deeds) while your divorce case is still pending. The more you accomplish before the decree is signed, the less you have to fight about later. Uncooperative spouses are usually easier to deal with while the case is pending because they often feel that the judge is "watching."

If problems develop after your divorce, you can proceed in different ways. Regardless of what you do, remember that you'll be asked to prove your claims, so be prepared to document the problems you're having.

For example, you can establish a paper trail in several ways: by confirming in writing any verbal agreements or other communications with your "ex," by using certified or registered mail when you send things to your former spouse, and by always using checks rather than cash whenever money changes hands between you and your "ex." For problems with visitation, consider bringing along a friend or relative when you pick up or drop off your kids. A neutral third party sometimes can calm a tense situation and can also serve as a witness if your case ever goes back to court.

If your efforts to resolve a problem fail, follow these guidelines:

➤ **Contact your attorney.** Even if you can't get through to your former spouse, your attorney might be able to. Ask your attorney to begin with a polite but firm letter or telephone call, and see whether there's a way to make some progress.

➤ **Use mediation.** Your divorce decree may describe some sort of dispute-resolution procedure, but if it doesn't, you may want to consider using a mediator to help resolve the problem. Although this service isn't free, it probably is cheaper than going back to court. It's also usually less traumatic than going through more court appearances. For more information about mediation, refer to Chapter 5.

➤ **Ask the court for help.** Remember that your divorce decree is a court order and that violation of its terms may put your spouse in contempt of court. Your lawyer can help you decide whether you should take this step.

Here's the most important thing *not* to do: *Don't retaliate against your "ex" by violating the decree yourself.* Refusing to allow visitation, for example, because your former spouse didn't send a monthly child-support check only makes matters worse. With this type of behavior, you give the court a basis to find you in contempt along with your spouse, you lose any sympathy the court may have felt for your problem, and you still won't have the child support you're owed.

If Support Isn't Being Paid

As you learned in Chapter 11, if your former spouse is not making the required maintenance payments, you have to try to collect the delinquent amounts in the same way as you would try to enforce any other judgment. You can enforce child-support obligations in this way, but additional resources are available to you as well.

Under Subchapter IV, Part D (or "IV-D") of the Social Security Act, the federal government appropriates money and other resources to state agencies so that these agencies can provide parents with assistance in obtaining and enforcing child-support orders. Each state administers its IV-D (pronounced "4-D") program in a slightly different way, so you have to contact your state's attorney's office or its Department of Public Aid for information about how to obtain this assistance in your state. These agencies provide their services free of charge to anyone, and the services are available regardless of your income level.

Whether child-support enforcement is pursued privately or through a IV-D agency, the problem can become even more difficult if the parents live in different states. The Uniform Reciprocal Enforcement of Support Act (URESA) now enables you to enforce a child-support order against someone in another state. The current process is slow and confusing, and there's been a continuing push in state legislatures and in Congress to make child-support enforcement easier.

At this writing, Congress is working on the Uniform Interstate Family Support Act (UIFSA), which, if passed, would make it significantly easier to enforce child-support orders across state lines. Many states have already adopted their own modified versions of UIFSA, but if it becomes a federal law, procedures in all states would be the same. Another significant feature of UIFSA is that it can be used to enforce spousal-support orders.

OOOOOH…

Tip
If you use the services of one of these government agencies, don't expect a miracle. A IV-D agency will try to enforce the child-support order, but the process takes time. The agency probably has thousands of cases, so you shouldn't expect results overnight. It can be frustrating dealing with this system, but keep in mind that the system you're dealing with is on your side.

Change Is the Only Constant

People don't return to court only because they're having problems enforcing the terms of their divorce decree. They may return to court and ask that their divorce decree be modified because of a major change that has taken place.

Whether a court agrees to modify part of your divorce decree depends largely on the basis of your request. If a substantial change in circumstances has occurred, the court is more likely to approve the change.

If you find out that your child has a learning disability and will have to attend special classes, for example, you would be justified in asking a court to increase the amount of child support you receive based on your child's special needs. On the other hand, if you ask the court to increase the amount of child support because inflation rose last year, you probably won't get the increase.

Legal Pitfalls

Only certain portions of a divorce decree can be changed at a later date. Typically, only the provisions dealing with child custody, visitation, child support, and spousal support can be modified after a divorce is final. All other provisions, including the property settlement, are not subject to later modification.

Modifications aren't always increases; support payments can also be lowered in appropriate situations. If your ex-spouse gets laid off and is working only part-time until a better job is available, for example, she can ask the court to temporarily lower the amount of the child-support payments.

It's the Law!

If you're under an order to pay support, don't make any payment changes without getting a new court order, even if your former spouse agrees to the changes. The clerk of the court and some government agencies keep track of support arrearages, and they won't know about any private agreements you have with your "ex." Side agreements and cash payments that don't go through proper channels will cause incorrect arrearages to appear on your records. This in turn can result in credit problems and even the forfeiture of your income-tax refund.

The Least You Need To Know

➤ You can use a variety of ways to deal with a former spouse who won't comply with the terms of a divorce decree. The most drastic way is to return to court and ask the judge to hold the person in contempt of court.

➤ Your local IV-D program can help you enforce a child-support order.

➤ Some portions of your decree can be modified after your divorce, if you can show that there's been a substantial change in circumstances.

Part 3
Dollars and Common Sense

After family, what's the next biggest area of concern for most people? You got it on the first try: money. This part of the book deals with a variety of money-related issues: from applying for your first credit card to filing bankruptcy; from getting a job to retirement. And, of course, we can't leave out a look at that venerable government institution, the IRS.

This part of the book doesn't tell you how to manage your money—plenty of good books on the market can teach you how to do that, especially The Complete Idiot's Guide to Managing Your Money, *by Robert K. Heady and Christy Heady (published by Alpha Books). This part of the book tells you about your legal rights and gives you some practical advice for dealing with creditors, employers, and, yes, the tax man.*

(And to any Internal Revenue Service agents who read this book, I want simply, as a citizen, to thank you for the fine work you do.)

To Your Credit

In This Chapter

➤ What a creditor can consider when you apply for credit

➤ What your credit report says about you

➤ How to fix problems and mistakes in your credit report

➤ What to do about common credit-card problems

Unless you've been stranded on a remote desert island for the past decade, you know that it's becoming more and more difficult to function in today's society without using credit cards and other credit accounts. And "credit" doesn't just mean those little pieces of plastic in your wallet. It includes long-term financing, such as car loans and home mortgages. As the volume of credit transactions increases, so does the number of federal and state regulations regarding credit. And even though most of those regulations and laws are designed to protect us as consumers, many people are not aware of the credit rights they do have or how to exercise them.

This chapter explains how you can make the most of your credit opportunities and how to deal with credit-report mistakes and credit-card problems when they occur.

Your Rights When You Apply for Credit

When you apply for credit, two federal laws (and probably your state's laws) protect you from unfair treatment. The two federal laws are the Equal Credit Opportunity Act and the Fair Credit Reporting Act. The first law, the Equal Credit Opportunity Act (ECOA), is geared toward protecting consumers by stopping discrimination by creditors. According to the ECOA, you cannot be denied credit or be discouraged from applying for credit because of the following factors:

➤ Your gender.

➤ Your race, color, or national origin.

➤ Your religion.

➤ Your marital status.

➤ Your age.

➤ The fact that you receive public assistance as part of your income.

When you apply for credit, you generally should get an answer from the creditor within 30 days of making your application. If your application is approved, you might get a letter notifying you, but you'll probably just receive your new credit card in the mail. If the creditor denies your application, the creditor must provide you with a written denial letter. That letter must contain the following information:

➤ A statement reminding you that federal law prohibits discrimination in granting credit.

➤ The name and address of the appropriate government agency that enforces the ECOA.

➤ The specific reason your application was denied.

Most of the time, a denial letter says that your application was denied because of information in your credit report. If you think that you've been discriminated against, you should contact the Federal Trade

Commission (FTC), which is the government agency that enforces the ECOA. The denial letter you receive from the creditor may tell you which FTC office to contact, but you can also locate the nearest district office by checking your telephone book, under Government Offices—Federal or a similar heading. The agency will help you make a complaint and investigate your claim. If the evidence supports your claim, the creditor may be fined or punished in some other way, but be aware that the government agency will not file a discrimination suit on your behalf. You have to hire your own attorney if you want to bring a private action against the creditor.

This Is Your (Financial) Life!

Although I'm sure that your mother has always told you what an honest face you have, that's not enough to get you credit. A creditor's only concern is that you can repay the money you owe, so before you can sign on the dotted line for that new car, computer system, or stereo, the creditor understandably wants to know something about you. And the way it finds out about you is by reviewing your credit report.

Items that normally appear on your credit report include the names of your current creditors, the credit lines (amounts) available to you, the amount you owe each creditor, your late payments, debts that have been sent to collection, prior bankruptcies, and the highest balance you've had on each account. Obviously, it's important that the information provided in your credit report is accurate and fairly reported. That's where the second important federal law comes in—the Fair Credit Reporting Act (FCRA).

> **WHAT!?**
>
> **Legal Pitfalls**
> A **credit report** is a detailed summary of your credit history. The report is prepared by a private agency that gathers information about you from your current and past creditors as well as from such sources as court files and other public records.

The FCRA regulates how credit bureaus prepare and distribute credit reports. This law protects you in these important ways:

➤ **The FCRA regulates who has access to your credit report.** You can obtain a copy, and so can someone with a legitimate business interest (a creditor considering your loan application, an employer, or an insurance underwriter, for example). Your nosy neighbor, however, can't see your report.

➤ **Credit reports can contain only relevant, timely information.** Most negative information on your credit report, such as late payments, defaults, and collections, can be reported for as long as seven years, and then it must be removed from your report. The exception is a bankruptcy, which can be reported for as long as ten years before it must be removed.

➤ **You have the right to challenge mistakes.** If you see incorrect information in your report, you have the right to—and you should—have it removed or corrected. See the next section for information about how to ask for corrections.

How To Find and Fix Mistakes in Your Credit Report

You've seen that the FCRA gives you the right to get a copy of your credit report and to have incorrect information corrected or taken off. Mistakes are more common than you might think, and you might be surprised at what's on your report. The last time I checked mine, the credit bureau had my previous home address and my employer's name wrong, and it listed a charge account as open when it had been closed for four years. These errors were relatively harmless, but the lesson is clear: Make sure that you review your credit report every year or two, just to be safe.

Tip
When you're getting ready to buy a home, car, or other large item, make sure that you review your credit report before making the loan application. That way, you have time to find and fix any errors before they can cause problems with your purchase.

You can order a copy of your credit report at any time. I've listed three of the largest credit-reporting agencies next, but you should be able to find others in your area by looking in the Yellow Pages. Some agencies provide you with one free report per year, but most of them charge anywhere between $2 and $20 per report. Each agency may have different (correct or incorrect) information. You don't know which of the three a creditor will use, so you should make sure that all three are correct.

➤ **Trans Union:** P.O. Box 390, Springfield, PA 19064; (312) 408-1050.

➤ **TRW:** P.O. Box 2350, Chatsworth, CA 91313; (800) 392-1122.

➤ **Equifax:** P.O. Box 740241, Atlanta, GA 30374; (800) 685-1111.

Your request for a report must be in writing and have your signature on it. (A simple letter will do.) It should also include your full name, Social Security number, current address, telephone number, and the name of your current employer. Call the credit-reporting company before sending your request to find out the cost of a report (you have to send a check or money order along with your request) and to see whether any other information is required in order to process your request.

Tip
If you have been denied credit because of negative information in your credit report, you are entitled to a free copy of the report used by the creditor. The creditor's denial letter tells you where to write for your copy.

OOOOOH...

You should receive your report within 30 days. When I saw my first credit report, I was surprised by its format. It looked like a cross between something off King Tut's tomb and a physics formula. It had columns—lots of columns. Some columns contained dollar amounts, some had number codes, and others were filled with letter codes and abbreviations. The report included a separate sheet that explained the abbreviations and codes, all 65 or so of them. It took a while, but I finally figured out what the report said about my credit. You'll probably be a little overwhelmed by the amount of data in your report, too. Just take your time when you're reviewing it, and keep a list of mistakes you see and questions you have. If you get stuck, review the instruction sheets again, or call the company's customer-service department.

You also receive with your report some specific directions for how to challenge information in the report. Under law, you have the right to request that account information be reverified and then corrected or removed from the report if appropriate. If information is corrected or removed, you can ask the company to send the updated information to any company that has received a copy of your report within the last year. Again, all of this must be done in writing.

A letter to a credit-reporting agency can help correct information.

TransUnion Credit Reporting
P.O. Box 390
Springfield, PA 19064

Re: Social Security # 333-33-3333

Your file # 11786WW

Dear Sir or Madam:

On May 10, I received notice that my application for a MasterCard from American Bank was denied. I requested a copy of my credit report from your company, and, after reviewing it, I found the following errors contained in the report:

1. My previous home address is shown as 1234 Pine Street; the correct address, however, was 1244 Pine Street.

2. My middle initial is *T,* not *E.*

3. There is a reference to a charge account with Sears, but I never opened such an account.

4. The VISA account listed on the report was paid in full on October 1, 1993, and the account was closed at that time. Your report says that the account is open.

5. The report refers to a judgment against me in the amount of $2,000; however, I know of no such judgment. In fact, I have never been sued.

Please review the information contained in my report and make the necessary corrections. If you need verification of any information, please contact me so that I can provide you with whatever documentation you need.

Very truly yours,

Robert T. Jones

What if negative information in the report is correct but you have a good explanation? For example, some of your credit-card payments may have been late because you were going through a divorce or because you were hospitalized. Each credit-reporting service has a way for you to add your own written explanations to your credit report. The instructions for how to prepare and send in your statement of explanation come with your report. Usually, the statement cannot consist of more than 100 words; and remember that those words are very important. They'll be read by people trying to decide whether to give you credit, so make sure that your explanation is concise, honest, and clear.

Handling Common Credit-Card Problems

You've read about how the ECOA and FCRA work to protect you when you apply for credit, but another federal law protects you after you've received credit. The Truth In Lending Act (TILA) requires that you be provided with an accurate and meaningful disclosure about the terms of your credit. TILA applies to almost all consumer-credit transactions.

A consumer-credit transaction is simply a transaction in which an individual buys something for personal or household purposes and the payment is subject to a finance charge, or payable in multiple installments. If you finance the purchase of a computer for your office, for example, it's not considered a consumer-credit transaction; if you finance the purchase of a new refrigerator for your home, however, it is.

In addition to many other things, TILA requires a creditor to tell you the following information:

➤ The interest rate you're being charged.

➤ Your current account balance and how it was calculated.

➤ Whether the interest rate can vary and, if so, how it is calculated.

➤ How monthly finance charges are calculated.

➤ What other fees you may be charged, such as annual "membership" fees, late-payment fees, over-the-credit-limit fees, and returned-check fees.

➤ What your billing rights are and where to write if you find billing errors in your account.

You can receive statutory damages if a creditor is in violation of TILA, but because this statute is complex, you need an attorney to help you decide whether this type of claim is worth pursuing.

In addition to the disclosures just described, TILA protects you in two other common situations: unauthorized credit-card use and problems with defective merchandise. If your card is stolen and you report it to the company that issued the card, your maximum liability for unauthorized charges under the law is $50. And regarding defective merchandise, you can usually withhold payment for a product or service if you can't resolve the matter directly with the store.

Suppose that you buy a top-of-the-line tent from Crazy Chuck's Out-door Equipment and pay for it by using your MasterCard. On your first night in the tent, mosquitoes quickly chew their way through the mesh tent screen and then through you. A late-night rain shower reveals that the tent seams leak, and after it gets wet, you notice that the tent gives off an unusual (and disgusting) smell. After returning home, you tell Chuck that he *is* crazy if he thinks that you're paying for that tent, but he still doesn't issue you a refund or credit.

Unfortunately for Crazy Chuck, TILA says that if the following condi-tions exist, you can withhold your payment:

➤ The amount in dispute exceeds $50.

➤ The purchase took place in the state in which you live, or within 100 miles of where you live.

➤ You've made a good-faith attempt to settle the matter with the store.

The $50 minimum and the geographic conditions don't apply if you used a credit card issued by the store. So in this example, these condi-tions don't apply if you used your Crazy Chuck's Gold Card rather than your MasterCard to pay for the tent. You could withhold payment for the tent as long as you met the last condition (attempting to settle the dispute in good faith). As you'll see later in this section, you can continue to withhold your payment until your dispute over the mer-chandise is resolved.

To begin the process, write to your credit-card company within 60 days of the date of the billing statement that shows the charge. Be sure to tell them the name of the store, the date of your purchase, and the amount you were charged, and describe the problem with the mer-chandise.

While your claim is being investigated, remember that you still have to pay for the items on your charge bill that aren't part of the dispute. If you bought $200 worth of fishing gear the day before the infamous tent purchase, you still have to pay for that purchase under your normal credit-card terms, even if you bought the gear from Crazy Chuck. You are not charged interest or finance charges on the disputed part of your bill, and it is not reported on your credit report as a late payment.

You will receive a letter from the credit-card company within 30 days, letting you know that the claim was received and telling you what it intends to do about it and about how long it should take. Don't assume at this point that you've won, though. The credit-card company will contact the store for its side of the story. The credit-card company may decide that you do owe the money—as in a case where you failed to read the large sign next to Crazy Chuck's tent display that said, "AS IS—ALL SALES FINAL!"

> **Legal Pitfalls**
> Make sure that you give the credit-card company notice in writing. You can telephone the company as a follow-up measure, but calling does not preserve your legal rights.

You can see by this example that your rights under TILA are tied to other rights you may have as a consumer. Because this chapter deals primarily with credit issues, the discussion of other consumer rights is covered in Chapter 28, which looks at warranties, "as is" sales, and other issues you can encounter when you buy merchandise. When you get to that chapter, however, keep in mind that you may have some additional rights if you bought the merchandise on credit.

The Least You Need To Know

➤ Federal law protects you from being discriminated against when you apply for credit.

➤ Your credit report is confidential and can be released only to you or someone with a legitimate business purpose. Most of the time you give the credit-reporting agency permission to release your report to a creditor by simply signing the credit application.

➤ Review your credit report, especially before making a major purchase on credit, to make sure that it is accurate.

➤ Send your credit-reporting company a written request for reverification of any information you think is incorrect.

➤ Unless you notify a credit-card company of billing errors or other disputes in writing, you risk losing your rights under the law.

Chapter 14

I Am Not a Deadbeat— I'm Solvency-Impaired

In This Chapter

➤ Solving payment problems before your account goes to collection

➤ Learning about the laws that protect you from harassment by bill collectors

➤ Knowing what to do if a collector doesn't play by the rules

➤ Knowing what to do when you're sued by a creditor

"Creditors have better memories than debtors."

—Benjamin Franklin, *Poor Richard's Almanac,* 1758

As this accurate observation shows, Ben really understood human nature. It's almost good enough, in fact, to make me forget about his obsession with making the turkey, rather than the eagle, our national bird. Almost, but not quite. The turkey thing was just plain weird. But I digress.

Almost all of us have problems with a creditor at some time in our lives. It can be the result of a creditor's screwed-up records or a genuine dispute you have with a store over the quality of an item or the amount you were charged for it. Of course, it can also be that money was tight and you skipped a few payments on that student loan. (Hey, they can't repossess your college education, can they?)

When You Fall Behind in Your Payments

Most of us go through a time in our lives when things are grim financially, but there are things you can do to get a handle on the situation.

A letter to a creditor.

```
Mr. John Lender
BuyMore Credit Card Company
123 Pine Street
Anytown, USA


Dear Lender:

I am writing to you because I am having a difficult time
keeping up with the scheduled payments on my credit-card
account (#1234-56-7890). I recently lost my job, and the
bills have really begun to add up.

I am writing to you now, before I default on my payments.
Please understand that I fully intend to pay your company
the money it's owed, but I am asking you to consider making
some temporary arrangements that would help me get through
this rough period. I would like to preserve my good credit
rating if at all possible.

Is there a way I can reduce my minimum monthly payments,
possibly by refinancing the amount I owe? Or would it be
possible to stop or defer the late charges, interest, and
other penalties on my account so that I can apply my
payments toward my actual balance?

I am open to any suggestions you may have.

As I said, I am asking that these arrangements be made only
on a temporary basis. I fully expect to be back to work
soon, and at that time I will be more than willing to return
to my normal payment schedule.

I would like to discuss this matter with you further. Please
call me at 310-555-1111.

Very truly yours,


Sally Shopper
```

Call or, better yet, write to the creditor and explain your situation. Direct your call or letter to a manager, supervisor, vice president, or someone else with a title after her name. Remember that the person answering the customer-service line doesn't have the authority to change your current payment arrangements. Regardless of who you end up talking to, make sure that you get the name and job title of the person, and if you do work something out over the telephone, confirm your agreement in writing right away.

What should you ask for? It depends on your specific situation, but here are some ideas:

➤ Will the creditor agree to temporarily reduce your minimum monthly payment?

➤ Will the creditor agree to stop charging interest on a short-term basis?

➤ Will the creditor agree to a one-time waiver of late charges, finance charges, "over credit limit" charges, or other fees?

➤ Is there some way to refinance the debt so that your monthly payments are lower?

Any of these arrangements will let you catch up on your payments, either by making the amount of your payments more manageable or by putting the brakes on spiraling interest and finance charges.

If your situation is serious, some creditors will agree to discuss alternatives, for two reasons. First, you showed a willingness to pay (eventually) and acknowledged your responsibility for the debt before the creditor had to send the account for collection. Second, if your situation is serious, the creditor may be afraid of not collecting anything on the debt if you file bankruptcy. If negotiations are going well, ask the creditor to agree not to make any negative notes on your credit history if you abide by the terms of your agreement.

Be realistic when you talk to creditors, and don't make ridiculously low offers, or else you'll destroy your credibility. All creditors have different policies about how much of your bill can be negotiated, and it's often best to make general suggestions about what you want to see happen and let the creditor fill in the numbers.

Suppose that the first time you contact a creditor, you have no idea about what charges or penalties it might agree to waive. Ask, in general terms, whether it will make this type of accommodation, and, if it says that it will, ask what specific amounts it means. Keep in mind that the shorter the time involved, the more likely you are to get some cooperation from your creditor. The creditor is more likely to go along, for example, if you ask that your payments be restructured for the next three months, as opposed to six months or a year. And be honest with the creditor—don't negotiate an agreement you won't be able to keep.

What To Do When Your Creditor Brings In a Collection Agency

If you fall far enough behind in your payments, your creditor will send your account out for collection to one of two places: a collection agency or an attorney. Collection agencies usually contact you by telephone and by mail in an effort to get you to pay, and an attorney may do this too. But a creditor may ask the attorney to skip the phone calls and letter writing and just file suit to collect the amount you owe.

The lawsuit your creditor brings will be based on breach of contract, or, in English, it will say that you didn't live up to your side of the agreement. ("What contract?" you ask. Remember that written agreement you signed when you first applied for or received your credit card? *That* contract.) The lawsuit will claim that you owe a certain amount of money plus interest and that you have failed to pay it according to the terms of your agreement. You may want to refer to Chapter 4 for more information about lawsuits and to Chapter 27 for more information about contracts and breach.

It's the Law!

If your account is referred to a collection agency, things are bad, but all is not lost. On the negative side, the fact that your account went to collection will be reported on your credit report, and you may remember from Chapter 13 that this information can stay on your report for seven years. On the positive side, you may still be able to negotiate a payment plan with the collection agency. Negotiation usually becomes more difficult when your account goes to collection, because you're no longer dealing directly with the creditor. Unfortunately, even if you do work out a payment arrangement at this point, it's likely that the damage to your credit report will have already been done.

We have laws governing the way bill collectors operate, the most important of which is the Fair Debt Collection Practices Act. The FDCPA, a federal law, protects consumers when they deal with collection agencies; your state may have other laws that offer additional protection.

What Shouldn't Happen...

The FDCPA generally prohibits a bill collector from doing anything to harass or deceive you while it is trying to collect, and it also restricts the ways a collector can communicate with you. The statute covers a great deal of ground, and recent case law has expanded it even more. This section lists some of the biggest protections offered by the FDCPA.

> **Tip**
> The *Fair Debt Collection Practices Act (FDCPA)* applies to "third party" collectors the same as it applies to collection agencies or collection attorneys, but it does not apply to creditors attempting to collect their own accounts. If you are being harassed by a creditor, you may be protected under state consumer-protection law. For help, contact the consumer-complaints division of the attorney general's office in your state or your lawyer.

Under the law's restrictions against harassment, a collector cannot do the following:

➤ Threaten or use violence against you or your property.

➤ Use obscene or abusive language when it contacts you.

➤ Make anonymous or "hang-up" phone calls or do anything else that would be considered telephone harassment.

➤ Publish a list of people who don't pay their debts (this does not include reporting you to credit bureaus).

Under the FDCPA's sections on false or deceptive practices, a collector cannot do the following:

➤ Misrepresent the amount or type of debt owed.

➤ Falsely imply that you have committed a crime or can be arrested if you don't pay.

➤ Threaten to take legal action against you that it is not entitled to take.

➤ Make documents seem as though they were issued by a court when they weren't.

Finally, in the area of communication, a collector cannot do the following:

➤ Contact you, physically or by telephone, at any unusual time or place.

➤ Contact you at all, if you advise him that you are represented by a lawyer and tell the collector how to contact your lawyer.

➤ Contact you at work after you've told him not to do so.

➤ Contact you at any "inconvenient" time (generally considered to be between 9 P.M. and 8 A.M.) including weekdays and weekends.

➤ Contact anyone else about your debt, unless it is solely to find a way to contact you at home or work and the collector does not reveal the reason for its call.

As you can see, the law restricts the way collectors can try to get you to pay. Most of the rules discussed so far are aimed at protecting you from being harassed by a collector. But the FDCPA also considers that not every person knows her rights under the law. So rather than tell collectors what they can't do, the FDCPA goes one step further and requires collectors to do certain things when they contact a debtor. A collector must do the following things, for example:

➤ Send you a written notice within five days of contacting you for the first time, telling you how much you owe, who the creditor is, and what to do if you don't believe that you owe the money.

➤ Advise you that the debt will be presumed to be valid unless you notify the collector in writing within 30 days that you want verification of the debt or that you don't owe the money.

➤ Stop collection efforts if it receives within the 30 days a letter from you stating that you want verification of the debt or that you don't owe the money.

A final note about that last point: A collector can start its collection efforts again if, after receiving your written notice, it provides you with written proof of the debt.

What To Do When a Collector Won't Play by the Rules

It's 3 A.M., and you're fast asleep. Your phone rings—it's a collector from Arm Twisters Collection Services calling to demand payment on an overdue credit-card bill. He tells you that if you don't pay up, you'll be arrested for credit-card fraud. As you're hanging up, he adds that it would be most unfortunate if your dog Sparky had a serious "accident."

Okay, this example is a little melodramatic, but the point is that people do find themselves in situations in which they're harassed by a bill collector. If it happens to you, how do you fight back? You can start by contacting your creditor and advising it of what has happened, or you can contact someone in authority at the collection agency. If this doesn't resolve the problem, you can take the following steps:

➤ **File a complaint against the collector with a government agency.** The Federal Trade Commission is the agency that enforces the FDCPA. If your complaint is based on a violation of state law, take your complaint to the attorney general's office in your state. You can find the telephone number for this agency in the government "blue pages" of your telephone book.

➤ **Talk to an attorney about suing the collector.** The FDCPA allows you to sue a collector for violating the statute, and it allows you to recover any actual damages you incurred, your court costs and attorney's fees, and additional statutory damages that are determined solely at the court's discretion. In deciding the issue of additional damages, the court considers a number of factors, including how often the violation took place, how severe the violation was, and whether the violation was intentional.

Tip
As soon as you begin having trouble with a collector, begin keeping detailed records about each incident. You will need these records if you decide to file a complaint with the FTC or the attorney general's office, and your attorney will need them if you file a civil suit against the collector.

Working Out an Agreement with a Collector

As you learned earlier in this chapter, negotiating a payment plan with a collector can be more difficult than negotiating directly with the creditor. Don't be surprised if the collector tells you that it doesn't have the authority to negotiate—it probably doesn't. Generally, the only thing the collector can do is take your offer back to the creditor and see whether it will approve it.

This type of "middleman" situation can cause two problems for you as a debtor. First, it's difficult to be sure that the collector ever talked to the creditor about your offer or that the offer was explained correctly. Second, even if your offer got relayed to the creditor, you can be sure that the collector didn't spend much time arguing on your behalf.

Even if your account is in collection, always try to deal directly with the creditor. It's the only way you can absolutely guarantee that your message is heard, and you'll make the situation much more personal. You won't be just a faceless account number to be reviewed by the collector and creditor—you'll be a person who genuinely wants to work out some kind of arrangement with the creditor.

If you're having some problems negotiating on your own, you may want to get some help. An attorney with experience in debt collection and consumer rights may be able to help you, but of course you have to figure out how you'll pay the attorney.

Some companies offer credit and debt-counseling services, and you can locate the ones in your area by checking the Yellow Pages. Begin by looking for nonprofit services that offer free counseling. Some of these agencies, such as Credit Counseling Centers of America, have offices nationwide and enjoy a good reputation among creditors. They work with you to review all your debts, prepare a budget you can live on, and negotiate payment terms with your creditors—all free of charge or for a minimal fee.

If your debts are overwhelming, you may have to begin thinking about filing bankruptcy. Bankruptcy is described in detail in Chapter 15, but it's simply a process that frees you from most of, if not all, your debts and at the same time attempts to repay your creditors to the greatest extent possible. Bankruptcy can be useful in some situations, but it's no cure-all. It damages your credit report for as long as ten years, and it doesn't erase all types of debt. It's a serious decision, and you should talk to an attorney experienced in the field before jumping into the process.

What To Expect if a Creditor Sues You

If other collection efforts don't work, a creditor's final option is to sue you for the amount you owe. Collection suits are usually not complicated because they involve only a few real issues: Do you owe the creditor money? How much do you owe? Do you have any defense for not paying what you owe?

If you are sued by a creditor, you have to decide whether you want an attorney to represent you. If large amounts of money are involved, if you think that there's still a chance of negotiating a settlement or payment plan, or if you think that you have a defense to the creditor's claim, you should definitely talk to an attorney about your case. But if the amounts involved are small and you don't dispute the amount you owe, you may be reluctant to spend even more money (that you don't have) on an attorney. It's largely a matter of how comfortable you feel dealing with the situation; as mentioned, collection suits normally don't involve complicated legal issues. Review Chapter 4 for information about how the lawsuit will progress.

When a creditor has a judgment against you, it can do several things to enforce it. Remember that the judgment is only a piece of paper from the court showing the court's findings and orders. It's not cash, and it can't be deposited in a bank account, so after a creditor receives a judgment, it still has to do something to get its hands on the money you owe.

If a creditor doesn't know much about you financially, you may be served with a notice to appear in court and testify under

> **Legal Pitfalls**
> A complaint under the FDCPA or similar statute is a separate legal issue from the collection suit. Filing a complaint is not a defense to a creditor's claim, and it does not get you out of paying a debt you rightfully owe.

> **Legalese**
> A **judgment** is an official decision of the court determining the rights and obligations of the parties involved in a lawsuit. In a collection case, for example, the judgment could be that you owe your creditor $500.

oath about your assets, income, and other money matters. These hearings go by different names depending on where you live (for example, they can be called "debtor's hearings" or "citations to discover assets") but their purpose is the same: They give your creditor an opportunity to find ways to collect on its judgment.

After the creditor knows where you stand financially, it can ask the court for other orders enforcing the judgment. For example, a creditor may be able to seize a piece of property of yours and sell it in order to satisfy the judgment. The creditor may be able to obtain a court order turning over to the creditor all the funds held in your savings account. Or a creditor can garnish your wages.

> **WHAT!?**
>
> **Legalese**
> A **wage garnishment** is a court order directing your employer to withhold part of your wages every pay period and then pay that amount directly to your creditor.

As bad as this sounds, there are limits on what a creditor can do in its efforts to get paid. For example, state law provides that certain assets cannot be seized in order to satisfy a judgment, and there are statutory limits on the amount of your wages that can be garnished. If a creditor is trying to enforce a judgment against you, you should consult with an attorney about how you're protected under your state's laws.

The Least You Need To Know

➤ If you see that you're falling behind in your payments, take action immediately. Call or write to the creditor to explain your problem and offer ideas about how to work out a solution.

➤ Collection agencies and collection attorneys are governed by the Fair Debt Collection Practices Act and often by state law as well.

➤ Problems with a collector can be reported to the Federal Trade Commission or the attorney general's office in your state. You also may be able to sue the collector yourself for violations of the FDCPA.

➤ Creditors usually return to court to enforce a judgment. They may try to satisfy the judgment by seizing and selling personal property, seizing bank accounts, or garnishing wages.

➤ Each state has laws that protect you and some of your property when a creditor is attempting to enforce a judgment.

Chapter 15

Wiping the Slate Clean: Bankruptcy

In This Chapter

➤ Some alternatives to bankruptcy

➤ The basic process and the pros and cons of filing a Chapter 7

➤ The basic process and the pros and cons of filing a Chapter 13

➤ The risks involved in bankruptcy, including loss of property and denial of a discharge

Nobody likes to think about filing bankruptcy. It can be embarrassing for the *debtor* (someone who owes money), and it's almost always expensive for a *creditor* (individuals or companies to whom money is owed). It's a big decision to make, and it's not always the best option. Bankruptcy isn't a quick fix for all your money problems, and if you're not careful, you can end up worse off than when you started. Unless your case is extremely simple, don't jump into the process without hiring an attorney.

Having said that, don't rule out bankruptcy as an option if you're in serious financial trouble. Don't give up a chance to get a fresh start because you're too embarrassed. Everyone hits hard times at some point in life, and if you do file bankruptcy, no one will pin a scarlet *B* on your chest. Businesses look at bankruptcy as just another, although extreme, financial strategy, and you should too. Make a rational, business-like decision, not an emotional one.

If you're considering bankruptcy, make sure that you've looked at all your other options first. Here are some possibilities to consider:

➤ **Work out an agreement with your creditors.** Explain your situation, and make sure to mention that you're considering bankruptcy. That gets their attention, but be realistic. No creditor is likely to accept an offer of ten cents on the dollar, but most are willing to talk about a compromise. See whether the creditor is willing to temporarily reduce your minimum payment or stop interest accrual. Some will agree to waive accumulated late-payment fees or other finance charges.

➤ **Consolidate your debts.** If you have a large number of credit-card accounts with big principal balances, you're making high minimum monthly payments, but most of the money is being applied toward interest. You can get a debt-consolidation loan or a home-equity loan and use it to pay off your charge cards and lower your total monthly payments. With a home-equity loan, you may even be able to deduct the interest on your taxes. Be careful: Lots of scams are out there. Check out the lender thoroughly, and avoid terms that sound

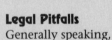

Legalese
Bankruptcy is a legal process designed to free a person from debt in order to start over financially and to make a fair distribution of her assets among her creditors.

Legal Pitfalls
Generally speaking, stay away from "debt consolidation" firms or "credit counseling" services. These services often cause more problems than they solve, not to mention that they don't do anything you can't do on your own. They also charge a fee for their services, further depleting your resources. You're far better off negotiating directly with your creditors than giving some stranger carte blanche over all your finances. The exceptions to this advice are the national not-for-profit credit-counseling services described in Chapter 14. These reputable agencies charge little or nothing for their services.

too good to be true, because they probably are. Also make sure that you close the charge accounts as soon as you pay them off. Otherwise, you'll be tempted to run the accounts back up, and you can end up owing twice what you did before.

➤ **Get professional advice.** Try talking to an accountant, a financial consultant, a reputable credit-counseling service, or an attorney experienced in collections and bankruptcy before making any final decisions about what to do. Stay away from debt-consolidation services that offer to negotiate with your creditors or set up a system in which you pay the service and they pay your bills. You just end up paying a service to do what you could do yourself, and odds are that the service won't get you any better deals.

Understanding the Bankruptcy Code

Bankruptcy is a legal process that is designed to do two things:

➤ Discharge, or free, a person from his debts in order to start over financially.

➤ Make a fair distribution of the person's assets among the creditors involved.

The idea of being debt-free and starting over always sounds appealing, but don't rush down to the courthouse yet. Bankruptcy has some serious side effects, not the least of which is that it will appear on your credit report for seven to ten years, depending on why the report is being done. If you have absolutely perfect credit for the first two years after a bankruptcy, you might be able to find a bank that will consider you for a mortgage or a credit-card account, but you'll probably be given a relatively low credit limit at a higher-than-normal interest rate.

Another thing to consider is that not all debts can be discharged. If most of your debts are the kind that can't be discharged, you don't gain anything by filing bankruptcy. The Bankruptcy Code contains the full list of nondischargeable debts, but here are some examples that occur regularly:

➤ Alimony and child-support obligations.

➤ Debts that have been reaffirmed.

Legalese
A **discharge** is a special type of court order that basically erases all your previous debts.

Tip
The code section that lists the nondischargeable debts (11 U.S.C. 523(a)), is amended frequently and is very technical in nature. Always consult an experienced bankruptcy attorney if you think that some of your debts may be nondischargeable. If many of your debts are in this category, you may want to explore alternatives to filing bankruptcy.

➤ Most student loans.

➤ Certain federal, state, and local taxes.

➤ Debts you don't list in the petition.

➤ Most fines and penalties owed to a governmental unit (for example, traffic fines and tickets).

➤ Debts incurred from the willful injury of another person or their property (for example, injuries caused by drunk driving).

Don't plan to go on a spending spree just before you file bankruptcy. Debts incurred on luxury items within 40 days of filing bankruptcy may not be dischargeable.

You can also be denied a discharge if you've been dishonest or even if you've been just plain uncooperative during the bankruptcy case. For example, any of the following can justify a court's refusal to enter a discharge:

➤ You failed to provide adequate financial records to the court, the trustee, or creditors. (A trustee is not like a judge at all, but I've included a sidebar anyway.)

➤ You filed a false claim or lied when you completed the schedules.

➤ You transferred or hid property to delay or defraud creditors.

➤ You refused to obey a court order.

➤ You failed to explain losses or otherwise answer important questions in court or at a meeting of creditors.

Legalese
A **trustee**, in terms of a bankruptcy case, is the person responsible for conducting creditors' meetings and liquidating (selling) the debtor's assets and distributing the proceeds among the creditors. The trustee is usually an experienced bankruptcy attorney.

Because bankruptcy is governed by federal statute (the one appropriately named Bankruptcy Code), the basic rules and procedures involved are fairly standardized from state to state. The Code addresses different types of debtors, including individuals, businesses, and farmers. Even municipalities (cities) can file for bankruptcy protection—just ask anyone who lives in Orange County, California. You can identify the different kinds of bankruptcy cases by their chapter numbers in the Code. This chapter discusses the two chapters, 7 and 13, that deal primarily with individuals.

Because bankruptcy is a technical field, it is easy to do more harm than good to yourself if you don't know what you're doing. The only people who should consider filing bankruptcy without an attorney are those who don't own a home, have only unsecured debts (such as credit-card accounts), and want to file a Chapter 7. Even these people may find that, by doing it themselves, they have bitten off more than they can chew. It's inadvisable for someone to attempt a Chapter 13 filing without consulting an attorney.

Who Said That Seven Is a Lucky Number?

Almost everyone has heard of "filing a Chapter 7." Chapter 7 cases are the most common kind of bankruptcy case filed by individuals, and for good reason. A Chapter 7 (or a "straight bankruptcy") gives you a simple and inexpensive way to get free from debt. As I've said, your goal in a Chapter 7 is to get a discharge. The Chapter 7 process usually follows these steps:

1. You file a petition that begins the process, and notices are sent to your creditors.

2. An automatic stay begins, protecting you and your assets. (A "stay" means that collection efforts must stop.)

3. The court appoints a trustee.

4. A creditors' meeting is held, in which you are questioned about your assets and debts.

5. Any reaffirmation agreements are approved by the court. (Reaffirmation agreements are discussed later in this chapter.)

6. The court enters the final orders, including an order of discharge.

Filing Your Petition

You start a Chapter 7 case by filing a petition with the clerk of the bankruptcy court in your area. To find out where your district's bankruptcy court is, check the blue pages of your telephone book. If you plan to use an attorney, he will provide you with all the forms you need and help you complete them. If you're not using an attorney, you need to know that you cannot get preprinted petition forms from the court but that you can usually find them at larger office-supply stores. The petition must be in the approved form before the clerk of the court will accept it for filing.

OOOOOH...

Tip

If you are confused about which forms to use or how to file them, you may want to talk to one of the clerks of the bankruptcy court. The clerks cannot give you legal advice, but they may be willing to let you see some petitions that have already been filed so that you can get some idea about what yours should look like. The clerks often have pamphlets or other materials that can tell you about local rules in your area.

The petition gives the court some general information about you and your finances, and it's made up of several separate forms, called *schedules*. Each schedule addresses a different part of your finances. For example, Schedule A lists real estate you own, and Schedule B lists personal property you own. Put together, these schedules describe all your assets, debts, income, and expenses.

You have to pay a fee for filing the petition and—I know that *this* will surprise you—the clerk's office doesn't take personal checks. After the petition is filed, the clerk's office mails notices about the bankruptcy to your creditors.

The Magic of the Automatic Stay

From the moment you file the petition, a strange and wonderful thing (at least if you're the debtor) called an *automatic stay* begins. The automatic stay puts you and your property under the protection of the bankruptcy court, and while the stay is in effect, no one can begin or continue any kind of legal action against you. The stay even prevents an order from a state court from taking effect. For example, a wage-garnishment order is ineffective while a bankruptcy stay is in place.

It's the Law!

If your former spouse is paying child support or alimony (see Chapter 10 for more information about these topics) and files bankruptcy, the rules concerning how the automatic stay affects the support payments get complex. There isn't just one rule in this area—there are several, and deciding which rules apply revolves around the specific facts of the situation. For example, whether your divorce case is over or still pending, what assets your spouse is using to make the support payments, and whether you're talking about arrearages or current support all make a difference. If you find yourself in this type of situation, talk to an experienced family-law or bankruptcy attorney to find out what your specific rights are.

The automatic stay applies not only to collection efforts but also to any kind of legal action against you, including ones that aren't directly related to the bankruptcy, such as a divorce. There are several exceptions to the automatic-stay rule, but, generally speaking, if you've filed bankruptcy in good faith, you're protected by the stay.

To Liquidate or Not To Liquidate

The Bankruptcy Code also protects you in another way. Chapter 7 is designed to give an honest debtor a fresh start, not to wipe her out. Because it's hard to get a fresh start when you don't even have change in your sofa cushions, filing a Chapter 7 does not require you to use every possible asset to pay off your debts. Instead, it allows you to keep a minimal amount of assets to use in starting over. These *exempt* assets, or *exemptions,* are excluded from liquidation. If you have assets in addition to the money and property classified as exempt, the additional assets are sold, and the money from the sale goes to pay your creditors.

Legalese
Liquidation is the court-ordered sale of assets in order to pay creditors.

Often the clerk of the court refers to a bankruptcy case as a "no asset" case, in which the debtor has only exempt assets and there will be nothing left to distribute among creditors. Most Chapter 7 cases filed by individuals are "no asset" cases.

For example, your state law might say that the following kinds of property are exempt from liquidation (they cannot be liquidated to pay your creditors in a bankruptcy):

➤ Necessary clothing and apparel.

➤ The right to receive veteran's or Social Security benefits.

➤ Your interest, not to exceed $1,200, in a car.

➤ The right to receive alimony or maintenance.

➤ Your interest, not to exceed $2,000, in any other property.

Though the Bankruptcy Code provides a list of exempt property, it also gives the states the right to create and use exemption lists. Each state can choose whether the bankruptcy courts within its borders will follow the Code or use the state's list of exempt property. This part of the bankruptcy law is one of the few that is not uniform around the country. At the time of this writing, only 14 states use the Bankruptcy Code list of exempt property; the others use state lists. Make sure that you know exactly which exemptions you're entitled to before you begin a Chapter 7. You can find your state's list of exemptions in your state statutes, and some of the preprinted form kits discussed earlier come with a summary of exemptions. It's probably easier and wiser, however, to consult an attorney if you have questions.

Reaffirming a Debt

No matter which exemptions your state allows, the list is always short, and it may not include all the property you might want to keep. Suppose that you bought a new stereo system on secured credit from Bob's Stereo Shack several months ago, but now you're thinking about bankruptcy. (Maybe you got carried away in the CD of the Month Club.) You have learned that the stereo system will not be considered exempt property under Chapter 7, but you really don't want to give it back. After all, you just learned how to use all 54 buttons on the remote, and what about all those new CDs?

Fear not, audiophile! What you need is a *reaffirmation agreement,* which is a new contract between you and a creditor, negotiated while the bankruptcy is still pending. It's used to remove a particular transaction from the bankruptcy proceedings. Under the new agreement, you continue paying the creditor as though the bankruptcy didn't exist. The creditor lets you keep the property (in this case, the stereo) rather than have it repossessed or liquidated. If you default on your payments, though, the creditor can begin collection proceedings immediately, and the automatic stay no longer protects you.

You and your attorney should discuss whether this type of agreement is right for your situation. Don't enter into a reaffirmation agreement just because a creditor offers you one (and believe me, they all offer you one). Remember why you're going through bankruptcy in the first place. The whole point is to get discharged from all your debts, or at least from as many as possible. Sometimes reaffirmation is necessary and practical, such as to keep a car from being repossessed or to keep a charge account open so that you still have access to some credit. But sign more than one or two reaffirmation agreements, and you risk having the worst of two worlds: a Chapter 7 on your credit history and several long-term obligations with large monthly payments.

Working with the Trustee

After you file a bankruptcy petition, the court appoints a trustee to the case. The trustee has two main jobs:

➤ Conduct a creditors' meeting.

➤ Sell off, or liquidate, any non-exempt assets the debtor may have and distribute the sale proceeds among the creditors.

As its name implies, a creditors' meeting gives creditors the opportunity to meet with you, your attorney, and the trustee. As a debtor, you are required to attend the meeting, even if none of your creditors intends to show up. These meetings are conducted outside of court and tend to be informal, but you still should expect to testify under oath about your finances. Your payment terms may be the same as the terms you originally had, but some creditors may be willing to restructure your payments to make them more manageable. You can be questioned by both your creditors and the trustee. Additionally, a creditor or trustee can require that you bring in certain financial records for examination.

In a "no asset" case, the creditors' meeting usually marks the unofficial end of the case. After the meeting, the court sends a final notice to the creditors, advising them that no assets are available for distribution and fixing a cutoff date for creditors to object to entry of a discharge. Unless a creditor objects, the court enters the bankruptcy discharge, and the bankruptcy case is closed. After the discharge is entered, previously entered judgments against you are void, and creditors are prohibited from beginning or continuing any collection suits against you.

If you have already been sued by a creditor and already have a judgment against you (see Chapter 14 for more information about judgments), don't worry. The discharge order makes previous judgments against you void, or, put another way, the creditor can't ever enforce the judgment, because of the bankruptcy discharge. With some assets left and all (or most of) your old debts gone for good, you have your new start.

And Speaking of Unlucky Numbers...

The other kind of bankruptcy that individuals can choose is a Chapter 13, also called a "wage-earner plan." In a Chapter 13, you work out a payment plan to be confirmed by the court, in order to repay a portion of your total debt. The trustee receives your payments and then distributes them among your creditors. After completing your payments under the plan, the remaining debts are discharged just as they are in a Chapter 7.

To be able to file a Chapter 13, you have to have "regular income," and as of the date of the filing of your petition, your unsecured debts cannot exceed $250,000 and your secured debts cannot exceed $750,000. Additionally, your regular income must be sufficient to cover your normal monthly living expenses, with enough left over to make regular, scheduled payments under the payment plan.

How Chapter 13 Works

In a Chapter 13, you file a petition just as you would in a Chapter 7. Additionally, you must file a payment plan that meets the requirements of Chapter 13 and have a statement showing your monthly budget and how much of your income is available to fund the plan. You may be able to prepare the payment plan and budget on your own, but even if you can, I recommend against it. An experienced bankruptcy attorney can help you with your Chapter 13 filing by doing the following:

➤ Prevent you from underestimating your budget requirements.

➤ Prevent you from overestimating the payments you can make under the plan.

➤ Guide you through all the technical aspects of the Chapter 13 procedure.

I know, you wouldn't be considering a Chapter 13 if you had extra money to spend, but hiring an attorney for a case such as this is a good investment.

Many people who would like to use Chapter 13 find out that they simply don't have enough monthly income to qualify.

Just how much money will you need under a Chapter 13 plan? This list shows you the requirements:

➤ The payment plan you submit must be completed within 60 months. You need special court approval, in fact, if your plan will run for more than 36 months.

➤ The plan must provide that each creditor holding an unsecured claim receives at least as much as it would have received if you had filed a Chapter 7.

➤ The plan must also provide that each secured creditor receives payments equal to the value of its secured property as of the date of the plan or that you'll give up the property.

➤ The plan must also provide that each secured creditor receives at least as much money as the secured property is worth. If your car is worth $5,000, for example, the payments to the bank that financed your purchase must be at least $5,000.

Legalese
A secured **creditor** is a creditor who has some interest in a piece of your property. When you finance a new car, for example, you use the car as collateral and give the bank an interest in the car—in case you don't repay your loan. An **unsecured creditor** is a creditor with no specific interest in your property.

Got it?

The rest of the Chapter 13 proceedings are much the same as they are under Chapter 7. You have the benefit of the automatic stay from the time the petition is filed through the time the discharge takes place. A creditors' meeting will be held, and the only difference is that a creditor can object to the plan you have submitted. Assuming that you made all the payments required under the plan, you receive a discharge order at the end of the case, just as you would in a Chapter 7.

So Which One Should I Choose?

Every situation is different, but people opt for Chapter 13 over Chapter 7 for two main reasons. First, Chapter 13 allows you to keep all your property; in Chapter 7, you will probably be required to return or liquidate property that's not considered exempt. Second, a Chapter 13 tends to do less damage to your credit rating than a Chapter 7 does. Credit managers aren't thrilled to see any bankruptcy on a credit report, but they prefer someone who at least tried to repay what she owed over someone who opted for a straight discharge of debts under Chapter 7. You'll probably have an easier time reestablishing your credit after filing a Chapter 13.

Tip
You've probably noticed by now that the calculations required under Chapter 13 can get pretty involved. If you're seriously considering Chapter 13, get some advice from an experienced bankruptcy attorney. Most Chapter 13 cases that get filed aren't successfully completed, sometimes because the debtor just doesn't follow up with the plan requirements, but many times because the debtor used an unrealistic budget and overestimated what he could pay under the plan.

Your existing creditors certainly like Chapter 13 better. Even if they don't receive every dollar they're owed, under a Chapter 13 plan they usually get more of what they're owed.

The Least You Need To Know

➤ Always begin by considering the alternatives to bankruptcy.

➤ The basic points in the bankruptcy process are filing a petition, starting the automatic stay, appointing a trustee, filing a payment plan (if it's Chapter 13), holding the creditors' meeting, approving any reaffirmation agreements, and entering the order of discharge.

➤ When you prepare to file under Chapter 7, remember that some of your property may have to be liquidated or sold during the bankruptcy process. Before you begin, make sure that you know which assets will be exempt.

➤ A reaffirmation agreement can remove a specific creditor or transaction from the bankruptcy process, allowing you to keep a piece of property or retain a line of credit.

➤ If you file Chapter 13, make sure that your budget is as accurate as possible and that you've set up a realistic plan.

➤ If you file a Chapter 13, make sure that you stay current in your payments under the plan. If you don't, you've gone through a great deal of work for nothing.

Chapter 16

Working for a Living

In This Chapter

➤ Why it matters whether you're an independent contractor or an employee

➤ What to be aware of during the hiring process

➤ What to do if you've been discriminated against or sexually harassed

➤ What you can expect if you're fired

Let's face it: Unless you manage to pick the right Lotto numbers this Saturday, you'll be back to work on Monday. And although our jobs may be similar to the ones our parents had, new rules govern hiring, firing, benefits, and other workplace issues.

In this chapter, you learn about some of those rules and see how they define and protect your legal rights on the job.

The Difference Between Employees and Independent Contractors

Almost everyone who works can be classified as either an employee or an independent contractor. Years ago, the great majority of people were employees. For example, you may have a written agreement with someone which says that you're working as an independent contractor, but that agreement is only one of the factors considered by the IRS. The IRS wants to know which you are—employee or independent contractor—not just what you call yourself. But today, because an increasing number of people do freelance work and run businesses from their homes, the number of independent contractors continues to increase.

It can be difficult to accurately define the differences between the two, and even the IRS looks at several factors in deciding how to classify a taxpayer. So rather than use textbook definitions, let's use two workers as examples: Alan, who works the drive-through window at the local BurgerWorld, and Alice, an architect.

The following list looks at some general factors the IRS considers when it decides whether someone is an employee or an independent contractor. Look it over, and then you can see how Alan and Alice measure up.

➤ **Employees have a steady relationship with their employers and independent contractors do not.** Employees are hired to do work on a continuing basis, and in return they receive payment based on the amount of time they work. Independent contractors are hired to perform a specific task, and they're paid a set amount for that task. In this example, Alan's pay is based on the hours he works, and he works at BurgerWorld for an unspecified amount of time. Alice, on the other hand, gets paid for a specific task, such as designing a new office building. After that design is finished, her relationship with the building owners is finished too (unless she agrees to handle an additional project).

You should note that even if Alan was summertime or part-time help, he's still considered an employee. That's because even though his employment might be for a short or temporary period, he's still not being hired to complete only a specific job or project.

His work is ongoing in nature (people always drive through at lunchtime), unlike Alice's which is a specific task (design the building).

➤ **Employees have little control over how the work is done, but independent contractors have almost total control over their work.** Alan is completely under BurgerWorld's control—he's told when he has to work, what uniform he has to wear, and exactly how to cook those golden fries. But Alice can set her own hours, wear what she wants, and do the work in whatever way she wants, as long as she meets certain basic standards and delivers her drawings on time.

➤ **Employees are generally provided with everything they need in order to do the job, and independent contractors usually provide their own tools and equipment.** Alan doesn't have to go buy his own fryer or shake machine, but Alice has to buy equipment and drafting tools for her office.

By now the Alans and Alices of the world are saying, "I see the differences, but who cares?" At least three people care: you, the person you're working for, and your friendly, neighborhood IRS agent.

Employers control almost everything about their employees and the job, but it also means that if an employee injures someone while on the job, the employer generally can be held liable. An independent contractor is liable for his own mistakes and negligence, and generally no liability is placed on a person who contracts for his services.

While we're on the subject of getting hurt, independent contractors are not covered by workers' compensation, like employees are. If employees are injured while working on a job, an independent contractor will end up making a claim on her own medical or disability insurance.

As far as taxes are concerned, employees have taxes withheld from their paychecks, and they receive a W-2 form at the end of

> OOOOOH...
>
> **Tip**
> If you're going to do work as an independent contractor, use a written agreement to define your own responsibilities as well as those of the person contracting for your services. Whether you call it a retainer agreement, an engagement letter, or something else, a written contract helps to prevent misunderstandings later.

the year showing how much they earned and how much they paid in taxes. Independent contractors must pay all their taxes on their own, and it's normally done by sending in estimated payments to the IRS every quarter. When they complete a job, they may receive a 1099 statement at the end of the year that shows only how much they were paid for their work.

Your Workplace Rights, or "I'm Sorry— I Thought They Abolished Slavery"

Independent contractors are governed largely by basic contract law, but the employer-employee relationship is heavily regulated by state and federal statutes. There are regulations on hiring, firing, and everything in between.

If these regulations are violated, you can contact the Equal Employment Opportunity Commission (EEOC), the Department of Labor, or your state's human-rights commission. The EEOC has branch offices throughout the country and handles alleged violations of the Equal Employment Opportunity Act. (Check the blue government pages in your telephone book to find the office near you.) Your state can also help with this type of complaint—usually through its Department of Labor or the state's Human Rights Commission. You can find any of these offices in the blue pages of your telephone book. Another option is to consult an attorney experienced in the field of labor law.

Getting Hired

Most people are aware that the law protects you from discrimination in hiring. This protection extends even to the questions you're asked during your interview. You can be asked questions about your qualifications or your ability to do the job, but you cannot be asked about your religion, marital status, plans to have children, age, nationality, or political or sexual orientation. Basically, any personal questions that might lead an employer to discriminate are prohibited.

In addition to a physical, your prospective employer can require other tests. Testing is something of a gray area, but if the test is relevant to the job, is given to all new employees in the same way, and is required only after a job offer has been made, the employer usually has the right to require the test. For example, a medical exam, psychological test, drug test, polygraph, and a background check all are reasonable steps in the hiring of a police officer. The same procedures probably wouldn't be reasonable if you were hiring a receptionist.

If you think that a prospective employer is acting improperly during the hiring process, you can politely point out that her questions are improper under the law and refuse to answer. Or you can give the employer the benefit of the doubt and answer the questions. Even if a question seems to be technically improper under the law, it might be an innocent attempt to "break the ice." After all, not every employer has a hidden, discriminatory agenda.

> **Tip**
> You also can't be asked about any disabilities during your interview, but you can be asked about your ability to perform a specific task (for example, "Can you lift an 85-pound box?"). Additionally, a potential employer can require you to take a physical after you've been offered a job to determine whether you have any serious health problems that would make you unable to perform the work.

If it seems that the employer is really out of line, you can file a complaint with the Equal Employment Opportunity Commission (EEOC).

After You're on Board

The number of lawsuits and administrative complaints filed over alleged discrimination, sexual harassment, and other workplace problems has skyrocketed in recent years. To help protect against unfounded charges, many savvy employers provide employees with a handbook detailing company policies on a variety of topics—everything from benefits to disciplinary actions. If your employer has this type of handbook, make sure that you read it and become familiar with its terms—you're bound by them.

If the company has no handbook, some general rules still apply to you. With benefits, for example, you generally don't have a "right" to any benefits from your employer. If your employer does provide benefits, the only real requirement is that the benefits must be offered in a nondiscriminatory manner. It's all right for an employer to provide all employees with basic health-insurance coverage; it's not all right if you're the only employee who has to pay for coverage.

Your employer may also place certain conditions on your employment—for example, you may be required to sign an agreement not to compete directly with your employer if you're fired or you quit. Or you may be asked to sign a confidentiality agreement that prohibits you from revealing trade secrets, software programs, client information, or other sensitive material to anyone when you leave. These agreements are generally enforceable, and you can be sued for violating their terms unless they are overly restrictive or will apply for an unreasonably long time.

If you're asked to sign one of these agreements before or after you've been hired, think twice about saying "no." If the same agreement is required of every employee, your refusal to sign could be sufficient basis for the employer not to hire you or to fire you (see the section "Going Your Seperate Ways," later in this chapter). Discuss the matter with your employer, and explain your concerns about the agreement—just realize that you may have to make a big decision if the employer doesn't waive the requirement.

There's one other related point to think about, especially if your job involves the use of your creative efforts. If you create something, whether it's a story, photograph, song, or even a new invention or process, while working within the normal scope of your employment (that is, your employer told you to), your employer owns any copyrights or patent rights that may become attached to your creation. This rule doesn't apply to things you create on your own time—you own all the rights to those creations.

When You're Asked To Do More than Just Your Work

Sexual harassment is to the '90s what discrimination was to the '60s. And because so much of the law in this area is relatively new, many people are confused about what constitutes harassment and what to do about it if they're victims.

Harassment can take different forms—from generally offensive or degrading language and posters that can make it difficult for you to do your work to unwanted physical contact or insistent requests for dates or sex.

Defining sexual harassment can still be a little vague. Part of the difficulty is that harassment can take place directly or indirectly—an improper grab or pinch can be considered harassment, but so can the pasting of explicit centerfolds all around the break room. And it's just as difficult to try to say what's *not* harassment. Few people would argue that an honest compliment about your appearance or a joke of questionable taste is equal to harassment, but people have different sensitivity levels.

So what can you do if you think that you have a claim of harassment? First, confront the individual involved, and let him know that his conduct is causing a problem. Keep a written log of any incidents so that you can document your claims. If the situation doesn't improve, take the matter to a superior. If your complaints don't generate a response, you may want to contact your local EEOC office to file a formal complaint. As in discrimination cases, your state also has an agency that handles these kinds of complaints.

Legalese
Sexual harassment occurs when improper sexual advances (verbal or physical) made in the workplace interfere with an employee's work or create an offensive or hostile work environment for an employee.

Legal Pitfalls
EEOC rules are complicated, and the process can be confusing. If you don't follow the procedures correctly, you can jeopardize any claim you might have. For example, after the EEOC issues a "right to sue" letter, you have only 90 days to begin your lawsuit. It's often wise to hire an attorney at the beginning of a claim to help guide you through the entire process.

The agency receiving your complaint will investigate the matter with your employer and attempt to reach some type of resolution. In theory, the agency can file suit against the employer, but in practice it rarely happens because of the tremendous backlog of cases. It's much more likely that the agency will issue you a "right to sue" letter, allowing you to bring your own action against the employer in federal court.

Going Your Separate Ways

There are normally only four ways to leave your job: get fired, quit, be laid off because of your employer's downsizing, or retire. To begin with, unless you have a written employment contract that states otherwise, most people are considered to be employees at will.

Legalese
Employment at will means that an employer can fire an employee for almost any nondiscriminatory reason and, generally, without notice.

Tip
Under certain circumstances, even an employee at will may have a wrongful-discharge claim. If you're fired because you notified the EPA that your company was dumping toxic waste in the local lake at night, you probably have a pretty good basis for a wrongful-discharge suit because you were fired in retaliation for turning in the company.

An employee at will works without a contract and can be fired for almost any reason. Suppose that you're one of my at will employees and that you called in sick for work yesterday. While I was out for lunch, I drove past the local golf course and saw you teeing off. This morning when you come in, I can fire you immediately—no probation, no warnings, no notice. But don't panic; this doesn't mean that an employer's ability to fire an employee at will is unlimited. An employer must still comply with federal discrimination, harassment, and other labor laws, so even an employee at will cannot be fired simply because he's Asian or won't sleep with the boss.

A few states have enacted laws changing the traditional "at will" relationship and prohibiting an employer from firing you unless she has just cause to do so. Some examples of just cause are poor job performance, chronic tardiness, stealing company property, and drinking on the job. If you're not an employee at will, either because of state law or a specific agreement with your employer, and you're fired without just cause, you can sue your employer for wrongful termination. You can find out whether your state is an "at will" or "just cause" state by calling your state's Department of Labor or by calling a labor-law attorney in your area.

Regardless of whether you're an employee at will, you generally have the right to be told why you're being fired; in fact, some states require your employer to tell you. As a practical matter, this rarely becomes an issue, because most employers want to document the reasons for the firing to protect themselves from claims of discrimination, harassment, or wrongful termination. By the way, you have to be paid only for the work you did. Just because you've been fired doesn't mean that you automatically get severance pay. Check your company's handbook or ask your employer about the severance-pay policy where you work.

The Least You Need To Know

➤ Independent contractors have much more freedom in the way they do their work than employees do.

➤ Federal laws prohibiting discrimination apply from the moment you are asked the first question in a job interview.

➤ The EEOC investigates complaints of discrimination and harassment at any stage during your employment—at the time of hiring, while you're working, and when you're fired.

➤ Under normal circumstances, you can be fired for almost any reason if you're an employee at will.

Thinking About Your Golden Years

Even though some of us may live in a constant state of denial, we're all getting older. Someday we'll be ready to retire, but it'll be a little late at that point to start worrying about what we're going to do for income. Financing your retirement is important, and it requires careful planning.

This book isn't about financial planning, so the discussion here is limited to the retirement benefits you may receive through your employer and the benefits you'll receive from Social Security.

Getting More Than a Watch When You Retire

Pension and profit-sharing plans are an attractive way for companies to give you additional compensation without increasing your salary. Under most standard plans, your company makes some type of contribution for you, but you don't receive any of the money until you retire or leave the company.

> **WHAT!?**
>
> **Legalese**
> A benefit **vests** when your right to receive it becomes permanent.

Profit-sharing and pension plans can be "win-win" situations for you and your company. If the plan your company uses meets certain requirements set by the IRS, the company gets a tax deduction for the amounts it contributes. On your side of the coin, you aren't taxed on any of this money until you actually receive it, and most people receive their distributions at a time when they fall into a lower tax bracket because they've just retired.

A profit-sharing plan and a pension plan have some important differences between them. First (and probably most obvious) is that under a profit-sharing plan, your company's contribution is based on a percentage of its profits, whereas a pension plan provides you with income that's not related to the company's profits.

Second, disbursements under a profit-sharing plan can be made in different ways and at different times during your employment. If you leave the company before retirement age, you'll probably receive one lump-sum distribution. Under most pension plans, however, disbursements are simply paid in installments when you reach retirement age, even if you've left the company before reaching that point.

A third difference between pensions and profit-sharing plans is that, under a pension plan, it usually takes longer for your benefits to vest.

Put another way, you risk losing any benefit amounts you've accumulated if you quit or get fired before your benefits have vested. After they've vested, you receive disbursements according to the terms of your plan, whether or not you remain with that company.

The amount of time it takes for your benefits to vest depends entirely on your company's specific plan, but you can usually assume that it will take anywhere from three to seven years for your benefits to vest.

Figuring Out Which Benefits You Have Coming

Chapter 16 pointed out that an employer is under no legal obligation to provide any benefits to its employees, but if it does provide benefits, the employer may be subject to various federal and state regulations. The same thing is true about retirement benefits. Employers providing retirement benefits are subject to ERISA, or the Employee Retirement Income Security Act. This act sets out various rules for employers that govern how they administer their retirement plans, and it also requires that certain notices and disclosure statements be given to the employees participating in these plans.

Under this federal law, your employer must provide you with a written explanation of the benefits you may be eligible for under the company's retirement plan. You should be provided with information concerning how to qualify for the plan, how long it takes for your benefits to vest, and how and when you can claim your benefits.

ERISA classifies all retirement plans in one of two ways: either as *defined-benefit* plans or as *defined-contribution* plans. Under a defined-benefit plan, your company pays out retirement benefits based on a set formula that factors in your years with the company and your salary. Under federal law, your company must set aside enough money to be able to make these payments when you retire. These plans are also federally insured so that if you retire and your company can't make the required benefit payments, the federal government will.

Under a defined-contribution plan, your company contributes a certain amount of money each year into your individual account, and the money is then invested. The amount you get when you retire is determined by how much the company contributes and by how well the company's investments perform. Under certain defined-contribution plans, you can also contribute directly to your individual account. A profit-sharing plan is an example of a defined-contribution plan.

> OOOOOH...
>
> **Tip**
> Most employers give you different options concerning your retirement benefits, and the choices you make can significantly affect your tax liability. Before choosing one plan over another, it's wise to get all the details from the plan administrator and review your options with your accountant.

157

Unlike the defined-benefit plan, your account is not federally insured, so a defined-contribution plan involves more risk. Under a defined-contribution plan, however, you generally have more control over the way your money is invested (under a defined-benefit plan, you have no say at all). It may not be as good as insurance, but it's something.

The Basics of Social Security (Assuming That It Hasn't Gone Bankrupt by the Time You Read This Book)

Social Security is a horribly complicated and confusing piece of federal legislation. The system provides benefits in three main ways:

➤ Under the Old Age, Survivors and Disability Insurance program, which provides benefits to workers and their families.

➤ Through Medicare, which provides medical care for people over age 65.

➤ Through Medicaid, which provides medical care for people with low incomes.

The first program in the list, often referred to as just OASDI, is the part of Social Security that's similar to the private retirement plans described earlier. You and I fund OASDI through the FICA taxes that are withheld from our paychecks. The theory is that, after we hit retirement age, we start getting back the money we paid into the system. (Oh, don't be so cynical.)

To receive benefits under OASDI, you must be at least 62 and you must be considered a "fully insured" worker. Don't sweat it, though: Being "fully insured" just means that you've worked at least 40 calendar quarters and that you've earned a certain minimum amount each quarter. The exact amount changes annually, but it's always very low.

Qualifying for Social Security benefits under OASDI is easy, but calculating the amount of benefits you're eligible for is another matter entirely. The formulas used in determining benefits are so complex that they border on the ridiculous. Unless you're a Mensa candidate and want to show off, take the easy way out: Call or visit your local Social Security office and ask for a "Verification of Earnings and Benefits" form (Form #7004, if you want to impress the person at the counter). This form is a written request to the Social Security Administration for a verification and report of your total contributions to OASDI over the years. When you receive the verification statement, you'll see that it also provides you with some basic information about which benefits you're currently eligible for under the program.

Here are some basic rules you should keep in mind about OASDI benefits:

➤ The benefits you receive are income; consequently, they may be subject to both federal and state taxes.

➤ The amount of your benefits is unaffected by other retirement benefits you may be receiving.

➤ The amount of your benefits can be affected, however, if you go back to work after you've retired and begun to receive benefits.

➤ You qualify for full benefits if you retire at age 65, but you do have the option of retiring at 62 and receiving reduced benefits.

➤ Your spouse will also receive benefits based on either actual earnings or one-half the amount of your benefits, whichever is greater.

For more information about these issues, see Part 5, "Your Life and Legacy."

Other Benefits if You Can't Work

Social Security can also pay you benefits if you become disabled and can no longer work. No age requirement is involved, as it is with retirement benefits; to receive disability benefits, however, you still have to qualify as an insured worker (that is, you still must have worked for 40 calendar quarters, as described in the preceding section). You also have to meet the administration's standards for being disabled.

The definition of a "disability" is relatively strict. Basically, any physical or mental condition that substantially keeps you from earning a living is considered a disability under Social Security rules, provided that the condition is expected to last at least a year or result in your death. (There's a cheery thought—and you thought that the *IRS* was cold-hearted.) To find out how to apply for disability benefits, contact your local Social Security office. It can provide you with the necessary forms and explain what else you have to do to qualify.

All This and Health Insurance Too?

Soon after receiving my law license, I visited my grandfather on a weekend afternoon. Pleased to have a lawyer handy (and a free one at that) he dumped a pile of paper into my arms and asked whether I could help him understand why his recent Medicare claim had been turned down. After a couple of minutes of paper-shuffling and mumbling, I began to think that I had wasted the preceding three years of my life, not to mention all that law-school tuition money. (My grandfather wasn't overly impressed either.)

Medicare, our national health-insurance system, is designed to cover people over 65 and some disabled people. It can pay a large portion of your health-care costs, but, as my grandfather can tell you, it doesn't cover everything. Coverage is broken down into two parts: hospital insurance (called "Part A" coverage) and medical insurance (called "Part B" coverage). As its name suggests, hospital coverage helps pay your hospital costs. It covers primarily your inpatient hospital care, but under certain circumstances it can also include other types of skilled care, such as the services provided by some home health-care agencies. Medical coverage helps pay for outpatient care, X-rays, blood and other lab tests, surgery, and other similar medical costs.

If you think that all this sounds like a good deal, you obviously didn't notice that I said Medicare "helps" pay for things. Medicare doesn't cover certain medical services at all, and even when it does offer coverage, there's usually a string or two attached. One of the strings is your deductible. You have to pay a deductible whenever you claim Part A or Part B Medicare benefits, and if your stay in the hospital is lengthy, it can really add up.

You can purchase a special type of insurance, called *Medigap*, that pays your Medicare deductible in addition to many costs not covered by Medicare. Several versions of this coverage are available, and your insurance agent can explain the different programs to you. Be advised that even Medigap doesn't cover absolutely everything, so even with this additional coverage, you may still find that you have to pay certain bills (or at least parts of them) on your own.

Contact your local Social Security office for information about enrolling in Medicare, but don't wait until you turn 65—begin the process at least three to six months before your birthday. Enrollment in Part A costs nothing, but you have to pay a premium for Part B coverage, as you would when you buy any other kind of insurance.

The Least You Need To Know

➤ You don't have the right to collect on benefits accumulating under a retirement plan until the benefits vest.

➤ ERISA is the federal law governing how employers administer and fund retirement plans for their employees.

➤ The Social Security Administration will provide you with a statement verifying your total contributions to OASDI and telling you which benefits you're currently eligible for under the program.

➤ Medicare pays many, but not all, health-care costs. You should talk to your insurance agent about whether a Medigap policy makes sense in your situation.

Chapter 18

The Infernal—
I Mean, Internal—
Revenue Service

In This Chapter

➤ How to reduce mistakes in your return and lessen your odds of being audited

➤ The importance of keeping records

➤ What to do if you're audited

"Of all debts, men are least willing to pay the taxes."

—Ralph Waldo Emerson

As I was opening the mail one afternoon last summer, I saw an envelope with a return address that read "Internal Revenue Service, Kansas City, MO." This was it—I was going to be audited. My stomach tied itself in knots as I considered the possibilities. Penalties. Interest. Leavenworth.

But after I settled down and read the letter, I realized that the IRS was notifying me of a mistake on my return and advising me that I would soon receive a $320 refund check under separate cover. To prove that the letter really came from the IRS, fine print at the bottom reminded me that if, at an unspecified later date, it was determined that this refund had been issued in error, I would be responsible for repaying it, with interest. What the IRS giveth...

This chapter gives you some suggestions about what to do to avoid an audit, explains the different types of audits, and teaches you what to do if you are audited.

Doing It Right the First Time

The Internal Revenue Service is not a government agency to toy with— it has a great deal of power. In addition to being able to require you to endure lengthy audits, the IRS also has the power to lien property and freeze assets in certain circumstances. You can challenge the IRS by litigating your dispute before the United States Tax Court, but even if you win, you may find that you've spent a large amount of time, money, and emotional energy on the process. All in all, it's best to do your taxes promptly and accurately, thereby reducing the chance of any problems down the road.

Despite constant cries for reform, the tax code (the fancy name for tax laws) remains an incredibly complicated piece of legislation. It has thousands of pages of rules and regulations, and thousands more pages that interpret the rules. But even so, there are still some things you can do to avoid paying more taxes than necessary and to reduce your chances of an audit:

➤ **Get organized!** Whether you prepare your own return or hire someone to do it for you, good recordkeeping is essential. Are your tax and financial records complete and stored in an organized way? Your records are the key to the following:

   Cutting the amount of time it takes to prepare your return

   Reducing the number of mistakes in your return

   Providing a defense in case of an audit

➤ **Don't wait until 10:00 P.M. on April 14 to begin working on your tax returns.** Waiting until the last minute creates all kinds of problems, and it makes it more likely that your return will have errors. It can be difficult to find the forms you need and still more difficult to get an appointment with a professional tax preparer if you need one. (My own mother would be among the first to tell you that I have no right to lecture anyone on the evils of procrastination. I feel, however, that my vast experience in this area makes me especially qualified to make this point. Besides, it's my book, and I can lecture about whatever I want. Let Mom write her own book.)

➤ **Use the correct forms, and read all the instructions.** Using the wrong kind of form or forgetting to attach a schedule will delay the processing of your return. Find out which forms you need before you begin preparing your return, and remember that not all forms can be used by all taxpayers. For example, you can use the EZ forms, such as the 1040EZ and Schedule C-EZ, if you meet certain specific criteria.

➤ **Know when to call in a pro.** The IRS distributes free booklets on a number of topics, and you can call your local IRS office to get a list of current titles. These publications are useful if you have general questions, such as which records to keep or how to deduct the business use of your car. But if you have specific or technical questions, you should talk to the IRS (it has a toll-free line with tax help), a professional accountant, or a tax preparer.

➤ **Make sure that your pro is a pro.** Find out about your tax preparer's background and experience. Does she do tax work all year, or is this just a "side job" every spring? Be certain to get a clear statement about the preparer's fees and other policies.

➤ **Keep your records.** Hold on to copies of your tax returns (state and federal) and all corresponding documents for six years (including canceled checks, W-2s, 1099s, and all the receipts on which you based your figures). Also be sure to keep copies of any correspondence you may have had with the IRS or your state department of revenue.

➤ **If you need to make estimated tax payments, make sure that you're making them on time and in the right amounts.** This rule doesn't apply to everyone, but it does apply to most self-employed people.

> OOOOOH...
>
> **Tip**
> Find out exactly what will happen if there's a mistake on your return. Will the preparer pay any penalties assessed against you? What if you're audited? Will the preparer represent you at no charge if the audit involves his mistake? Think twice about using a preparer who won't stand behind his work.

Self-employed people earn income, but there's no employer to withhold income tax. If you are in this category, you have to make quarterly payments of income tax based on what you estimate your total year's income will be. You have to be somewhat accurate in your estimation—unless you pay in at least 90 percent of what you ultimately owe this year or 100 percent of what you paid last year, you'll be charged an underpayment penalty by the IRS.

Here's a sample 1040 form.

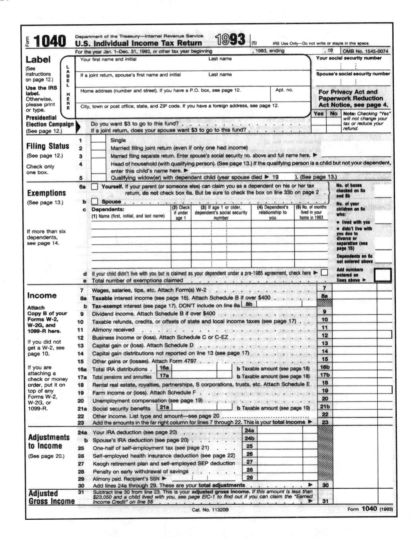

Proving That You Did It Right: The Audit

IRS audits are the stuff of legend. Just the word *audit* conjures up visions of a poor, defenseless taxpayer being placed under a giant magnifying lens, enduring a process that makes the Spanish Inquisition look like a day at the beach. Although some audits can be agony, many are not.

The IRS performs different types of audits, and the simplest is done by mail. This type of audit is usually conducted if your return has an error in it or if the IRS wants only to verify a specific part of your return, such as a medical deduction. If you get audited this way, you receive a letter in the mail describing the information the IRS is requesting and advising you about how you can respond by mail.

If you end up being audited by mail, be certain to follow all the instructions fully and keep copies of everything you receive and send back. You may want to take the extra precaution of sending replies back by certified or registered mail, but of course that still doesn't guarantee that your correspondence will get to the right person after it reaches the IRS office, and it may take a little longer for your correspondence to get there.

If the problem with your return is more serious or if the IRS wants to review a larger portion of your return, you'll probably be told that your audit will be conducted in a local IRS office. These *field audits,* as they're sometimes called, can also be held at your office or your tax preparer's office, if necessary.

Finally, a small percentage of Americans are selected for a special type of audit that occurs every few years and isn't even based on actual tax returns. These audits are conducted to give the IRS a way to measure "taxpayer compliance"—that is, to see how truthful people generally are in preparing their returns. These incredibly comprehensive audits cover every aspect of a taxpayer's return.

Legalese
An **audit** is the process of reviewing and verifying all, or just a portion of, the information contained in your tax return.

WHAT!?

These last two types of audits can be intense. You may want to bring an accountant or tax attorney with you, but first read the audit notice thoroughly to see what the real issues are before you make that decision. If things get tough during the audit, you can ask the IRS agent to stop and reschedule it for a later time so that you can bring a tax professional with you. When you receive notice of the audit, the IRS will tell you what documents you should bring with you. If you have any questions about what you should (or shouldn't) bring, talk to your accountant or attorney beforehand. Good preparation, documentation, and attention to detail are important, just as they are when you initially prepare your taxes. Make sure that you have all your financial ducks in a row before you go to the audit.

No matter which kind of audit you go through, the IRS always makes the same demand: Prove that the information on your return is correct. The only effective way to do this is by keeping good records. But how long do you have to keep them?

Generally speaking, the IRS can audit or review any return for as long as three years after its filing date, but in certain circumstances, it can go back six years rather than the normal three. In cases of fraud, no time limits are placed on the IRS and its investigations. Keep your records for at least six years (I'm assuming that you're not participating in any fraud), and make sure that you store them in a safe place. You can normally order a copy of your tax return from the IRS if you need to, but remember that the return alone isn't much help in an audit. You need supporting documentation, and after two or three years it can become difficult to replace lost or destroyed receipts.

What—Me, Worry?

The odds of being audited vary from person to person. Middle-income people generally have a 1-in-100 to a 1-in-200 chance of being audited. Your odds of being audited increase as your income level increases, and they also increase depending on what you do for a living. For example, an auto assembly-line worker has a lower chance of being audited than does a self-employed insurance agent who uses a home office. The reason is that the IRS "flags" the returns of self-employed people, especially those who work from their homes.

If you're feeling a little paranoid, don't panic. Keep in mind that we're talking about all audits, not just grueling field audits. Remember that it's still considered an audit if the IRS sends you a letter asking for documentation of that contribution you made to the American Cancer Society last year.

What To Do if You're Audited

First, review the IRS notice thoroughly. Figure out exactly what it's asking for, and get the necessary records together to review. If the audit covers only a specific part of your return or if it asks only for basic documentation, you probably can answer it yourself, either by mail or with an office visit.

If the audit looks more serious and a tax professional prepared your return, you should contact the preparer to discuss the situation. If you prepared your own return, you have to decide whether you want to spend the money to hire an accountant or tax attorney to go with you and represent you at the audit.

An audit can produce only three results:

➤ The IRS owes you money.

➤ You owe the IRS money.

➤ Your return was correct, and neither side owes money.

If you owe money, you'll be told the amount and how to pay it. Ask for a breakdown of the total amount that shows how much tax you owe as well as the interest and penalties that have been added to it. Depending on the problem with your return and the amount of money involved, you may be able to negotiate with the IRS and get it to waive some of the interest or penalty charges.

You'll probably have to pay within 30 days, but if the amount you owe is large, talk to the IRS agent about using some type of payment schedule. The terms of this type of schedule vary from case to case, based on how much you owe, your income, and the assets you own. Even if the IRS agrees to let you make payments, don't be surprised if it puts a tax lien on property you own, possibly including your home. This lien essentially makes your property collateral for the amount you owe, and it gives the IRS some assurance that you won't suddenly skip town without making your payments.

If you disagree with the outcome of your audit, you can ask that a supervisor review the auditor's findings or you can ask for more time to bring in additional records in support of your return. You can also contact your regional IRS office and ask that it review the matter. Ultimately, you can take the issue to court in one of two ways:

➤ Pay the disputed amount, and then file suit in U.S. District Court for a refund.

➤ Refuse to pay the disputed amount, and file a petition in U.S. Tax Court.

Although a lawsuit is an option, most people aren't prepared to undertake one without professional help, and it's often difficult to justify the additional costs involved in pursuing these types of actions.

The Least You Need To Know

➤ When you hire someone to prepare your taxes, find out what that person will do in case a mistake in your return leads to an audit or IRS penalties.

➤ Keep organized records, and hold on to them for six years after filing your return.

➤ Not all audits are long and involved; some involve narrow issues and can even be done by mail.

➤ You can file suit in U.S. Tax Court or U.S. District Court to challenge an audit, but you'll probably need professional help, and it can be an expensive process.

Part 4
A Roof over Your Head

I recently saw a television commercial for an extermination service that asks viewers whether they realize that there are hundreds of places in a home where pests can breed. Not to be outdone by an exterminator's marketing efforts, I now ask you, "Do you realize that there are hundreds of places in your home where legal problems can breed?" (Good thing I didn't say "where lawyers can breed"—you'd really be scared.)

Maybe that was a little dramatic, but it is true that many legal problems can develop right in your own home. This part of the book looks at some of the areas in which problems commonly arise, including leases, buying and selling a home, and disputes between neighbors. It also looks at homeowner's and renter's insurance and how the right insurance policy can protect you from all sorts of disasters.

Chapter 19

When Your Home Is Your (Rented) Castle

In This Chapter

➤ Why a written lease agreement is necessary or desirable

➤ What provisions should be in your lease

➤ How eviction proceedings work

➤ Why you might want an option to purchase as part of your lease

Almost everyone leases property at some time in their life, whether it's a house, an apartment, or a single room. Landlord-tenant courts are full of tenants who have had problems with their landlords, and vice versa. As in most other contract situations, one key to minimizing your chances of ending up in court is to have a well-drafted, clear agreement. Earlier chapters described how circuit or district courts are broken into separate divisions just for the sake of convenience and organization. Landlord-tenant court is one of those divisions.

In this chapter, you learn why you should have a written lease agreement, what should be in your lease, and how to handle common problems that come up between landlords and tenants. The primary focus of this chapter is on your rights as a tenant, but if you're a landlord, you'll probably learn a few things too.

Do You Need a Written Lease?

The simple, one-word answer is "yes," for two good reasons. From a legal standpoint, most state statutes say that a lease must be in writing if it's for one year or more. Chapter 26 covers this principle, technically referred to as the Statute of Frauds, in more depth. From a common-sense standpoint, a verbal lease agreement can cause a great deal of trouble, just as many other oral contracts do. Although it may not seem like a big deal at first, a verbal lease agreement invites arguments down the road. And, of course, if the disputes are serious enough, you can easily find yourself in landlord-tenant court.

At a minimum, your written lease agreement should contain the information listed in the following section, "The Ten Most Important Lease Provisions." You and your landlord can write your own lease, but if neither of you has any experience with leases, get yourselves some lease forms from an office-supply store rather than start from scratch. A standardized form gets you headed in the right direction, and you can still change or delete sections of it to reflect your particular agreement. If the forms you find seem too complex or if unusual circumstances are involved (such as an option to purchase), have an attorney draft the lease for you. It costs much less to have an attorney draft a good lease agreement than to hire one later to litigate a bad one.

If you're unfamiliar with leases and want to get an idea of what one looks like before you move on, check out the sample lease in Appendix B.

The Ten Most Important Lease Provisions

Make sure that any lease you sign covers, at minimum, the following points to ensure that your rights are protected (remember that these are just some basics and that your lease should be detailed enough to cover the facts of your particular situation):

1. **Rent.** Okay, you probably won't forget to put this provision in writing, but make sure that the payment terms are clear. When are

your payments due? Is there a grace period for late payments? Will you be charged a penalty for late payments? What forms of payment can you use? What happens if your check gets returned because you don't have sufficient funds in the bank to cover it?

2. **Term.** How long will you lease the property? Your lease agreement should, at the very least, set out your initial term. You also might want to consider adding a paragraph about renewing the lease at the end of the term. Note any notice requirements that will apply when you move out. Failure to give proper notice under the lease might mean that you'll end up paying a penalty or an extra month's rent.

3. **Security deposit.** Most leases stipulate that the security deposit is security for any damage you may cause to the property and that it cannot be used as the last month's rent payment. Does your lease clearly state when the security deposit can be forfeited and when it must be refunded? Will you have any right to notice before the landlord uses part or all of your deposit?

4. **Condition of premises.** Make sure that you inspect the rental property before signing your lease and before moving in. Go through the property with the property manager or the landlord, and make written notes of anything that appears broken or damaged. When you're finished inspecting the property, both of you should sign the notes and each keep a copy for your records. This precaution helps you avoid disputes over repairs or maintenance when you move out. Noting that the refrigerator was dented when you moved in, for example, will prevent the landlord from claiming that you did the damage during your stay.

> **OOOOOH...**
>
> **Tip**
> Many state laws and even some local ordinances say that, under certain circumstances, a tenant must be paid interest on her security deposit. Check your state landlord-tenant statute and your city ordinances to see whether you qualify.

5. **Repairs.** Appliances break, walls need painting, carpets wear thin, and pipes clog. Make sure that your lease spells out who is responsible for which repairs and under which circumstances the landlord can charge repair costs to you. Usually, a tenant is charged only for repairs that are beyond "normal wear and tear." It's one

thing if the pipes under your bathroom sink leak because they're old. It's another if they leak because you've been dumping chemicals from your "Develop It Yourself" darkroom lab down the drain.

6. **Pets.** Some landlords simply do not allow pets, but many allow them under specific conditions. Your landlord may put a weight limit on the pet (forget that Saint Bernard) and limit the number of pets that can live in the property. You should also expect to pay more in rent or be charged a higher security deposit for the privilege of having Fluffy live with you.

7. **Sublet or assignment.** Your lease should state whether it is transferable to another person if you want to vacate before the term is up. You can handle this type of transfer in two ways: through a sublet or an assignment.

Legalese
When you **sublet**, *you* simply lease the property to another person for part of your original lease term.

When you sublet, you are still legally a tenant, even though you don't live in the property, and you still have all the same responsibilities you did under the original lease, including the payment of your rent. In other words, even if the person to whom you sublet doesn't pay you one month's rent, you are still legally obligated to pay the landlord. The difference is that you are also a "landlord"—you collect rent from the new tenant. Subletting can cause many problems unless both lease agreements are well drafted. Disputes can easily arise over who has the responsibility of making repairs and what happens if one tenant or the other doesn't make his rent payments. Have an attorney draft your leases if you are considering subletting.

Unlike a sublet, where you end up acting as the "middle man," an assignment removes you as tenant and a new person takes your place. All the original lease terms normally stay the same after the assignment, and the new person finishes the term of the lease with the same rights and responsibilities you had under the agreement. In other words, the person you assigned to must pay the rent directly to the landlord.

When in doubt, err on the side of being too detailed in your agreement or get an attorney. Don't just assume, for example, that your landlord will let you run a home-based dog-grooming business from your new apartment. (Any business use of the property that involves customers or clients coming to your home is expressly prohibited by many residential leases and by municipal zoning codes.)

8. **Utility bills and taxes.** Your lease should state clearly which utility bills, taxes, and other charges are included in the rent amount and which are your responsibility.

9. **Default.** Your lease should spell out what the landlord can and can't do if you default under the lease. As explained in other chapters, a *default* is a failure to comply with the terms of your agreement. A lease usually provides for different penalties based on what the default is. If you pay your rent five days late, for example, you might be charged a $50 late payment fee. On the other hand, selling heroin from your apartment will typically result in an eviction. Review your lease to see what rights you and your landlord have if you default, and pay attention to what kind of notice you are entitled to under the agreement.

> **Legal Pitfalls**
> If you assign a lease, make certain that your landlord releases you from any additional liability under the lease. Unless you have this assurance, in writing, you can be liable for something the new tenant does, such as missing a rent payment.

10. **Insurance.** You may not find insurance specifically listed in your lease, but you will almost certainly find a statement limiting the landlord's liability in case of damage to the property and in case someone gets injured on the property. Your landlord's insurance covers the building in case of fire or other disaster, but it doesn't cover loss of your possessions. Likewise, the landlord's insurance also covers her if someone is injured on the property, but it doesn't protect you if you are also sued individually.

To fully protect yourself, you should purchase renter's insurance. Renter's insurance gives you the kinds of protection you're missing under the landlord's insurance, and in many ways it's similar to a standard homeowner's insurance policy. It covers the loss of your personal property and protects you if you are sued by someone who was hurt on the property. Contact your local insurance salesman for information about pricing and see Chapter 22 for more information about insurance.

To Sign or Not To Sign

If you have a roommate, how can you be sure that he won't violate the lease and leave you to deal with the landlord? One way to protect yourself is to insist that your roommate sign the lease as a tenant. If you're both tenants, you're both equally responsible for abiding by the lease terms and the landlord can sue both of you for violations of the lease. That won't help you much if your roomie moves out in the middle of the night just before the rent payment is due, so you may want to write up a short agreement between the two of you clarifying what your responsibilities are. Even this precaution doesn't completely protect you from a "roommate from hell," so the best advice I can give you is to choose your roommates carefully. If you don't know the person well, ask for a credit report first.

Evictions

Generally speaking, a landlord can evict a tenant for any serious violation of the lease. Not paying the rent is a good way to become familiar with landlord-tenant court, but you can be evicted for other reasons too. Violating a "no pets" clause, installing or removing appliances without the landlord's permission, subletting or adding new tenants without permission, and staying in the property after the lease term has expired are all grounds for an eviction suit.

The eviction process begins when the landlord gives you written notice that you have violated the lease agreement and that she intends to file suit for eviction. The notice may give you a short amount of time (usually around five days) to fix the problem, such as catching up on your past-due rent. If you do nothing, the landlord can then file suit.

Like any other lawsuit, an eviction suit begins when the landlord files a complaint and sends formal notice to you advising you when and where to appear in court. Both the complaint and notice forms, as well as general information about how eviction suits are handled in your area, are available through the office of the clerk of the court for your county (check the blue pages in your phone book). An eviction complaint typically asks for two things: that you be removed from the property, and that a monetary judgment be entered against you. Your case is given a hearing date, at which time you can present any defense you think you might have.

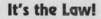

It's the Law!

One situation that normally provides a legal defense to an eviction is when a landlord lets the condition of the property deteriorate to the point that you just can't live there anymore. If the place is overrun with mice or roaches, for example, or if no running water is available, you would probably be justified in moving out and making a claim of "constructive eviction," or, in English, that the property was simply uninhabitable and it was necessary for you to move out. If you think that you have a defense for the nonpayment of your rent, contact an attorney for guidance about what you should do, preferably before you just move out or refuse to write your next rent check. Your lawyer can advise you about the best way to handle your legal claims.

Options To Buy

If a homeowner or condominium owner is having trouble selling a property, she may decide to rent it to help reduce the costs of maintaining it. Many times, these owners offer tenants an option to purchase the property at the end of the lease. An option to purchase is a separate part of the lease agreement, and it says basically that the tenant is paying an additional amount of money at the beginning of the lease to have the option of buying the property later.

Legal Pitfalls
Unless you can settle the eviction case quickly with the landlord, consult an attorney for advice. Local rules for evictions vary widely, and the cases move rapidly through the court system. You can easily find a default judgment entered against you if you miss a court date.

An important thing to keep in mind about these types of arrangements is that everything is negotiable. Some landlords let you apply some of your rent as part of your down payment if you decide to buy; some consider rent a separate issue and don't give you any credit for rent paid when you buy. A landlord who's motivated to sell the property, either because of its condition or because he just doesn't want to be a landlord anymore, may offer you an attractive deal—as much as 25 or

30 percent of your rent may be applied toward your down payment when and if you decide to buy. On the other hand, a landlord who has minimal interest in selling probably won't offer you any better terms than what he would offer a prospective buyer who just walked in off the street.

My point is that there are no hard and fast rules about crediting rent toward an eventual purchase, and like any other contract, you should try to negotiate the best deal you can.

Keep in mind that if you're the tenant, you're simply buying the right to buy the property under certain terms at a later date. If you do not buy the property, you do not get your money back. If you do buy the property, the amount you paid is (normally) not credited against the purchase price. The landlord is simply guaranteeing that he will not sell the property to anyone else until you have decided whether you want to buy it or until the option expires.

Although it might seem like money for nothing at first glance, an option to purchase can be the right choice for some people. If you really want a particular property but can't afford the down payment right now, a lease with an option to purchase puts you in the property today and "reserves" it for you for the length of your lease. That may give you enough time to save more money for the down payment, clear up past credit problems, or solve whatever other problems are keeping you from buying your dream home today.

The Least You Need To Know

➤ Always use a written lease to avoid confusion and disputes about your agreement.

➤ Start by using a form lease and make necessary changes as you go. That way, it's less likely that you'll omit an important term.

➤ For complicated leases, unusual situations, or leases with options to purchase, consult an attorney.

➤ Eviction suits usually contain both a demand that you vacate the property and a claim for monetary damages.

Buying and Selling a Home

Buying a home is often the biggest investment you make during your lifetime, and if you're a first-time buyer, the process can be overwhelming. You've got contract negotiations, property inspections, title reports, surveys, mortgages, tax prorations, escrows, insurance, and more to think about. And that's just the legal side—it doesn't include such important issues as figuring out how to load all the stuff from your spouse's closet onto a moving truck without breaking the rear axle or figuring out how much pizza and beer it will take to bribe your friends into helping you move. After all that, the closing—the signing over of your check in return for the seller's deed—can seem somewhat anticlimactic.

Before you get into this chapter, two cautions are in order. One is that because real-estate law is a huge field, it's impossible to cover every aspect of it in one chapter. If you want additional information about any of the topics covered here, try checking out (shameless-plug alert!) *The Complete Idiot's Guide to Buying and Selling a Home,* by Shelley O'Hara (published by Alpha Books). Another caution is that because real-estate laws and customs vary widely among states, and sometimes even among regions of the same state, this chapter covers only basic terms and concepts. If you have specific questions (and you will), talk to a real-estate attorney in your area.

What the Buyer and Seller Have in Common: The Contract

You've been shopping around for weeks, either on your own or with the help of a real estate broker, when you finally find the perfect place. Now what? In a normal situation, it's up to the buyer to make an offer to the seller. Mechanically, this process can be done in a couple of different ways, depending on the agreement you and the seller have with the real estate broker (or brokers). The real estate broker you're dealing with has almost always been hired by, and works for, the seller. At times, however, you, as a buyer, may want to hire a broker too, especially if you're trying to find a specific type of property or just property in an unfamiliar location.

Legal Pitfalls
Real-estate sales contracts must be in writing to be legally enforceable. If you're interested in why, check out the section on the statute of frauds in Chapter 27.

Almost every local board of Realtors has a standard contract form for its area, but if neither you nor the seller has been working with a Realtor until now, you should hire an attorney to help you write a purchase offer, which becomes an enforceable contract after the seller agrees to its terms and both parties sign it.

Regardless of who helps you complete the contract forms, the following basic points must be included:

➤ An identification of the parties and the property.

➤ A clear statement of the price and a description of how it will be paid.

This description includes such things as your down payment, the mortgage financing you plan to apply for, an assumption of the seller's current mortgage, and seller financing. This part of the contract also requires you to deposit money with the Realtor in order to give the seller some assurance that you'll carry out all your obligations under the contract. You receive a credit at closing for this deposit (called *earnest money*), but if you refuse to or can't complete the purchase, your earnest money deposit may end up being forfeited to the seller.

Sellers always want a large amount of earnest money for their own protection; buyers always want to keep it to a minimum so that if they do lose their deposit, they're not out thousands of dollars.

➤ The kind of deed that will be used to transfer the title to you.

A *deed* is a document that transfers ownership of the property from the seller to you. There are several different kinds of deeds, but when you buy property you should always insist on receiving a *warranty deed*. This type of deed guarantees that the seller has a clear, marketable title to the property and offers the buyer the most protection. (Marketable title is discussed more fully later in this chapter.)

➤ The kind of title evidence the seller is required to provide.

➤ Whether the seller will have to provide you with a survey, title insurance, termite inspection, or other documentation.

➤ Whether you have the right to have your own professional inspection of the property.

These inspections are performed at the buyer's expense, and you can choose from a variety of services. Some home-inspection services offer a general inspection of the entire house, including the structure (walls, roof, foundation, and so on) and all the major systems (such as heating, electric, and plumbing). Additionally, some services specialize in a certain type of inspection. For example, some services test only for radon gas, others look for termites and other pests, and still others do only well and septic-system tests. Your real estate broker or attorney can tell you which inspections are commonly done in your area and can refer you to qualified inspectors.

➤ A description of which personal property will be included in the sale.

This list contains all the items included in the sale that aren't technically considered part of the "real estate." For example, your list might include such things as the dishwasher, stove, refrigerator, and other appliances.

➤ A description of when, where, and how the closing will occur.

➤ A statement about the condition of the property—for example, whether it's being sold "as is" or whether the seller is making any representations about the working order of major systems and appliances.

➤ How taxes, insurance, water or fuel bills, and so on will be pro-rated at closing.

Suppose that I'm selling my house to you, that my property taxes for the current year were due in March, and that I paid them on time. If we close in July, I should receive some money back from you at closing because I paid a full year's worth of taxes but lived in the house for only a little less than half the year.

If the bill is $3,650, for example, we would begin by dividing that number by 365 to see what the tax bill is on a per-day basis. In this example, it's $10 per day. If closing occurs on July 1, we would count how many days are left in the year (183) and multiply that number by the $10 per day, which produces a total of $1,830. You would owe me this amount at closing for your share of the property taxes. I will have paid a net amount of $1,820 toward the taxes, and you will have paid $1,830. Splitting the bill in this way is fair to both of us because the figures are proportionate to the amount of time each of us owned the property during the year.

➤ Who will bear the risk of loss if the property is damaged or destroyed between the time the contract is signed and the time of closing.

➤ Whether the contract is contingent on anything.

You will probably want to make the purchase contingent on your ability to get a mortgage so that if you don't qualify for financing, you can get out of the contract without losing your deposit. You can also make the contract contingent on the outcome of a professional home inspection or your ability to sell your current home, but you should remember that the more contingencies you add, the less likely it is that the seller will accept your offer. Your Realtor or attorney can advise you about which contingencies are customary in your area.

These are just some of the points to cover in your agreement; even though the preceding list looks long, it's not complete by any means. Don't try to use it to draft your own contract.

After your offer is submitted to the seller, it is either accepted or rejected. If it's accepted, you have a contract. After you've deposited your earnest money, you're ready to move on to the next stage of the process. If the offer is rejected, the seller will probably make a counteroffer on one or more points, and negotiations will continue until either you reach an agreement or one of you gives up on the process.

> OOOOOH...
>
> **Tip**
> One common contingency to include is that the contract will be subject to attorney approval. This contingency gives your attorney and the attorney for the seller a few days to review the contract and to propose any changes they might feel are necessary. Considering the amounts of money and liability involved in real-estate transactions, it's important to have this added protection whether you're buying or selling.

A Word of Caution About Buying "On Contract"

Some buyers may find that they can't afford the mortgage payments on their dream house because bank interest rates are too high. Other buyers may not be able to get a loan from a bank or savings and loan because of past credit problems. But these problems don't necessarily mean that they're doomed to rent for another year or two.

One way around problems like these is to ask the seller about *seller financing*. Two types of seller financing are commonly used, and they're relatively simple. The first type is the simplest: You sign a mortgage with the seller, and after closing you make payments to her just as though a bank held the mortgage. In this situation, the entire process, from sales contract through closing, is the same as normal. At the end of the process, you own the land and the seller has a lien on the property (the mortgage).

The other type of seller financing involves an *installment contract,* in some areas called a land contract, a contract for deed, or even articles of agreement. No matter what it's called, it works the same way. Under an installment contract, you still negotiate a sales contract as you normally would, and you still end up making payments to the seller rather than to a bank. Unlike the situation in which the seller simply holds a mortgage on the property after closing, however, under an installment contract the seller doesn't give you a deed until you make all your scheduled payments. If your payment schedule under an installment contract lasts ten years, for example, you don't receive your deed (making you the legal owner of the property) for ten years.

One concern that occurs with an installment contract is, "What happens if you don't make your payments?" You run the risk of losing both the money you already paid to the seller *and* the house. This situation may seem extreme, but it's still the traditional common-law rule that is applied to installment contracts. Because of the sometimes harsh results of this rule, many states have enacted statutes that change the rules about defaults and installment contracts.

Some of these states (such as Illinois, Florida, and Maryland) make the seller follow rules similar to those that apply to banks trying to foreclose a mortgage. Under these rules, the buyer has a statutory right to catch up on his payments and avoid a complete forfeiture under the installment contract. In other states (such as California, Wisconsin, and Montana), the buyer has even more protection if he defaults on the installment contract. In these states, the buyer may be entitled to receive a refund of at least some of the money paid to the seller.

Installment contracts can be complicated, and if you and your seller are interested in using one, you should be sure to have it reviewed thoroughly by your respective attorneys. Also be sure to ask your attorney about your state's rules in the event that you default on your payments, so that you know exactly what kind of risk is involved.

LAW OFFICES OF
BRENT W. TERRY
SUITE 300 · GOLF PLACE
449 TAFT AVENUE
GLEN ELLYN, ILLINOIS 60137

June 8, 1995

Mr. and Mrs. Robert Homeseller
9650 W. 71st Street
Springfield, IL 60448

RE: Sale of 9650 W. 71st Street, Springfield

Dear Mr. and Mrs. Homeseller:

Please be advised that I will be representing Jack and Marie
Housebuyer in their purchase of your home. Pursuant to the
attorney approval contingency of the contract, I would ask that
the following changes to the contract be made:

1. Subparagraph (g) of paragraph 2 shall be deleted.

2. Paragraph 5 of the "Conditions and Stipulations" shall be
modified to state that in the event of a default by the Buyers,
the Sellers' remedies will be limited to forfeiture of any
earnest money actually deposited by the Purchasers prior to the
default.

3. Paragraph 9 shall be modified to include facsimile
transmissions during regular business hours as an acceptable form
of notice.

If you are in agreement with the above modifications, please
acknowledge that fact by signing the enclosed copy of this letter
and returning it to my attention at your earliest convenience.

Very truly yours,

BRENT W. TERRY
Attorney at Law

Your attorney may ask for modifications to a sales contract, as shown here.

Things To Do Between the Signing of the Contract and the Closing

After the contract is signed, both the buyer and the seller must begin getting ready for the closing. On the buyer's side, the main concern is the mortgage financing; on the seller's side, it's document preparation and clearance of any title problems.

If You've Got the Money...

If you're a first-time buyer, be aware that shopping for a mortgage can be a time-consuming project. Not all mortgages are created equal, and

Legal Pitfalls
A prequalification letter is not the same thing as a loan commitment. Prequalification is usually based solely on unverified information you provide to the lender, so expect to go through the normal loan-application and approval process when the time comes. Even if you have a prequalification letter from a lender, your loan application can still be denied.

you need time to become familiar with the financing programs that are available. As with anything else, the only way to get the best deal on a mortgage is to shop around and compare. Here's food for thought while your loan officer is explaining the affordability of your financing: The word *mortgage* is Latin for "death pledge."

After you've decided on a lender, the approval process can take another 30 to 45 days, and sometimes more. Make sure that you begin looking for a lender as soon as the seller has accepted your offer so that you don't have any problems meeting the contingency dates in the contract. Many lenders can help you shop for a mortgage even before you've shopped for a house, through a process known as prequalification.

During *prequalification*, you give the lender much of the same information as you would if you were actually applying for a loan. After the lender reviews it, you receive a letter explaining which kind of loan programs you qualify for and the amount of financing you can receive. You can use prequalification to do the following:

➤ Determine how much home you can afford to buy and the likely total cost of your financing.

➤ Educate yourself about different types of loan programs.

➤ Speed up the loan-approval process because you'll already have done much of the necessary paperwork.

➤ Make your offer more appealing to the seller because you'll have proof of your ability to get financing.

A federal law, the Real Estate Settlement and Procedures Act (or RESPA, for short) gives borrowers certain rights and protections in applying for and obtaining mortgage financing. RESPA applies to any first mortgage on a one- to four-family residence made by a federally insured or regulated lender. In English, unless you're borrowing money from Mom and Dad or the seller is providing your financing, you're probably covered by the act. Here's why it's important:

➤ Within three days of making your loan application, you should receive a copy of the HUD booklet *Settlement Costs and You.* Make sure that you get a copy, and *be sure to read it.* It contains an incredible amount of information about settlement fees and costs and about the settlement process. You receive an additional HUD booklet about adjustable-rate loans if you've applied for that kind of mortgage.

➤ You should also receive a good-faith estimate of your closing costs within three days of making your application. This form shows what your settlement costs are expected to be, but keep in mind that all these numbers are estimates. Your final figures may not match the good-faith estimate dollar for dollar, but they should be reasonably close.

➤ You will receive at the time of closing a Uniform Settlement Statement that should detail all your actual closing costs. It also shows any credits provided to you by the seller in addition to the seller's closing costs.

After your mortgage application has been approved, you have to purchase insurance for your new home, and you also have to take care of any conditions your lender put on your loan commitment. Common loan-commitment conditions include such things as paying off a credit-card account prior to closing and providing a gift letter from your parents showing that they gave you $3,500 to use as a down payment.

...I've Got the Deed

While the buyer is working on his financing, the seller also has things to take care of to get ready for closing. As the seller, you're obligated to deliver a *marketable title*, or a title that's free from defects, liens, or other problems. You or your attorney must order from a local title or abstract company some type of title report that shows the current condition of the title to your property.

If you review the title report, you'll see that it identifies you as the current owner, provides a legal description of the property, and gives other general information about the property. More important, it shows any liens affecting the property in addition to anything that

Legal Pitfalls
Different areas of the country use different documents to report and guarantee the condition of title: title insurance, abstracts, opinion letters, or certificates of title. Your attorney or real-estate broker can tell you what's customary where you live.

restricts the use or transfer of the property. These restrictions and liens are collectively referred to as *encumbrances,* and each one must be reviewed. Certain encumbrances are generally considered permissible, and the buyer is obligated to accept the property subject to these encumbrances on the title. Other encumbrances are not permissible; the seller must remove them before or at the time of closing. If it can't be done, the buyer is not obligated to buy the property.

This list shows some common permitted encumbrances:

➤ Real-estate taxes not due at the time of closing.

➤ Building and building line restrictions.

   These restrictions deal with the types of structures you can put on your lot and where you put them. They're used to help give a subdivision or development a neat, orderly appearance. A typical building line restriction might require that your house be set back at least 30 feet from the street.

➤ Public utility easements.

   These restrictions allow a utility company to come onto your property for a limited purpose, such as to repair a damaged line.

➤ Zoning ordinances.

   These city, county, or township ordinances can regulate the appearance of your property. For example, your city may have an ordinance that prohibits you from building fences taller than eight feet high on residential property.

➤ Restrictions and rules of a homeowner's association.

And here are some common encumbrances that aren't permitted:

➤ The seller's existing mortgage.

➤ Mechanic's liens.

Suppose that the seller had a new roof put on last month but never paid the contractor. The roofer can record a lien against the property for the value of his services and materials.

➤ Tax sales or tax liens.

For example, if the seller forgot to pay his 1993 property taxes when they were due, the county will have a lien on his property for this unpaid amount plus interest.

➤ Judgments against the seller that have been recorded against the property.

If I had sued your seller and obtained a judgment against him for $2,000, I could record the judgment against his property and create a lien in my favor. (Refer to Chapter 4 for more information about enforcing judgments in this way.)

In addition to providing the title report, you may be required to provide the buyer with a survey, a termite report, a well and septic report, or other reports about the condition of the property. These requirements are in the contract terms.

Last, your attorney must prepare the necessary documents for closing. At minimum, you'll have a deed to convey title to the real estate and a bill of sale to transfer the personal property that's included in the sale. You'll probably be asked to sign an affidavit saying that you haven't done anything to encumber the property since the time that the title report was prepared. Many attorneys provide their sellers with a separate closing statement, showing them the costs they've incurred in the sale as well as the amount of the proceeds they'll receive. Again, the form and number of documents you'll be asked to sign as the seller depends largely on your state's real-estate laws and on local custom.

The (Not So) Big Moment: The Closing

At the beginning of this chapter, I said that the closing could be anti-climactic, and by now you've probably figured out why. By the time a closing is scheduled, both the buyer and the seller (and the Realtors, attorneys, and lender) have already done the most difficult part of their respective jobs. The closing is simply an exchange of paperwork (the basis for the term for real-estate closings: "passing papers"), checks, and keys. Depending on where you live, closings in your area may even be conducted through escrow companies, with none of the parties present for the final disbursement.

Before closing, you should go to the house and check everything thoroughly. You want to make sure that the property is in the same condition it was in when you signed the contract, unless the seller agreed to make certain repairs. In that case, you want to make sure that the repairs were made. Ask the seller whether the work came with any guarantees, and, if so, get a copy of the guarantee as well as a copy of the paid receipt for the work.

If you discover problems with the house after closing (the roof leaks, for example, or the garbage disposal doesn't work), you may or may not have a legal claim against the seller. Although a seller doesn't normally guarantee the condition of the house or its contents after closing, a seller can be held liable for problems under certain circumstances. For example, if the seller knew about a problem and tried to hide it (such as paneling the basement to hide cracks in the foundation), he usually is liable for the cost of repairs.

Your lawyer can advise you in situations like these and help you figure out whether you have a valid claim against your seller.

The Least You Need To Know

➤ Regardless of who drafts your real-estate contract, make certain that it is detailed and that you understand all your obligations under it.

➤ Prequalification can help you get a head start on the financing of your new home and can make your offer more attractive to a seller. (Just remember that it's still not an actual loan commitment.)

➤ RESPA requires your lender to provide you with some good, comprehensive disclosures and explanations at the beginning of the loan-application process.

➤ The seller must make sure that title to the property is marketable and that she can provide proof of that to the buyer at the time of closing.

Chapter 21

No Home Is an Island

In This Chapter

➤ Common restrictions on your property

➤ Nuisances and how to get rid of them

➤ Liability concerns for homeowners

If you're a fan of "The Honeymooners," you're probably familiar with Ralph Cramden's frequent speech about how "A man's home is his castle, and in his castle, he is the king." To a large extent, Ralph was right, but you and your property don't exist in a legal vacuum, either. There are neighbors to consider, zoning laws to obey, city ordinances to comply with, and homeowners' association rules to follow. As though that's not enough, liability issues can arise if someone gets hurt while on your property. It looks as though Ralph may have oversimplified the concept of home ownership, as you'll learn in this chapter.

It's My Property, and I Can Do What I Want (Kind of)

If you just bought a home, you probably aren't pondering the responsibilities and restrictions that come with it. I'm not talking about just mowing the lawn and trimming the hedges—I'm talking about the legal responsibilities that are part of home ownership.

As you learned in Chapter 20, a person buying property is provided with information concerning the title to the land. In addition to telling you who the current owner of the property is, the title report also gives you information about restrictions that may apply to the property. For example, if the title report shows that a homeowners' association governs the property, you are subject to the association's by-laws and rules when you buy the property. For this reason, it's important to know what the association's by-laws and rules are before you purchase. If you plan to erect a 15-foot-high stockade fence around your property and the homeowners' association rules prohibit any kind of fencing, you obviously have a problem.

The following list shows some things that can affect the way you use your property and that normally show up on a title report:

➤ **Homeowners' associations.** As just mentioned, your use of the property may have to conform with a homeowners' association's by-laws. An association can have rules concerning the appearance of your home, and it can restrict what you put on your lot, such as fences, pools, or sheds. Additionally, associations normally charge their members some type of assessment fee to pay for the landscaping or maintenance of common areas (parks, ponds, and subdivision entrances, for example). You should take these restrictions seriously: An association can sue an individual homeowner in order to enforce its regulations, and it can place a lien against a homeowner's property for unpaid assessments. Even though it's unlikely to get this far, the association could actually foreclose on the lien (just as a bank forecloses on an overdue mortgage) and get a court order forcing you to sell the property to pay off the lien amount.

Legal Pitfalls
Condominium owners are always part of an association and are governed by its rules and regulations. As in the case of a homeowners' association, condo owners can be sued for violating the rules, and a lien can be placed against their unit for unpaid monthly assessments.

➤ **Easements.** An easement is the right to enter onto someone's property for a limited purpose. Different kinds of easements exist, but the most common is a public-utility easement. This easement gives a utility company access to your property for service installation or repairs. Easements vary in size, but they usually run along the sides and back of your lot. You are required to keep the easement clear so that the utility company can have free access.

Most utility companies will try to work around objects that might be in the easement, but if they can't, they have the right to remove the object. This is no big deal if the offending object is a small bush or a lightweight chain-link fence. It's a completely different matter if you've built an in-ground pool in an easement. The part of the pool crossing the easement (or, to be technical, *encroaching* on the easement) can be removed, and the utility company may have no obligation to pay for the damage.

➤ **Shared property.** If you live in a condominium or a townhouse, you probably share at least one of your walls with your next-door neighbor (the kitchen wall in Unit 302, for example, also serves as the living room wall in Unit 304). Walls that are shared between property owners are called *party walls* (don't get excited—they sound more fun than they are), and both property owners have a duty to maintain the wall. Sometimes the owners prepare and record a "property wall agreement," which is a written document establishing each person's rights and responsibilities concerning the wall and its maintenance and repair, although this step isn't necessary. Unless some other agreement is made, the cost of maintaining or repairing the wall is shared equally by the property owners. This basic principle—sharing the expense of upkeep and repairs for shared areas—also applies in cases in which adjacent land owners share a common driveway.

➤ **Zoning or use restrictions.** Your title report may also describe certain restrictions on how your property can be used. For example, use restrictions commonly require that a particular property be used only as a residence and not for commercial or business purposes. The way you use your property is probably also restricted by city ordinances on zoning and other related matters.

The things listed can obviously have an effect on the way you use your property—that's why it's best to review these issues before buying (as you learned in Chapter 20). But if you've already bought your home, there is a chance that you can get the rules changed. If you want to install a pool, for example, but find that a telephone company easement is messing up your plans, call the telephone company and have it review the easement. Most utilities will release their easement rights if they no longer need the easement. Likewise, a homeowners' association may agree to waive a specific restriction for you, and a city or town may even agree to waive a zoning requirement in rare cases. It never hurts to ask, but don't get your hopes up. If an exception were made for every homeowner, there would be no point in making the rules in the first place. Contact your lawyer for advice about handling problems in these areas because it's often difficult to get special exceptions made for a single piece of property.

Issues Between Neighbors

Almost every homeowner has a run-in with a neighbor at one time or another. Most of these problems work themselves out, but if the problem is serious enough (or the people are stubborn enough), the issue can end up in court. If you experience any of the common problems described in this section, keep your sense of perspective. Proving that you're right may not be worth the time and money involved in litigation, not to mention the general hard feelings you'll create.

This Land Is My Land, That Land Is Your Land

It's relatively easy to avoid lot-line disputes with your neighbors, but these problems still occur all the time. Disputes typically arise when a neighbor puts something on your land or vice versa. How bad the dispute gets often depends on what the "something" is—a rose bush planted 18 inches into your yard probably won't upset you nearly as much as a new driveway that overlaps by the same amount.

Legally, you have the right to demand that your neighbor remove whatever is encroaching over the lot line, including things that may overhang your property line, such as tree limbs. If your neighbor refuses, you can remove the encroachment yourself, but depending on the nature of the work involved, you can inadvertently make yourself liable for damages to your neighbor's property. If your neighbor puts up an aluminum shed in the backyard, for example, and you determine that part of it is in your yard, you can move the shed if your neighbor refuses to do it himself. But if you damage the shed when you move it, you'll probably be held liable for the damage you cause. A little ironic, isn't it?

The same rule applies if you hire someone to do the job for you. You can demand that your neighbor pay for the expense you've incurred, but you're also responsible for any damage done to your neighbor's property by the person you hired.

I doubt that anyone has made a formal study of boundary disputes, but if someone ever does, I'm willing to bet that improperly placed fences are ranked as the number-one cause of all lot-line disputes. It can be expensive to move a misplaced fence, so make sure that you have your lot surveyed and staked before the work begins. Also ask the fence company about its policy if the fence is placed incorrectly.

> **Legal Pitfalls**
> Before you begin dragging things across your respective yards, be certain that there is actually an encroachment. Call a surveyor if necessary. Second, ask your neighbor in writing to correct the problem. Third, if the encroachment is large or the offending item is expensive, contact your attorney before you do anything rash. You probably wouldn't want to jackhammer off a section of your neighbor's driveway without getting a court order authorizing your action.

Loud Noises, Strange Smells, and Other Nuisances

The law recognizes your right to use and enjoy your property without interference from others, including your neighbors.

A nuisance can be caused in a variety of ways. If your neighbor's kid plays bass for the band Six Drunk Demons and the band likes to practice in the garage at 3:00 A.M. or if the person next door has so many cats that the entire block smells like a giant litter box, you're probably the victim of a nuisance.

> **Legalese**
> A **nuisance** is any act or condition that seriously interferes with another person's right to use and enjoy his property.

You can sue to have a nuisance removed, but before you rush to the courthouse, consider other alternatives you might have. To use the examples I just gave, you may be able to handle your problem with the band by filing a complaint with the police. And you can contact your local animal-control agency or health department

197

for help with the "cat freak." In both situations, the nuisance gets removed and you don't incur any legal fees.

If you have a nuisance problem, discuss the matter with your attorney to see how to handle the problem in the quickest and most cost-effective way.

Common Liability Issues for Homeowners

As mentioned in this chapter, you and your property don't exist in a legal vacuum, and this principle becomes most obvious if someone is injured while on your property. Personal-injury suits are part of a larger area of law known as torts (no, not the law of pastries).

A *tort* is simply a wrong or injury that's been done to someone. It's an extremely broad definition that covers many different types of injuries, everything from defamation (you injured my reputation) to assault and battery (you injured my face) to negligence (I was injured because you drive like a complete goof). One thing to note, however, is that breach of contract (see Chapter 27) is not one of the civil wrongs included under tort law.

Legalese
A **tort** is a civil wrong or injury for which a court awards money damages.

Legal Pitfalls
If you're sued for negligence, contact your attorney right away. You should also contact your homeowner's insurance company and advise the company of the lawsuit because the cost of your defense may be covered by your policy. See Chapter 22 for more information about liability insurance.

To prove a tort claim, the plaintiff (the injured party) must show that the defendant had a legal duty of care to the plaintiff, that the duty was breached, and that the plaintiff was injured as a result.

So what does all this have to do with a homeowner? Under your state's law, you have a duty to protect from harm those who come onto your property. If you breach this duty (in other words, if you're negligent) and a person is injured as a result, you could be liable for that person's injuries.

Let's use snow shoveling as an example. Generally speaking, you have no legal obligation to shovel your walk, but if you decide to shovel, you have an obligation not to shovel it in a negligent manner. If you shovel but don't remove all the underlying ice and I slip on the ice and fall and break my arm, my lawsuit will claim that your negligence caused my injuries. Would I win this type of suit? Maybe, but it depends on your state's laws as well as on the other facts in the case. If I was drunk when I hit your sidewalk, for example, it might change your liability.

Rover Versus the Mailman

Pets can be another source of liability to you as a homeowner. In the good old days, man's best friend was given the benefit of the doubt. The law recognized a principle known as the "one bite" rule, which said essentially that an owner was not liable for a dog-bite injury unless the dog had bitten someone in the past or had previously shown vicious tendencies. This rule gave Rover one free bite, so it was important to make the most of it.

Today, many states have gotten rid of the "one bite" rule and hold a pet owner responsible for any injuries the dog causes, even if the noble beast doesn't have a checkered past.

Swimming Pool Problems

A swimming pool can add to your potential liability problems as a homeowner. Pools are unique because they are considered attractive nuisances. An attractive nuisance is an object or condition normally considered dangerous to kids but that attracts them anyway. An unattended pool obviously can be deadly to a small child, but that doesn't mean that the child won't play in or around one if given the chance.

The law in this area varies widely from state to state, and if you're installing a pool, you should discuss the issue of liability with your insurance agent or attorney. In addition to the guidance they offer, check with your city to see whether it has special cover or fencing requirements for pools.

The Least You Need To Know

➤ Restrictions concerning how you use your property can come from various sources, including homeowners' associations, city ordinances, and recorded easements.

➤ Depending on the situation, you may be able to get rid of a nuisance without having to file a lawsuit.

➤ Taking matters into your own hands in a lot-line or nuisance dispute with a neighbor can often backfire and create liability problems for you in the long run.

➤ If you're negligent and someone on your property gets hurt because of it, you can be held liable for that person's injuries.

Chapter 22

C.Y.A. (Cover Your Assets)

Chapter 21 pointed out some of the liability issues homeowners can be exposed to, but another kind of risk is involved in home ownership as well: damage or destruction of your property. The property damage and loss caused by a fire, tornado, or even a burglar can cost tens of thousands of dollars to repair. A good homeowner's insurance policy from a reputable company can protect you from these potentially devastating losses.

Getting the Protection You Need

If you took out a mortgage when you purchased your home, it's a safe bet that you were required to purchase homeowner's insurance before your closing took place. The requirement of insurance isn't the result of your lender's deep concern for you—the bank simply wants to know that its loan will be repaid no matter what happens to the property. Under the terms of a standard mortgage, your house is the collateral for your loan. If it was destroyed and you were to stop making your mortgage payments, your lender would be left high and dry. To protect itself from this situation, a lender wants to be named as an "additional insured" on your policy and will require that you insure the property for at least the value of the loan.

What's in Your Homeowner's Policy

A standard homeowner's insurance policy protects you in two ways: with property coverage and with liability coverage. The property coverage in your policy protects you from loss in case the property or its contents are damaged or destroyed. Your insurance agent can explain the different coverage options available through her company, but typically you'll discuss these points:

Legal Pitfalls
Don't assume that the coverage your lender requires is adequate for your protection. The lender typically requires just enough coverage to pay off your loan, but keep in mind that you probably didn't finance 100 percent of your home's value. Talk to your insurance agent to make sure that the coverage you're buying not only meets your lender's requirements but also enables you to replace your house and possessions.

➤ **What risks do you want to insure against?** You can choose, to a certain degree, which risks you want to be insured against. The broader the coverage, of course, the more expensive your premium. You may even need an additional, separate policy to cover certain serious risks, such as floods or earthquakes.

➤ **How will value be determined if there is a loss?** The best way to cover yourself on this point is to ask for "replacement-cost coverage." This coverage requires the insurance company to pay a claim based on the current cost of replacing the damaged item.

➤ **What extra coverage do you need for the contents of your home?** Review the basic coverage included in your policy, and be aware that certain valuables, such as furs, expensive camera equipment, jewelry, antiques, and certain collectibles, won't be adequately covered by the basic policy limits. Make a list of all your particularly valuable possessions for your agent, and get additional coverage for these items. You may have to document the value of these items for your agent with appraisals, photographs, and so on.

Legal Pitfalls
If you run a business from your home, be sure to ask your agent about getting additional coverage for your computers or other equipment. Items you use for business purposes aren't normally covered under a standard homeowner's policy.

The second part of your policy, liability coverage, protects you primarily in case someone is injured while on your property. If your kid leaves his Super Ninja Robot Mutant Dinosaur Warrior toy on the stairs, causing your mother-in-law to swan-dive into the basement, your liability coverage protects you when she sues for her injuries. When you discuss liability coverage with your insurance agent, be sure to ask the following questions:

➤ **How much coverage do I need?** Each policy has a limitation on its coverage, often $100,000 per claim. If your mother-in-law's hip replacement cost $125,000, for example, you could be liable for the additional amount.

➤ **What's included in the coverage?** Under most policies, all your mother-in-law's medical bills are covered (up to the policy limit), and so are your legal fees if she sues you. But, again, policies differ, so have your agent show you what is and isn't included in yours.

➤ **What kinds of incidents are covered?** Basic negligence, such as leaving toys on a staircase, are covered, but if you're concerned about any particular hazards or risks, ask your agent.

Just as with property coverage, the more options you add to your policy's liability coverage, the higher your premium will be.

A Special Warning to Condo Owners (and Apartment Renters)

If you own a condominium unit, you still need your own insurance. The condo association has a master policy that insures the association itself and covers the buildings and common areas. This coverage does not protect you directly, and it doesn't cover the interior or contents of your unit.

For example, if there's a fire in your building and your unit is gutted, the condominium association's master policy would pay for the structural repairs necessary to rebuild your unit. But it probably doesn't cover much of the repairs to the inside of the unit, and it definitely doesn't cover any other losses you had. Your furniture, clothes, stereo, Sega system—everything would be gone, and the association's policy wouldn't pay you a dime. Likewise, if someone inside your unit falls, breaks his hip, and later wants to sue you for his injuries, you won't be covered by the association's liability insurance because the injury took place inside your unit.

So what can you do to protect yourself? The answer is not "roll the injured person into a common area and run back inside your unit." The answer is "buy adequate insurance coverage for your unit, just as you would if you owned a house." Talk to your insurance agent about the different types of coverage available, but be sure that you buy a policy which provides both property coverage and liability coverage.

If you rent an apartment, the same warning applies to you. Regardless of what insurance your landlord may carry on the building, it's a safe bet that if disaster strikes, you'll be left high and dry. Contact your insurance agent and ask about renter's insurance. It's usually not that expensive, and the protection it offers is important.

What To Do if You Have a Claim

If something happens that might be the basis for a claim under your homeowner's policy, there are certain basic things to remember:

➤ **Report the incident.** If you fail to notify your insurance company promptly of a possible claim situation, you can jeopardize some or all of your coverage.

➤ **Document the event.** Whether it involves a property-damage claim or potential liability, keep a good record of what happened. Write down the details of the incident so that you don't forget anything when you contact your insurer. Taking pictures can also be helpful. Keep claim forms, reports, appraisals, receipts, estimates, and other paperwork together in one place for easy reference.

➤ **Follow instructions.** Your insurance adjuster or agent will need your cooperation, and the terms of your policy obligate you to assist the insurer with the processing of your claim.

➤ **Keep records of your conversations with your insurance agent or adjuster.** If the claim is large or seems complicated, you may want to confirm in writing your telephone conversations with the adjuster to lessen the chance of a misunderstanding later.

A good friend of mine in the insurance business is fond of pointing out that no insurance company makes a profit by paying claims. If you jeopardize your coverage by making an inflated claim, failing to report a claim promptly (usually within 48 to 72 hours), or by being uncooperative with the insurance company, you are providing the company with a valid reason not to pay.

If you have complaints about your insurance company or the handling of a claim, contact your state's department of insurance. If it can't help you resolve your problem, you may have to hire an attorney to pursue the matter with the insurance company.

Tip
Less reputable companies in the industry will try, of course, to avoid paying on any claim—including a valid one.

The Least You Need To Know

➤ Homeowner's insurance protects you by providing both property-damage coverage and liability coverage.

➤ You should review your policy thoroughly with your agent before signing on the dotted line, because many people need more than just basic coverage.

➤ It's important to report a claim promptly and keep good records so that you can document the claim.

➤ Complaints about your insurer should be taken to your state's department of insurance, or you can consult an attorney.

Part 5
Your Life and Legacy

Even though most of us hate to admit it, we're all mortal. Someday we all have to face old age, illness, and even the Reaper himself. In case that thought doesn't depress you enough, each of these things brings with it a unique set of legal issues and problems. For example, how can you control what medical treatment you receive if you're too ill to tell the doctors what you want? What legal rights do you have as a patient in a nursing home? How can you make sure that your money and property go where you want them to after you're dead? Should a lawyer represent you when you go to meet St. Peter at the Pearly Gates? The chapters in this part help guide you through these and other legal issues (okay, maybe not that one about St. Peter).

Serious medical problems or the death of a loved one can be a tremendous financial and emotional strain on anyone. This part of this book can help lighten the load, by showing you how to minimize or avoid some of the legal complications that commonly come up.

Matters of Life and Death

If you think that the law doesn't have much to do with your next stay in the hospital or trip to the doctor, think again. Health-care reform, medical malpractice, patient's rights, "right to die" questions—you see these issues in headlines every week, and they're just some of the areas in which the law and medicine become entangled with each other.

In this chapter, you'll learn what your rights are as a patient and how to protect yourself in the areas of medical malpractice, long-term care, and decisions about life-sustaining treatment.

The Legal Side of Being a Patient

Imagine that you're sitting in a hospital emergency room because your new vegetable slicer tried to make julienne fries out of your fingers rather than that potato. You might be thinking about how many stitches you need, whether the doctor will prescribe pain killers, or how cool your scar will look. Chances are, you won't be mentally reviewing your legal rights as a patient.

Whether or not you're aware of them, you do have certain rights as a patient. Some states have passed laws specifically establishing these rights; in other areas, doctors and hospitals follow standards set by the American Medical Association, the American Hospital Association, and other professional organizations.

Your Rights as a Patient

Many hospitals and clinics provide you with a written statement of their policies and your rights as a patient when you first come in for treatment. You'll probably receive it, in addition to various insurance forms and a general release form, when you're admitted for treatment. The hospital release form will probably talk about such things as your responsibility to pay for the services provided (whether you have insurance coverage) and how the hospital cannot guarantee the results of any treatment.

The exact form and content of these releases vary widely, but they all are written primarily for the benefit of the hospital. On the other hand, the statement of patient rights and hospital policies is written primarily for your benefit as the patient. You will probably be required to read and sign both kinds of documents in order to be admitted. This section lists some of the basic rights you have as a patient:

➤ **Unless it's an emergency, you have the right to be informed and actively consulted about your condition and its treatment.** You have the right to receive and discuss information about your condition, the specific kinds of treatments available, the doctor's experience with your type of condition, and the risks and benefits involved in treatment. You also have the right to get second opinions.

➤ **You have the right to choose which treatment to accept and, generally speaking, to refuse treatment altogether.** The right to refuse treatment is not absolute, especially in cases in which you don't have the mental capacity to make that type of decision or your condition presents a serious threat to others. (You probably wouldn't be allowed to refuse treatment if you were found to be carrying the Ebola virus, for example.)

➤ **You have the right to make an informed decision about whether to try any experimental treatment or drug.** You must be fully advised of all the risks involved before you make your decision.

➤ **You have the right to have a properly prepared living will or power of attorney honored by the doctor and the hospital.** This chapter discusses both these documents later so that you can "properly prepare" one if you want.

➤ **In an emergency, you have the right to be treated at any hospital, and you also have the right to expect continuity in your care.** A hospital cannot have you transferred or discharged, for example, without notifying you in advance and discussing it with you. Likewise, your doctor can't suddenly end her professional relationship with you without first giving you reasonable notice and a chance to find another doctor.

In non-emergency situations, a private hospital can refuse to treat you if you cannot offer proof of insurance or your ability to otherwise pay for the its services or if you refuse to comply with its admissions procedures (such as refusing to sign its general release form). A public hospital (one that's funded largely if not entirely by the government) is generally required to accept patients for treatment, even if they are unable to provide proof of insurance or their ability to pay.

➤ **You have the right to be informed about costs and payment methods.**

If you think that your hospital has violated one or more of these policies, contact the hospital's administration department and explain your complaint. The hospital will have some type of internal dispute-resolution process and will review the situation and tell you what (if anything) it intends to do about your complaint. If this step doesn't resolve the issue or if you or your loved one can't effectively use this method because the medical problem is too severe, contact your lawyer for advice.

You may have additional rights under state law or under your hospital's policies, but you should remember that there can always be valid exceptions to any of these rules.

Who Knows What About You

You have a basic right to privacy concerning your condition, treatment, and medical records. Additionally, the communications you have with your doctor are considered privileged, and doctor-patient privilege works in much the same way as attorney-client privilege does. (See Chapter 3 for more general information about privilege.)

It's the Law!

Just as there are exceptions to attorney-client privilege, there are exceptions to doctor-patient privilege. Every state requires doctors to report cases of child abuse, gunshot wounds, deaths, and other serious matters to the appropriate governmental authorities. Doctors also must report cases of AIDS and certain other types of disease.

As far as records go, your doctor can show your records to other doctors, nurses, and other health-care professionals. They can also release your records to your insurance company when you've made a claim under your policy. Other than that, your records are generally considered confidential, even to family members, unless you do something to cause their release. If you file a malpractice claim against your doctor or hospital, for example, your records would be part of the evidence used at a trial.

When the Treatment Does More Harm Than Good: Malpractice

Everyone has heard horror stories of medical malpractice—cases of the wrong limb being amputated or surgical instruments left inside patients' bodies, for example. Not all cases of medical malpractice are so dramatic, although they can be just as damaging. For example, a missed or incorrect diagnosis might also be considered malpractice.

Doctors can't (and don't) guarantee the results of any treatment, and malpractice cannot be blamed for every unfortunate outcome. If you need a liver transplant, for example, and you go to a skilled surgeon who follows all accepted procedures and takes every normal precaution, there's still no guarantee that you will be cured or even that you won't die during surgery.

Legally, malpractice is a complex area. It becomes even more complicated because expert witnesses and technical medical terminology are involved. If you think that you or a family member might have a malpractice claim, consult as quickly as possible with some attorneys experienced in this particular field. They can help you evaluate your claim and advise you about how to protect your rights. Bring with you to the consultations any medical records or documents you have so that the attorneys can get a clearer picture of what has happened. For more information about choosing an attorney, refer to Chapter 2.

Legalese
Medical malpractice is negligence, an unreasonable lack of skill, or professional misconduct on the part of a doctor that results in injury to the patient.

WHAT!?

Legal Pitfalls
State laws (called statutes of limitations) limit how long you can wait before bringing a suit for malpractice. The way the time periods are calculated, and even the time limits themselves, vary from state to state. But regardless of which state you live in, if you don't file suit within the statutory time limit, it's likely that your claim will be barred.

Using Powers of Attorney and Living Wills

Earlier in this chapter, you learned that you normally have the right to be fully informed about your treatment options. Even more important, you have the right to make your own decisions about whether to accept treatment.

Legalese
A health-care power of attorney is a legal document that gives someone (your "agent") authority to make some or all medical decisions for you in the event that you cannot make them yourself.

Tip
If you're incapacitated for a considerable amount of time, other problems can occur concerning your finances or other legal matters. Your attorney can advise you about other types of powers of attorney you can use to delegate authority in these areas as well.

This is all fine and good, assuming that you're conscious so that you can hear the explanations and make the decisions. If you are unconscious or otherwise unable to make decisions about your treatment, the doctor or hospital will look to your spouse or nearest relative. A problem arises here: What your spouse, parent, or adult child decides about your treatment may not be what you would have decided. This can be especially true when it's a real life-or-death decision: for example, a decision about whether to use artificial life support. You can make your wishes known, however, before the situation ever occurs. One way to do so is to use a health-care power of attorney.

Although you can probably find fill-in-the-blank forms and prepare a health-care power of attorney yourself, you may want to have yours drafted by an attorney. The cost is usually low, and an attorney knows which technical requirements state law places on these documents (for example, the number of witnesses necessary or limits on what authority can be given under the document). An attorney can also answer any specific questions you might have about the document.

Before you see an attorney about drafting a health-care power of attorney, review the following questions so that you don't feel any pressure to make such critical decisions on short notice (you may also want to talk to your doctor if you have medical questions):

➤ Whom will you name as agent (the person who has the decision-making authority under this document)? Can you trust that person to follow your wishes? Name a second person in case the first agent can't or won't accept the responsibility.

Please note that terminology in this area (as in many others) can vary depending on which state you live in. You may find that in your state the person you give legal authority to is called an "agent," or she may be referred to as "attorney in fact." Don't confuse "attorney in fact" with "attorney at law"; an attorney in fact is anyone (lawyer or non-lawyer) to whom you give authority to act on your behalf, and an attorney at law is always a lawyer.

Legalese
A **living will** is a document that indicates whether you want various life-support methods used if you are in a permanent coma or if your condition is terminal. It can also be used to indicate whether you want to make any organ donations.

➤ Do you want your agents to have full discretion, or do you want to limit their authority?

➤ Are certain medical procedures unacceptable to you, for religious or other reasons?

➤ Would you ever want life-sustaining measures withheld? If so, under what circumstances?

➤ When should the power of attorney become effective, and when should it end?

In addition to the health-care power of attorney, you can also use a living will to let people know your wishes concerning treatment, although a living will doesn't cover nearly as many situations as a health-care power of attorney does.

A health-care power of attorney gives much broader authority to the person acting on your behalf than does a living will. Generally, a living will applies only to situations in which the patient is terminal or in an irreversible coma and a decision must be made about sustaining life. On the other hand, a health-care power of attorney can be used to authorize or refuse a wide range of treatments whenever the patient is unable to make decisions on his own (his condition doesn't have to be terminal).

A basic living will lets you specify whether heroic means should be used to sustain your life.

DECLARATION

TO MY FAMILY, PHYSICIAN AND MEDICAL FACILITY:

I, JOHN DOE, being of sound mind, wilfully and voluntarily make known my desire that my dying shall not be artificially postponed under the following circumstances, and I do hereby declare:

If at any time I should have an incurable injury, disease, or illness judged to be a terminal condition by my attending physician who has personally examined me, and it is determined that my death is imminent except for life-sustaining procedures, I direct that such procedures be withheld or withdrawn, and that I be permitted to die naturally with only the administration of medication, sustenance, or the performance of any medical procedure deemed necessary to provide me with comfort care.

In the absence of my ability to give directions regarding the use of such life-sustaining procedures, it is my intention that this Declaration be honored by my family and physician as the final expression of my legal right to refuse medical or surgical treatment, and I accept the consequences from such refusal.

I understand the full meaning and import of this Declaration and I am emotionally and mentally competent to make this Declaration.

I make this Declaration this ___5ᵗʰ___ day of ___May___, 19_95_.

John Doe
JOHN DOE

1220 Maple Avenue

Chicago, Illinois

ATTESTATION

The Declarant has been personally known to me and I believe him to be of sound mind. I did not sign the Declarant's signature above for or at the direction of the Declarant. I am not related to the Declarant by blood or marriage, entitled to any portion of the estate of the Declarant according to the laws of intestate succession or under any will of Declarant or codicil thereto, or directly financially responsible for Declarant's medical care. I further certify that on the date it bears, this Declaration was signed in my presence and I do hereby sign our names as witness thereto.

_____
WITNESS

_____
WITNESS

Whether you use a health-care power of attorney or a living will, there is always a chance that the hospital or doctor involved in your treatment may ignore the document. This can occur for different reasons (if doctors disagree about your condition, for example). In this type of case, your family can do the following:

➤ Seek assistance from other doctors or appeal to the hospital's review board.

➤ Transfer you to another facility where your requests will be honored.

➤ Obtain a court order enforcing your power of attorney or living will.

What You Need To Know About Nursing Homes

The decision to place a parent or grandparent in a nursing home is difficult for any family. Both the people being admitted and their families often have fears or concerns about the treatment the resident will receive in that type of facility. It does help to know that residents of nursing homes are protected under both state and federal laws. In fact, federal law requires that a nursing home make its residents aware of their legal rights. Some of the rights residents have include:

➤ The freedom to choose, and to refuse, medical treatment.

➤ The freedom from restraints, except under doctor's order if necessary to keep the resident from injuring herself.

➤ The freedom to manage his own finances.

➤ A basic right to privacy, which extends to the nursing home's records and communications.

➤ Various rights concerning discharge or transfer from the facility, including a minimum 30-day notice.

In addition to how the nursing-home resident will be treated, the next biggest concern the resident and her family have is paying the bills. Unless you've become independently wealthy by the time you need to start thinking about nursing homes, this concern is a genuine one.

Medicare, our national health-insurance system, does not cover the cost of a nursing home. Consequently, most people (unless they can pay for the care out of their own pocket) look to Medicaid for assistance. Medicaid covers primarily medical costs, including the costs of nursing homes, for people with low incomes and few assets. It can also cover medical costs for people over age 65 and disabled people, depending on the amount of their incomes and assets. Funds are disbursed by the federal government to each state, which in turn administer their own Medicaid programs.

The rules for applying and qualifying for Medicaid can fill several of these books, and they're not half as entertaining. It's not an area to venture into without professional advice, especially because qualification depends so heavily on your income and assets. You may be able to transfer some of your assets to qualify for Medicaid, but you should review the technicalities involved with an attorney experienced in estate planning or elder law. And don't wait until the last minute, either—your state Medicaid office can inquire about transfers of property you made as far back as three years before you applied for benefits.

The Least You Need To Know

➤ As a patient, you have certain basic legal rights, especially when it comes to accepting or refusing treatment.

➤ If you think that you have a medical malpractice claim, consult experienced attorneys about the situation promptly to avoid any problems with your state's statute of limitations.

➤ A health-care power of attorney covers a broader range of situations than a living will does, but both documents can help make your wishes known if you're unable to communicate them at the time.

➤ Medicaid may pay nursing homes costs for you or a loved one, but you should get professional advice because the process of applying and qualifying for benefits is extremely complicated.

Chapter 24

Old Age Is Not for the Timid: Estate Planning

In This Chapter

➤ Why estate planning is important

➤ The basic, but important, parts of a will

➤ Using a trust agreement as an alternative to a will or as a supplement of a will

---

The Wisdom of Planning Ahead

Estate planning. Wills and trusts. Probate. Death. These things probably aren't among your favorite topics of conversation. Besides, you're young, you're healthy—estate planning is for old people. Wrong. Estate planning, the legalese for deciding what happens to all your property when you die, is not just for old people. And if you have small children, it's even more important that you plan ahead.

This chapter looks at estate planning from two angles: how your property will be handled and how your children will be taken care of after you're gone. Almost everyone has strong feelings about each of

> **WHAT!?**
>
> **Legalese**
> Your **estate** is simply all the property you own at the time of your death. It includes all kinds of property, including real estate, cash, vehicles, bank accounts, stocks, and personal property.

these subjects, but it's important to realize that now is the time to make your wishes and intentions known. If you die without any form of estate plan, a court may have to decide what will happen to your property—and who will raise your children. I know that it may sound like a cheap scare tactic, but it's true: You can see that your wishes are carried out only if you plan ahead.

No one particularly enjoys thinking about his own demise, but death is still a fact of life. (Oxymoron alert!) And if you have a family, you can't ignore the legal consequences your death will have on your family members. No law requires you to make a will or set up a trust, but the benefits of doing so are enormous. Good estate planning can do the following:

➤ Allow you to control how your property and money are distributed when you die.

➤ Give you the chance to make a special bequest to a certain family member, friend, or organization.

➤ Enable you to have some control over who raises your minor children by nominating a guardian.

➤ Let you choose who handles and distributes your estate.

➤ Help a family business or other business partnership deal with the impact of your death.

➤ Help reduce tax liability for your survivors.

Notice that I said *good* estate planning. The issues in this list can get complicated, and it's important that you seek professional advice when you are working on an estate plan. And, for once in this book, "professional advice" doesn't just mean advice from your attorney—it includes advice from your insurance agent, accountant, tax advisor, financial planner, personal banker, and any other professional who might have valuable advice. Your estate-planning decisions will touch every major part of your life, so make certain that you have all the information you need before you make your choices.

If you're still not convinced that you need to think about an estate plan, consider this: If you die *intestate* (legalese for "without a will"), a court distributes your estate according to state law. The statute doesn't make exceptions for special circumstances, and the judge won't spend any time trying to guess what you would have wanted.

Can you write your own will? Sure, and you can also build an airplane from a kit. But if either one is put together incorrectly, it won't do what it's supposed to do. (If you want to get an idea of what a will looks like, look at the sample will in Appendix B.) Plenty of do-it-yourself estate-planning kits, books, and computer software are on the market, and some are pretty good. But before you rush out to the store, review the section in Chapter 2 about drafting your own legal documents. Unless your estate plan is extremely simple, play it safe and consult an attorney for advice.

> OOOOOH . . .
>
> **Tip**
> Taxes shouldn't be a big factor in your estate planning unless your estate is large. The federal estate tax doesn't apply unless your estate is at least $600,000 or more, but if the tax does apply, it is payable before any part of your estate gets distributed according to your will. States usually have their own taxes too, but the rules on these taxes are far from uniform. Your attorney can help you decide whether taxes will be a big factor in your estate and, if so, give you options for how to minimize the tax liability on your estate.

It's the Law!

In some advertisements for estate-planning kits or services, you hear people say that the state can get your property if you die without a will. Although it's technically true that if a person dies without a will and absolutely no heirs, her property goes automatically to the state, the odds of it happening are small. Very few people die without leaving a single relative somewhere down the family tree who can inherit the estate by law. This does not mean, of course, that you don't need an estate plan—just that you shouldn't panic when you see these ads.

It's the Law!

State laws vary on the technical requirements for a valid will. Some states require two witnesses, and others require three. Many require the witnesses to sign a formal statement (called an *attestation*). Some state statutes allow a *holographic* will (one that's written in your own handwriting and not witnessed) under certain conditions, and possibly even an oral will. In other states, these kinds of wills are absolutely invalid. Make sure that you know your state's laws for signing, witnessing, and so on before you try to write your own will. Check your local library for information, or, better, consult an attorney.

Be careful if you're using a kit or a software program—witnessing, notarizing, and attesting are all different things, and you must be certain that your will complies with your state's requirements.

What's in a Will

The financial aspects of estate planning are far too complicated to try to fit in a single chapter, but you should at least be aware of how the basic will format works. Except for the technical requirements that vary from state to state, all wills look pretty much alike (see the sample will in Appendix B). They begin with an opening paragraph that identifies you as the maker of the will, says where you live, whom you're married to, and who your children are. This introductory paragraph is then usually followed by a statement that you revoke any previous wills or codicils.

Legalese
A **codicil** is a written amendment to an existing will. A codicil must be signed and witnessed in the same way as a will is, so whatever your state's requirements are for a valid will, the requirements are the same for a codicil.

You can add to the introduction any details about how you want your body disposed of and arrangements for your funeral, for example, but it's usually better to handle these kinds of concerns in a separate written document. This process helps guarantee that your requests are honored, because your will may not be the first thing on your family's mind immediately after your death.

Do I Get a Key to the Executor's Washroom?

That's executor (or executrix, for a woman), not executive. Anyway, naming an executor is the first important decision you make. An executor carries out the instructions you leave in your will, though he can use some of his own discretion as well. The person you name obviously should be someone you trust, but it doesn't have to be someone who's a financial genius or who has experience in this kind of thing. It's common for an executor to hire an attorney to help with the estate distribution and provide guidance throughout the legal issues that can arise during the process.

Legalese
An **executor** or **executrix** is the person who handles the distribution of your estate.

It's a good idea to talk to your prospective executor or guardian (see the following section) before including them in your will. This step gives you a chance to find out whether that person is willing and able to handle these matters for you. Some people may not feel comfortable accepting the responsibility, and you should encourage them to be honest with you in your discussions. It's certainly better if they just tell you that they don't want the job now, while you can still be the one to choose someone else.

The guardian you name doesn't have to live in the same state as you, but you should remember that your child would probably end up moving out of state in that type of situation. This may be a major factor in your decision depending on where the rest of your family lives, your child's age, and so on.

You should name at least one other person whom you would want as executor, in case your first choice can't do the job for some reason. The role of the executor is discussed in more detail in Chapter 25.

While You're Naming Names...

If you have children who are minors, the next thing you have to do is nominate a guardian for them. The guardian of your children will have both responsibility for and control of your children. She will make all the decisions about raising them, just as you would if you were alive. Most people nominate the child's other natural parent as the first choice for guardian, but this choice can vary in cases of divorce and remarriage. Consult an attorney if you have any concerns or questions about who should, or can, be a guardian. Just as you do with an executor, name an alternate guardian to avoid any problems.

WHAT!?

Legalese
A **guardian** is a person who is legally responsible for another person—in this case, your child.

You probably noticed the use of the word *nominate* in the preceding paragraph. In most jurisdictions, the court enters an order making the guardianship official. Unless the guardian you name is the natural parent of the child, the court will probably hold a hearing to determine whether the guardian you named in your will can, or should, be officially made the child's guardian.

Some people prefer to split the authority over their children. You can do this by naming a "guardian of the person" (who physically takes care of the kids and makes all the routine day-to-day decisions) and a "guardian of the estate" (who distributes and controls the money you have willed to your children).

Splitting authority over your children has certain advantages, and the greatest one is that it provides a system of "checks and balances" on both guardians. Suppose that your brother is your choice for guardian of the person: He's loving, he's caring, and you think that he would do a great job of raising your child. There's only one problem, though: He's rotten at managing money. To make sure that the money you leave your child isn't wasted or spent foolishly, you could also name your sister as guardian of the estate. That way, your brother would have to go through her in order to get money disbursed from the estate.

If you split authority over children in this way, you have to choose people who can, of course, work reasonably well together. Serious disputes can end up being litigated in probate court—the exact thing you're trying to avoid.

Giving It All Away

Another main section of your will contains all your *bequests*. In this part of the will, you give away your assets. Your bequests can be as general ("all my personal property to my son Johnny") or as specific ("my emerald ring to my niece, Nancy") as you want to make them. This section includes any special bequests to charities, schools, or individuals, and it also contains any specific directions you have concerning a piece of property. For example, you could say, "I give $1,000 to my alma mater, Dewey Teachum High, provided that it uses the money to buy books for the library." You should talk to an attorney if you're interested in putting specific conditions or restrictions on bequests or if you're interested in preventing someone from inheriting part of your estate.

Unless a small amount is involved, it might be wise to express a bequest of money to a person or charity as a percentage of your estate's total worth or to put some other type of condition on it. Think about this example: While you're young, healthy, and working, it might seem like a good idea to include in your will a bequest of $10,000 to the Humane Society. But if 40 years and thousands of dollars in medical bills go by, leaving you with only $10,200 to your name, would your wishes be the same?

You Can "Trust" Me

Another common estate planning tool is a *trust agreement.* A trust that's part of a will is called a *testamentary trust,* and a trust set up while you're alive is a *living trust,* or, if you want to impress your friends, an *intervivos trust.* And you thought Latin was a dead language.

Mechanically, a trust can do pretty much everything a will can, and there is virtually no difference between the two from a tax standpoint. One advantage to a trust is that it can be used to manage your financial affairs while you're still alive, which can be important if you become seriously ill. Another advantage to using a trust is that it is not subject to probate when you die. For more information about probate and estate administration, see Chapter 25.

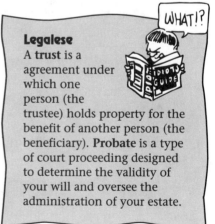

Legalese
A **trust** is a agreement under which one person (the trustee) holds property for the benefit of another person (the beneficiary). **Probate** is a type of court proceeding designed to determine the validity of your will and oversee the administration of your estate.

It's the Law!

Legally speaking, a trust can be used to do almost everything a will can, including nominating guardians and making specific bequests. Be careful, though: Depending on the provisions of your trust, it may have to conform to the same technical requirements as a will. This is true, for example, if you're using the trust to nominate guardians. Now you're back to all the mechanical issues you read about earlier: the number of witnesses needed, attestation language, and notary requirements. Make sure that your trust complies with your state's technical requirements so that it can do the job you want it to do.

Tip

Talk to your attorney about your state's probate procedures and the typical costs involved. Many people (often those selling trust services) rank the probate process just slightly under eating broken glass as a painful experience. But after reviewing your particular estate and your state's probate requirements with your attorney, you may find that the probate process isn't much of a factor in your planning.

To create a trust, you first have to determine who the beneficiaries are, and then you must choose a trustee. The trustee can be a person, or it can be a corporate entity, such as a bank or trust company. After creating a trust agreement with the trustee, you have to transfer your assets and property into the trustee's name, making the trustee the legal owner of your property. The trustee then holds the property according to the terms of your agreement. Corporate and professional trustees charge a fee for their services when you first create the trust, and they also charge you annually to maintain it. Corporate and professional trustees often have their own trust-agreement forms, but they can be complex. If you have any questions about this type of agreement, take it to an attorney for review.

Before and After Your Will Is Prepared

This section describes a few things you should do before you see your attorney for help with your estate plan so that you get the most from your office meeting:

➤ Call ahead to find out whether you need to bring any documents with you to your appointment. During your meeting, your attorney may want to review with you such documents as deeds, insurance policies, bank statements, appraisals, and tax returns.

➤ Decide on an executor and an alternate, as well as a guardian and an alternate if you have children.

➤ Write down any special bequests you want to make and any conditions or restrictions you want to put on the bequest.

➤ Think about what you want to happen if a beneficiary of your will is younger than 18 when you die. Whom do you want to hold the money or property until the person reaches legal age? Can the money be used for any reason if the beneficiary is under age 18?

After you have your will or trust prepared, you have to keep it somewhere safe. A locking fireproof box kept in your home is ideal.

You should have your will or trust reviewed every time there's a major change in your life, such as buying or selling property, having a child, or getting married or divorced. Even if nothing major seems to be happening in your life, you should still review it at least every three years.

Be sure to have your will reviewed if you move to another state. As you've learned throughout this chapter, states have different requirements for a valid will, and it's important to verify that your will is valid in the state you're moving to.

> **Legal Pitfalls**
> Your family or executor must have easy access to your original will when you die, so don't store it in a bank safe-deposit box. This precaution avoids problems with bank hours, bank holidays, and bank restrictions on who has access to the box. Many people leave a copy of their will with their attorney.

The Least You Need To Know

➤ Estate planning can be a complicated process, and it's best to consult an attorney, as well as other financial advisors, when you're setting up a plan.

➤ A will allows you to name an executor to handle your estate, to name a guardian to care for your children, and to make the bequests you want.

➤ A trust serves much the same purpose as a will, but it can also be of some value while you're alive, especially if you need help managing your finances during a serious illness.

➤ Whatever form of estate planning you use, it should be reviewed and updated regularly.

Chapter 25

Someone Named Me Executor, and I Don't Have a Clue Where To Begin

In This Chapter

➤ Things that need immediate attention after someone dies

➤ What an executor does

➤ How the probate of a small estate works

➤ What happens to an estate if there's no will

If you read Chapter 24, you'll remember that it briefly discussed the probate process. Again, probate is the process of determining the validity of a will and administering an estate; the "administration" part is really the heart of the process. It includes such tasks as locating and collecting assets; paying creditors of the deceased and any taxes that might be due; and distributing the remaining property according to the will or according to state laws of inheritance if no will exists.

Probate has a bad reputation, but not all of it is well deserved. It can be a long and costly process, or it can be a quick and inexpensive one—it all depends on your state's laws and the size of the estate involved. For example, many states have adopted special probate rules for small estates, making the process cheaper and relatively simple.

What To Do First When Someone Has Died

Despite the grief that comes with the death of someone close to you, many practical decisions must be made; some, quickly. Some of the more common decisions and arrangements you have to make are shown in this list:

Legal Pitfalls

If someone with a trust dies and leaves you in charge of handling her estate, don't assume that you have less work to do than if she had left a will. You may want to review the trust with an attorney to determine the estate's tax liability, for advice about what to do about creditors and any property not included in the trust.

➤ Make arrangements for the care of minor children.

➤ Get a copy of the death certificate or other medical reports regarding the cause of death because you'll probably need this kind of documentation when it's time to begin handling the estate.

➤ Make sure that any gift provisions under a living will (see Chapter 23) or organ-donor card are followed.

➤ Check and secure any property belonging to the deceased, including his home, vehicles, and business.

➤ Follow any funeral instructions that have been left by the deceased, or, if there are none, contact a funeral director to make the necessary arrangements.

➤ Prepare an obituary and notify family, friends, and clergy of the death. (A funeral home often prepares the obituary for you, if you provide basic information.)

➤ Begin assembling all of the deceased's important papers to keep them from becoming lost. In all the confusion that occurs after someone close to you has died, it's easy for papers to become misplaced or even destroyed accidentally. If the deceased kept important papers in a safe-deposit box, find out whether anyone else has access to it. If not, you have to contact the bank involved or your attorney to find out the rules for getting access to the box. Each state has slightly different procedures about opening a safe-deposit box in this kind of situation.

➤ Contact your attorney for help with any urgent questions about estate administration—for example, if there's an immediate need to use cash from the estate.

You can handle a need for immediate cash by opening a checking account in the name of the estate and depositing the deceased's cash on hand. If the deceased had little cash on hand, locate any joint checking or "payable on death" accounts the deceased might have had. If you still can't find a source of cash, the estate's representative can take out a loan from a family member on behalf of the estate, to be repaid during the course of estate administration. If you do this, make sure that you use a written promissory note and treat it like any other formal business transaction. Also make certain that you keep detailed records of any amounts you disburse.

> **Legal Pitfalls**
> Disburse money only on an emergency basis until you've had time to thoroughly review the estate's financial situation and, if necessary, consult an attorney. Under IRS rules, if you pay bills or make other distributions before all taxes are paid and the estate doesn't have enough money left to pay the taxes later on, you can be held personally liable for the shortage.

Handling a Small Estate on Your Own

Most states have taken significant steps to try to simplify the probate process for small estates. To find out whether your state uses this kind of simplified process (sometimes referred to as *summary,* or *independent, administration*), call your local bar association or the clerk of the probate court in your county. Before this discussion of the probate procedure gets too involved, remember that you have to probate an estate with a will but that you don't have to probate an estate with a trust. You may want to refer to Chapter 24 for more information about this point.

> **Legalese**
> **Independent administration** is a simplified way to probate a small estate, involving much less court supervision of the process than normal. Because the court has a less active role in the process, fewer court appearances and paperwork are required, which helps make the process faster and cheaper.

If your state uses this or a similar process for small estates, the clerk of the court can provide you with the forms you need and guide you through the mechanics of filing them. But the simpler small-estate rules apply only under certain conditions. Here are some of the more common requirements:

➤ There's always a maximum dollar amount on what's considered a "small" estate, usually between $25,000 and $50,000, but the exact amount varies.

➤ There can be no dispute over the will itself. Don't plan to use independent administration if your sister shows up claiming that you're holding a forgery and that she has your mother's "real" will.

➤ All of the deceased's heirs must be known (even if you'd like to forget some of them).

Tip
By signing the small-estate affidavit, you're not only swearing that the estate meets the requirements for independent administration but also assuming full responsibility for the collection and distribution of the estate's assets. Be sure that you know what you're getting into before deciding to handle the process without an attorney.

OOOOOH...

Your state probably has additional conditions, so you have to talk to the clerk of the probate court or an attorney in your area. You'll be required to complete and sign a small-estate affidavit, certifying that all the necessary conditions have been met.

The Nuts and Bolts

Regardless of your specific state's probate laws, certain basic procedures exist for handling an estate. First, you have to file with the clerk of the probate court the deceased's will and an order to admit the will to probate. The will is usually filed in the county in which the deceased lived; however, there might be exceptions under your state's probate code. Additionally, the will must be filed within a certain amount of time under state law, as little as 30 days after the date of death in many states. If you don't know in which county to file the will or how much time you have to get it filed, contact the clerk of the probate court or an attorney.

IN THE CIRCUIT COURT OF SOME COUNTY, ANYSTATE

PROBATE DIVISION

Estate of

ROBERT FRANKLIN,

Deceased,

No. *95 P 237*

Docket: *141*

Page: *29*

ORDER ADMITTING WILL TO PROBATE AND APPOINTING REPRESENTATIVE

On the verified Petition of _____*MARY JAMES*_____

for admission to probate of the will of ____*ROBERT FRANKLIN*____

and for issuance of letters of office, the will having been proved as

provided by law.

IT IS ORDERED THAT:

1. The will of *ROBERT FRANKLIN*, dated *FEBRUARY 6, 1982*

be admitted to probate;

2. Letters of office as (executor) (~~independent executor~~) (~~administrator~~)

issue to *MARY JAMES* ;

ENTER:

_____

J U D G E

DATE: _____

You begin the probate process by filing the will with the clerk of the probate court, along with a form like this.

After filing the will, you have to begin preparing the documents you obtained from the clerk of the court or your attorney. Among the documents is an affidavit asking you to name all of the deceased's heirs. You'll also find notice forms that you have to send to the heirs and beneficiaries of the deceased, telling them that the will has been probated and that you've asked the court to allow you to handle the estate. If no one objects to your being in charge of the estate, the court issues letters of office.

Legal Pitfalls
Be certain to make several copies of the will before you file it with the clerk of the court. You'll need copies for yourself and for any beneficiaries named in the will, and making extra copies provides some protection in case the original will gets lost or destroyed.

Letters of office are notices issued by the probate court authorizing you to handle all the financial matters of the estate. Suppose that you're the executor of your brother's estate and you want to sell 200 shares of his IBM stock to me. You certainly don't own the stock, and the person named on the certificates is dead. I'd naturally want some proof that you have legal authority to sell me the stock before I fork over the cash. You can provide that proof by showing me your letters of office.

The clerk of the probate court may also provide you with forms you can use as receipts when a beneficiary receives money or property from the estate. You'll probably also receive some type of "final report" form to prepare for the court; the form summarizes the finances of the estate and the distributions you made as executor. This final report may require a court appearance, but depending on your state's rules and the circumstances, you might be able to simply mail it to the clerk of the court.

If There's No Will, Is There Still a Way?

If a person dies without a will (or dies *intestate*), the basic process is much the same as if she had died with a will. The estate goes through probate, although it's handled by an administrator rather than by an executor. The administrator is appointed by the probate court and is usually the spouse or an heir of the deceased. The court can appoint an administrator of its own choice if it feels that it's necessary or required under state law. To be appointed, you must file a petition with the probate court asking to be named administrator. After you're appointed, your job is pretty much the same as an executor's: You have to gather assets, notify heirs, pay creditors and taxes, and make the final distribution of the estate to the heirs. Remember that because no will is involved, the final distribution is made according to your state's inheritance laws.

If you're an administrator and you're not using an attorney (as in the case of a small estate), you can obtain all the necessary forms from the clerk of the probate court. In most cases, these forms are identical to those used by executors, and many simply require that you indicate on the form whether you're an executor or an administrator.

Some Final (Pardon the Pun) Thoughts

Probate, like almost anything else, can sometimes turn into an adversarial process. Controversies can arise over the validity of the will, the choice of executor or administrator, specific bequests or other provisions of the will, attempts at disinheriting someone, the way the executor or administrator handles the estate, and more. No estate is exempt from problems like these—just because an estate is small doesn't mean that it will be simple.

After you're dead, of course, there's not much you can do to stop your family members from going at each other like cats and dogs—except maybe haunt them. While you're alive, however, you can do a few things to minimize conflicts later on:

➤ **Make a will—don't make people guess at what you wanted.** Keep bequests as clear, simple, and specific as possible.

➤ **Keep your will current.** Make sure that it reflects any major changes that occur in your life, such as marriages, divorces, births, and deaths. If you move to another state, be sure to have an attorney review your will.

➤ **Talk to your intended executor, and let her know that she's named in your will.** If that person doesn't want the job or won't be able to do it for some reason, you can pick someone else right away. Do the same for someone you plan to name as guardian of your minor children.

➤ **If you're changing your will, make sure that the new one clearly revokes any prior wills or codicils.** To be even safer, destroy any old wills and codicils so that there can be no confusion about which document should govern how your estate gets handled.

➤ **Keep your will safe, but don't hide it as though it's a chest of pirate gold.** Tell people where you keep it so that someone in your family or your executor can easily locate it and other important paperwork in case of your sudden demise. You may even want to take one more step and give a copy of your will to close family members so that they know your wishes ahead of time.

The Least You Need To Know

➤ Probate is a court process that determines the validity of a person's will and manages the distribution of the person's estate.

➤ If your state has summary administration or a similar process, you may be able to handle the administration of a small estate without an attorney.

➤ If a person dies without a will, an administrator handles the estate according to rules and procedures that are similar to those for executors.

Part 6
Everyday Legal Issues

This last part of the book looks at all kinds of different issues people commonly run into. In case you haven't noticed, the law is everywhere; this part of the book looks at some areas of your life in which the law hits close to home. From the laws that govern you as a driver to the laws that protect your basic rights as a citizen of the United States, these chapters take you through topics you probably encounter on a daily basis but still don't think of as being "legal issues."

King of the Road

Driving is probably a part of your daily routine, even though you don't spend much time thinking about all the legal issues it presents—until you see red lights in your rearview mirror or you hear a loud crunch when you're backing out of your driveway.

Driving is a privilege, not a right. And because it is a privilege granted by the state, the state can set and enforce the rules of the road. Beyond that, though, are serious liability questions if you're involved in an accident, especially if someone gets injured. This chapter explains how to deal with things that go bump in the road.

What You Need To Know When You Buy Car Insurance

Just like other types of insurance, car insurance offers protection from different kinds of losses, and you can always add "extras" to your policy—for a price, of course.

Legal Pitfalls
Some states have laws that prohibit you from driving without liability insurance. Getting caught without proof of insurance in these states usually means a ticket and a hefty fine, but it can also mean the suspension of your driver's license. The amount and type of coverage required by law vary from state to state. Ask your insurance agent or attorney about your state's requirements.

The first kind of coverage your policy should provide is *liability coverage.* This portion of your policy covers injuries you may cause to someone else or the damage you may cause to that person's property. It's important to have adequate liability coverage because you can be held legally responsible for any amounts in excess of your policy limits. Talk to your insurance agent about the right amount of coverage for you.

The second kind of major coverage, called *collision coverage,* pays for damage you may cause to your own car in an accident. As with liability coverage, different amounts of collision coverage are available, and you can also choose the amount of deductible you want your policy to have. Raising the amount of your deductible generally lowers the cost of your coverage.

Although these two types of coverage offer basic protection against damage to your car, damage to the other car, injuries to the other driver, and injuries to any passengers or pedestrians who get hit, additional types of coverage are important to consider, including the ones in this list:

➤ **Uninsured/underinsured coverage.** Covers you if you're involved in an accident with someone who's not insured or who's insured but has only minimal coverage. State laws dealing with uninsured and underinsured motorists vary widely; talk to your insurance agent for advice about the best way to protect yourself in your state.

➤ **Medical coverage.** Covers injuries you sustain in an accident. Your health insurance may already provide substantially the same coverage, so make sure to compare the policies before signing up.

➤ **Comprehensive, or Other Than Collision (OTC) coverage.** Covers damage to your vehicle not caused by a collision (for example, damage caused by attempted theft, vandalism, or hail).

➤ **"Convenience" coverage.** Optional coverage can be purchased to cover towing your car, emergency roadside assistance, car-rental expenses, and so on.

> **Legalese**
> A **deductible** is the part of your insurance policy that says you'll pay the first part of a loss and the insurance company will pay the rest. If you had a $250 deductible on your collision insurance, for example, you'd be responsible for paying the first $250 worth of repairs, and your insurance company would be responsible for paying anything above the $250.

When You're on Vacation

Your plane has just landed at the airport. You vault from your seat, grab the kids, race through the baggage claim—Disneyland, here you come! But wait—one obstacle remains: the rent-a-car counter. The car isn't the problem, of course; it's deciding whether to buy the additional insurance they offer. You're inclined to refuse it, to the great disappointment of the person behind the counter. But then you're asked to initial certain boxes on the contract, boxes filled with words and phrases such as "limitation of liability," "waiver," and "Hey, we tried to warn you." What should you do?

The best way to avoid this type of dilemma, whether you're traveling for business or for pleasure, is to make your decision before you leave home. Review your auto policy. There's a good chance that it covers you when you drive a rental car, especially if you won't be using the rental for business.

> **Tip**
> Some credit-card companies offer free coverage when you rent a car using their card, but be sure to read the fine print. This offer may include only collision coverage, and if so you still need liability coverage.

If your policy doesn't cover rentals, contact your insurance agent before your trip to see how much it would cost to add this coverage. Adding coverage to your current policy is usually much cheaper than buying the coverage offered at the rent-a-car counter.

The Ten Commandments When You're Involved in an Accident

If you have ever been in a car accident, even a small one, you know how scary it can be. The shock of the crash and the chaos afterward can leave you feeling dazed and confused—even a little panicked. The things you do and say at the accident scene can seriously affect your legal liability down the line. Here are some things you should always do if you're involved in an accident:

1. **Thou shalt stop at the scene.** Failing to stop at the scene of an accident is a crime. Even if you're scared or feel that you were to blame for the accident, running won't solve anything and will only make matters worse for you in the long run.

2. **Thou shalt care for the injured.** Call an ambulance, the fire department, or a doctor immediately if someone appears to be injured. Don't move anyone who's injured—you might make their injuries worse.

3. **Thou shalt call the police.** This rule is important, even if there are no injuries. The responding officer will investigate the accident scene and file an official accident report, and she may also issue tickets to the drivers. Be sure to use flares, flashlights, or other signals to warn other traffic away from the wreck until the police arrive—the last thing you want is a second crash.

4. **Thou shalt write down everything.** Write down (at minimum) the other car's license plate number and its make, model, and year; the other driver's license number, address, and telephone number; and the name of the other driver's insurance company, insurance policy number, and insurance agent's name. You can use the tear-out card in the front of this book to organize this and other information, such as the names, addresses, and telephone numbers of any witnesses to the accident.

5. **Thou shalt admit nothing.** It can be natural to feel a little guilty after an accident. If you find that that's how you feel after a collision, the best advice I can give you is to *keep your mouth shut!* Admissions and statements you make at the accident scene may come back to haunt you (and your insurance company and attorney). Do not comment on the hows and whys of the accident except to the police officer on the scene. I can't stress this point enough: It's possible that even a simple, generic "I'm sorry" made at the accident scene can come back to haunt you.

6. **Thou shalt not offer to pay for anything.** Same principle as number 5.

7. **Thou shalt not accept any payments.** This rule is also known as "Thou shalt not let greed get the better of thee." Be suspicious of anyone who's just dying to write you a check. If you're approached by someone who's in a hurry to settle with you, be sure to contact your attorney or insurance agent before signing any releases or accepting any payments.

8. **Thou shalt contact thine insurance company promptly.** Report the accident to your insurance company as soon as possible, while your memory is still fresh.

9. **Thou shalt not make a self-diagnosis (medical or legal).** Consider seeing your physician for a thorough physical. Injuries may not appear serious right away, so it's important to pay special attention to what your body is trying to tell you. Contact your lawyer for advice about any legal problems that may arise from the accident. Again, don't accept settlement offers or agree to sign any documents without first reviewing them with your attorney.

10. **Thou shalt keep thy records organized.** If you've been seriously injured in an accident or suffered other losses, you have to add to your initial notes on the crash. Keep a notebook or diary of your care and the related costs, including information about hospital stays, doctors, and prescriptions. Itemize, and preferably photograph, any property of yours that was damaged in the accident. If the last time you saw your brand-new, state-of-the-art, automatic-everything Nikon camera was when you put it in your trunk, and now, after a loud crunch, it seems to be serving as a minivan's hood ornament, document that fact for your insurance company.

When Those Red Lights Appear in Your Rearview Mirror

Although some of us have more experience in this area than others, almost everyone has been pulled over at some time in his life. As mentioned at the beginning of this chapter, driving is a privilege, and the state has the ability to set down certain rules and restrictions about how we exercise that privilege. Traffic violations can be lumped into two general categories: moving violations and everything else.

Moving violations concern how you operate your vehicle, and they include such things as speeding, driving too fast for conditions, disobeying a stop sign, and making an illegal U-turn. Nonmoving violations, the "everything else" category, include a broad range of things. Parking tickets, failure to display a current vehicle sticker, and failure to wear a seat belt when required are all examples of this kind of offense. Although these offenses carry fines, they are relatively minor when compared to moving violations. Moving violations carry much stiffer penalties. Being convicted of serious or frequent moving violations can subject you to large fines, and a conviction on some violations, such as drunk driving, can even mean jail.

"But I Can Explain"

Traffic-court procedure varies greatly depending on where you live. If you get a ticket, begin by making sure that you read it carefully to see what you're required to do. Some tickets require that you appear in court; others give you the option of mailing in a check to cover the fine instead of going to court.

Legal Pitfalls

If you simply mail in your fine, you're admitting your guilt, and your driving record will reflect a conviction for that offense. Convictions for moving violations can cause your insurance premiums to rise, and multiple convictions can result in your license being suspended.

If you want to fight a ticket, you're free of course to do so. You can go to court, enter a plea of "not guilty," and request a trial. If it's a relatively minor offense, such as speeding, the trial is often conducted that same day. Most of these trials come down to the police officer's word (and radar gun) against yours, so don't count on being found not guilty.

If the charge is serious, such as drunk driving or reckless driving, and you're before the court for the first time, you'll be asked whether you need time to get an attorney. You should always hire an attorney to represent you in cases involving a serious offense. If you can't afford an attorney, ask the court to appoint a public defender. Don't just try to wing it on your own—remember that drunk driving and other serious charges can carry jail sentences as well as large fines.

The Least You Need To Know

➤ You definitely need adequate liability and collision coverage under your car insurance, but you may also want to add other types of coverage to the policy.

➤ Your existing car insurance may already protect you if you rent a car, but, if not, you can buy the extra coverage for a minimal fee.

➤ If you're in an accident, don't discuss the details of what happened with anyone except the police and your insurance company.

➤ Hire an attorney if you're charged with a serious traffic offense, because a conviction can carry with it a large fine, suspension of your license, and, in some cases, jail time.

Chapter 27

You've Got My Word on It: The Law of Contracts

In This Chapter

➤ How valid contracts are made

➤ The importance of putting it in writing

➤ How breach-of-contract claims are handled

You come into contact with contracts every day. The lease you signed for your new apartment is as much a contract as your membership in the Cookbook of the Month Club. Even the simple act of buying a newspaper from the guy on the corner involves a contract.

From simple verbal agreements to lengthy written documents brimming with legalese, all contracts operate on the same basic principles. This chapter introduces you to the way contracts work and explains the basic elements included in every contract.

All Contracts Are Created Equal

A valid, enforceable *contract* is an agreement that can be enforced through the courts. In other words, if you promise to do something under a contract (prepare my taxes, for example) and you don't do it or don't do it correctly, I can sue you for violating our agreement.

Legalese
A **contract** is simply an agreement between two or more parties that creates a binding legal obligation to do (or *not* to do) something.

Later, this section looks at what's necessary to form an enforceable contract; as you go through the list, however, keep in mind that if any of the necessary pieces is missing, your agreement isn't enforceable (you won't be able to win a lawsuit if the other person doesn't keep her end of the bargain).

If you and I have a valid, enforceable contract for you to prepare my taxes, I can sue you for my damages if you don't prepare them. It sounds obvious, but there are agreements that don't become enforceable contracts (if I promise to give you $100 as a gift, for example). You can agree—I'm sure you would—but no contract will be formed because the agreement is missing the necessary element of consideration (consideration is described later in this chapter).

Although this definition gets you headed in the right direction, it doesn't tell the whole story. A contract is made of up of the following parts:

➤ **Parties.** The *parties*, or people who enter into a contract, must have the capacity to enter into a contract, or, put another way, each person must be considered legally competent. Minors, for example, do not have the capacity to enter into an enforceable contract.

➤ **Subject matter.** You can contract for just about anything—as long as the subject matter doesn't involve anything illegal. A contract for the sale of cocaine is not legally enforceable.

➤ **Consideration.** This piece of legalese just means that each side must have some obligation under the agreement. For example, I could agree to sell you my car for $3,000. You're obligated to give me $3,000; I'm obligated to give you the keys and the title for the car. A promise to do or not to do something can also be sufficient consideration. For example, I give you $700, and you promise not to sue me for backing my car over your motorcycle. Even though you have only made a promise, consideration exists because you have given up your legal right to sue me.

➤ **Agreement (or assent).** Obvious maybe, but important. The parties must mutually understand and agree to the material (important or basic) terms of the contract. In a sales contract, for example, some material terms might include such things as the identity of the seller and buyer, the item being sold, the price, and the time for delivery. You could add more terms (and depending on the transaction, you probably would want to), but it's vital to have agreement on these basic terms in order to form a contract. This process is often referred to by lawyer types as the "meeting of the minds."

This last part, the necessity for agreement, needs a little more explanation. A contract begins with an offer—a proposal to do something or pay some amount according to some set of terms. "I'll paint your house for $800" is an offer, and it shows my willingness to enter into a contract with you. After you receive my offer, you can accept it, and if you do so, we have a contract. Of course, if your house was just painted two months ago, you can simply reject my offer. If you do, your rejection terminates my offer; in other words, you can't accept it at a later time. As a third possibility, you can make me a counteroffer and tell me that you'll pay me $600 to paint your house.

If you make a counteroffer, a contract is not formed until we reach a final agreement on terms. A valid contract requires an offer and an acceptance, and the terms of the two must match each other exactly. Suppose that I offer to paint your house for $800 and you say, "I accept your offer. Have it done by Tuesday." Your statement

> **Tip**
>
> OOOOOH...
>
> Are advertisements offers? The answer, maybe surprisingly, is no—they're legally considered to be an invitation (to you, the customer) to make an offer. This distinction is important because if you're the one making the offer, the store gets to decide whether to enter into a contract because it has the capability to accept or reject your offer.

249

isn't a valid acceptance because it adds a new term (completion of the job by Tuesday) to my original offer. Because your attempt at acceptance doesn't match my offer, you've only made me a counteroffer, and still no contract exists between us.

These different parts of a contract stand out when you're looking at formal, written agreements, but they're also present in simple transactions. When you buy a newspaper, for example, you have capable parties, legal subject matter (the paper), consideration (my 35 cents, the vendor's copy of the *Daily Planet*), and agreement (he will give me a paper, and I will give him 35 cents). In simple transactions, everything happens all at one time, so we often don't think about these types of situations as contracts.

To Write or Not To Write?

Does a contract have to be in writing? The answer usually is no, but keep in mind the saying about how an oral contract isn't worth the paper it's printed on. Agreements involving many conditions, confusing terms, or substantial amounts of money should be written down to prevent later misunderstandings. If the contract is complicated or a good deal of money is at stake, consult a lawyer. If your contract ends up in court, the judge will have only the contract to guide her decision. Make sure that your agreement contains enough detail so that a court won't have to guess about what you meant.

As mentioned in Chapter 2, many office-supply stores stock standard contract forms for less complicated transactions. You can usually find simple leases, basic sales contracts, and promissory notes (agreements used when you borrow money) among the selections, but it would be helpful to review Chapter 2 for the list of cautions about using these standard agreements before you buy.

In some limited situations, a written contract is required in order to make the agreement enforceable. These situations fall under an old (circa 1677!) English legal doctrine called the *statute of frauds*. Most states have adopted an updated, modified version of this doctrine, which says that certain types of agreements are not enforceable unless the contract is in the form of a signed writing. Agreements that fall under this rule typically include:

➤ Contracts for the sale of real estate.

➤ Contracts that cannot be completed within one year's time, such as a five-year office lease.

➤ Contracts for the sale of goods in an amount greater than $500.

➤ Contracts in which one person agrees to guarantee payment of another person's debt.

As stated, if these kinds of contracts aren't in writing, they are not enforceable. If I renege on a verbal contract to sell you my house, you probably will lose if you sue me in court. Even if all the contract parts were there, we still didn't meet the requirements of the statute of frauds.

Now That I Have a Contract, What Do I Do with It?

After a contract is created, the parties are under a legal obligation to carry out their respective duties. In the example earlier in this chapter, my obligation is to paint your house, and your obligation is to give me $800. The process of meeting the contract obligations is called *performance.*

There's always the chance, of course, that one of us won't do what we're supposed to do. I might simply refuse to paint the house, or you might give me a rubber check. If a party fails to perform his obligations under a contract, that person is said to have *breached* the contact.

The two extremes, performance and breach, are clear, but what happens if I paint most of the house and don't finish some of the detail work? Or what if you're short $200 when the time comes to pay me? Appropriately enough, this type of situation is called *partial performance*—one or both of us have done some, but not all, of what we were required to do.

Partial performance is sort of an odd thing—you did some of what you were required to do under the contract, but not all of it. The end result varies depending on the specifics of the situation (how much performance occurred, the amount of money involved, and so on), but you're generally responsible for whatever damage you caused to the other party. In the house-painting example, I can sue you for the balance you owe me. Or if I was the one who only partially performed, you can sue me for the cost of hiring another painter to finish the job I started.

As with most of the other areas discussed in this chapter, questions of breach and partial performance all come down to a question of what you can prove if you end up suing.

To protect yourself, begin by using a detailed, written agreement so that there can be no confusion about what's required of each person. Second, make sure to document problems and concerns as they develop. If I painted half your house on Saturday and you're still waiting for me to show up again on Tuesday, you'll probably want to contact me to find out what the problem is. As usual, if you're concerned about the situation, confirm verbal agreements or discussions in writing. Finally, don't overact. If you think that the other person is breaching the agreement or that he'll only partially perform, make a formal written demand that he comply with the contract terms. By giving the other person this final chance to correct the problem, you protect yourself from having the situation turned around on you.

In the preceding example, I may have a legitimate reason for not showing up to finish the job on Sunday or Monday—I may have run out of paint and your particular selection has to be special ordered, for example. If you march out Tuesday morning and hire a new painter to finish without giving me notice of any kind, I can make the claim that you were the one who breached the contract because you didn't give me an opportunity to complete the job when I was willing and able to do so.

"I Brought a Note from My Mother" and Other Excuses

Failure to perform under a contract isn't always a breach. The law recognizes that, in certain cases, performance should be excused. If your house burned to the ground the night before I was supposed to begin painting, for example, I'm no longer under any contractual obligation—with the house gone, my performance is impossible, and the homeowner's duty to pay me $800 also has ended.

Sometimes the duty of performance is never created. Suppose that you want your house painted in fluorescent orange-and-blue stripes. Obviously concerned about what the city might think, I agree to do the work on the condition that you obtain an appropriate work permit from the city. Needless to say, the permit never gets issued. Because you didn't meet the condition of obtaining the permit, I'm under no legal obligation to do the work.

Fraud or misrepresentation may also relieve me of any obligation to paint your house, and under certain circumstances a mutual mistake may be enough to get me off the hook. Let's use a different example (I'm tired of painting your house). Suppose that I've agreed to install an in-ground pool for you. We contract for the work, and, as part of the deal, I agree to dig the hole for the pool for a separate charge of $1,200. I begin digging, but after a few hours my equipment hits concrete. Unknown to both of us, there's a large, steel-reinforced, concrete slab under your yard, and it will take all kinds of special equipment to remove it.

If you're unwilling to pay more than the original price to have this hole dug, I can claim that we both made a fundamental mistake about the kind of work to be done. I shouldn't have to perform because the work to be done isn't even close to what we originally agreed on.

Paying Your Dues: Contract Damages

Ultimately, contract disputes that can't be resolved can turn into lawsuits. If the amount in dispute is small, you may end up in small-claims court, but if your case involves larger amounts, you can expect to go through the normal litigation process. Chapter 2 has information about small-claims cases, Chapter 4 discusses litigation, and Chapter 5 describes alternatives to litigation, such as arbitration.

If a party breaches the contract, or even if she only partially performs her obligation, the other party has the right to sue for compensation. The law of contracts, unlike the law of torts, awards money to people only to "make them whole"—in other words, to give them the benefit of their bargain. In contract law, these damages are called *compensatory damages*—they compensate a person for losses due to a breach of contract. In tort law, the court can also award money to the injured party primarily to punish the wrongdoer. These damages, known as *punitive damages,* are generally not allowed in breach-of-contract lawsuits.

In the house-painting example, suppose that I begin the work but walk off the job after painting only half the house. You then call another painter who agrees to finish the job but for $2,200, a substantially higher cost.

Assuming no other facts, you have a breach-of-contract claim against me for damages in the amount of $1,400, which is the $2,200 you had to pay the new painter minus the $800 you would have had to pay me anyway if I had done the work.

It's the Law!

In addition to money damages, certain kinds of contract cases are eligible for court-ordered relief. In these *specific-performance* cases, the court orders the other party to do what's required by the contract. Specific performance is reserved for cases in which the subject of the contract is unique and money just won't adequately repair the breach. Suppose that I agree to sell you an original Salvador Dali painting. If I breach the contract, you're stuck—you can't get another painting from somewhere else because it's one-of-a-kind, and even if the court awards you money, it doesn't solve your problem because you still don't have the painting. An order of specific performance would require me to sell you the painting at the agreed-on price.

When You Might Want To Breach a Contract Intentionally

Our legal system, as well as our economy, is founded on the basic principle of freedom of contract. You're free to enter into any agreements you want, and, conversely, you're also free to breach any agreements you want, provided that you make the other person whole. This concept may seem odd at first, but think about it for a minute. There may be a good reason for me to breach our painting contract.

Suppose that after I begin work on your house, I go back to my shop to get more paint. While I'm there, I receive a telephone call from Joe, who has seen some of the other houses I've done. He thinks that I'm the Michelangelo of house painting and offers me $6,000 to paint his house. The only problem is that he wants it done immediately. I accept his offer and walk off your job, leaving your house half painted.

Is this nice to do? Nope. Is it good business? Nope. Is it economically smart? Absolutely.

Assuming that you hire the same replacement painter, you've learned in this chapter that I'll probably be liable to you in the amount of $1,400 for compensatory damages. But by taking the new job, I've just received $6,000. Even if I compensate you for your losses, I still come out ahead.

Business is business, as the saying goes, and sometimes it can be to the advantage of a company to breach a contract. This maneuver can be done to increase profits, as in the example just described, or it can be used to cut a company's losses.

The Least You Need To Know

➤ All contracts require capable parties, legal subject matter, consideration, and mutual agreement.

➤ An offer can be accepted (creating a contract) or rejected (terminating the offer). As a third option, you can make a counteroffer (acts like a rejection and creates a new offer).

➤ A person who breaches a contract is liable for the other party's losses or compensatory damages.

➤ It sometimes can make good economic sense to breach a contract.

Chapter 28

Grab a Microscope: Looking at Warranties and Other Fine Print

In This Chapter

➤ What warranties are and how they're created

➤ Your rights under different kinds of warranties

➤ How a warranty can be limited or disclaimed altogether

Ask anybody in sales—consumers just aren't what they used to be. Today's consumers are smarter shoppers, and they pay attention to more than just the price of a product. They want to know how it's made, its ingredients, how safe it is, and what its effect may be on the environment. Another issue that concerns consumers today is whether a manufacturer will stand behind what it sells.

In this chapter, you learn about warranties—what they are, how they're made, and how they protect you, the consumer.

Your Word Is Fine, but Can I Get It in Writing?

Who hasn't bought a product that didn't work the way it was supposed to? Whether or not you realized it at the time, when you brought the product back to the store, you were exercising your rights under the product's warranty.

A *warranty* is a guarantee or, to put it even more simply, a promise about a product. Warranties can be extensive (promising a complete replacement of the product if you're not satisfied, for example) or limited (promising only to repair the product if it breaks within the first 30 days you own it), or they may not be given at all (you buy something "as is"). Warranties spell out your rights if you're not happy with a product.

A warranty made by a store or a manufacturer usually gives you one of three solutions if the product doesn't perform as it should: replacement of the product, repair, or a refund of the purchase price. Generally speaking, it doesn't matter whether you purchased the product yourself, received it as a gift, or even bought it used from your neighbor—the warranty terms stay the same. A warranty can limit coverage to the original purchaser of the item, but warranties for consumer and household products normally don't have this limitation.

Legalese

A **warranty**, by a seller or manufacturer, promises that certain things about a product are true.

Different kinds of warranties can be made, by either a seller (such as a store) or the product's manufacturer, and the rules governing warranties are primarily a matter of state law. Forty-nine of the 50 states have adopted a uniform body of law dealing with various commercial issues, most notably in the area of sales. This body of law, called the Uniform Commercial Code (or just UCC), includes provisions governing warranties: the way they're created, the way they can be disclaimed, and what they mean for a buyer. In case you're wondering, Louisiana is the only state that doesn't follow all the provisions contained in the UCC.

Two main types of warranties fall under the UCC: express warranties and implied warranties.

Express warranties are affirmative representations about the product, as shown in these examples:

➤ "This watch is waterproof."

➤ "This stereo comes with a one-year guarantee on parts and labor."

➤ "This shelving unit can hold 350 pounds."

➤ "This tire will last 50,000 miles."

As you can see, an express warranty is made when a seller does one of the following:

➤ Makes a promise about the product.

➤ States a fact about the product.

It's important to listen (or read) carefully—not every statement made about a product is an express warranty. For example, general sales talk ("This finish really holds up") and opinions ("This is a great value") are not considered warranties.

Even if an express warranty is given, be certain to review it thoroughly and find out exactly what's required to make a claim under the warranty. Suppose that you buy a new computer that comes with a ten-year warranty on all its parts. That sounds nice, but read carefully—it may not be such a great deal after all. Consider these questions:

➤ **If the computer needs to be repaired, who pays the cost of the labor?** (If the warranty is only on parts, you'll probably be picking up the tab.)

➤ **Where can the computer be serviced?** If the only authorized service center is in Okinawa, the shipping costs back and forth may be more than the cost of buying a new unit.

➤ **Are you required to do anything to protect your rights under the warranty?** Most warranties require you to at least send in a registration card that establishes the date you bought or received the item. The date on the card is considered the date that begins the warranty period. If you never get around to sending in the registration, you may void your coverage, especially if you want to make a claim after you've had the computer a long time.

➤ **Are there situations in which the warranty doesn't cover you?** Most warranties limit their coverage in some way or another. You may find that the warranty prohibits you from trying to make any repairs or upgrades on your own or from taking the computer to anyone other than a factory-authorized service center. You may find that the warranty doesn't cover certain uses of the product— if your computer is expressly designed for home use, for example, and not meant for commercial or business use.

In addition to making promises or stating facts, a seller can make an express warranty about a product by showing you a design, model, or sample. Cabinets, carpeting, decks, bathroom fixtures, and other home-improvement items are often sold in this way. The express warranty made by the seller is that the product you receive is the same as the sample you saw in the showroom.

You may also be protected by another kind of warranty when you make a purchase. These warranties, called *implied warranties,* are implied by law, and they can exist whether or not you've received any express warranties about a product. In other words, these warranties don't have to be "delivered" to you in any way—the seller can say nothing, do nothing, and give you nothing in writing, but an implied warranty may still exist. There are two kinds of implied warranties:

➤ Implied warranty of merchantability.

➤ Implied warranty of fitness for a particular purpose.

An *implied warranty of merchantability* requires that an item be reasonably fit for its normal, intended use. A food processor should chop food; a CD player should play music; a cordless screwdriver should be able to screw things together. This implied warranty doesn't require that the product perform its job perfectly or even that it perform well— the product just has to function. Everyone knows, for example, that a cassette player you buy for $14.95 doesn't have the same sound quality a top-of-the-line model has, but it still should be able to play your tapes. The implied warranty of merchantability doesn't change the fact that you usually get what you pay for.

The idea of "intended use" is important to all warranty coverage, including the implied warranty of merchantability. If you frequently use your new cordless screwdriver to pry the lids off paint cans, the implied warranty of merchantability no longer applies, and you may even void any express warranty coverage you have.

The second kind of implied warranty, the *implied warranty of fitness for a particular purpose,* exists in only certain situations. Unlike merchantability, this warranty can be made by any seller, whether he's a merchant under the UCC or not. In order for the warranty to exist, the following conditions must exist:

➤ The seller must believe that you are buying the item for a specific purpose.

➤ The seller also must believe that you're relying on his judgment, skill, or experience in your selection of the item.

Suppose that I'm about to build some bookshelves for my den. I know that I want to use oak for the shelves, but I don't really know which kind of blade I need to use on my electric saw. I go to my neighborhood hardware store and tell the clerk that I need a saw blade that can cut oak shelving, and I ask her to help me find the right one from among the dozens of blades in stock. If I use the blade she recommends and it wrecks the wood or my electric saw because it can't do the job, I have a claim for breach of the implied warranty of fitness for a particular purpose.

> OOOOOH...
>
> **Tip**
> Under the UCC, the implied warranty of merchantability applies only when you buy something from a "merchant." Simply put, the warranty exists when you buy something from someone who's in the business of selling—the store clerk, the Avon representative who comes to your door, or the celebrity on the cable-TV shopping channel. It doesn't apply to a one-time transaction between individuals—if I sell you my bike, for example.

More Warranty Protection for Consumer Goods

When you buy a consumer good (a product to be used for personal or household purposes) that costs $15 or more, you're protected by more than just the UCC. You're also covered by the federal Magnuson-Moss Act, which regulates how warranties are made.

Magnuson-Moss requires that if a product comes with a written warranty, the consumer must receive a written explanation of how the warranty coverage works. This explanation must tell you the following details:

➤ Who is covered by the warranty.

➤ Which parts of the product are covered.

➤ What will be done if there is a defect or problem.

➤ What charges or expenses you will have to pay (for example, the cost of shipping the product back to the manufacturer).

➤ Whether any type of informal dispute-resolution process is available.

➤ When the warranty begins (the date of purchase, when you send in the registration card, and so on).

➤ When the warranty coverage expires.

➤ What specific steps you must take to obtain remedial action under the warranty coverage.

Tip

Keep in mind that although the Magnuson-Moss Act does not require a store or manufacturer to give you a warranty, if a warranty is given, the Act regulates how it's done. Under the Act, you're entitled to review warranty terms before you buy a product. If the store doesn't have warranty information posted or if it's not marked on the product's packaging, ask to see it before you buy.

The Act additionally requires that you be told whether the warranty is "full" or "limited." A full warranty, as defined by federal law, requires the seller or manufacturer to repair any problems within a reasonable time and without charge to the consumer. If the product cannot be repaired after a reasonable number of attempts, the consumer is entitled to have the item replaced or receive a full refund. A warranty offering anything less than this kind of full coverage is considered a limited warranty.

When the Ticket Says "As Is," They're Not Kidding

As you've learned, manufacturers and sellers are normally under no obligation to give you a warranty when you buy their products, but many still do. Sometimes, however, a manufacturer or seller wants to limit its warranty liability, and under the UCC a warranty can be disclaimed. But the UCC spells out how a warranty can be disclaimed, and if the UCC requirements aren't met, the disclaimer has no legal effect and a warranty may still exist.

Under normal circumstances, most written express warranties don't get disclaimed—they simply aren't made in the first place. There are, however, some types of express warranties a seller or manufacturer may want to specifically disclaim. Suppose that you were shown a model of a hot tub. You've learned that the model acts as an express warranty—that the tub you receive will be just like it. To disclaim this express warranty, the seller can add to your sales contract a statement that says, "Any samples or models were used only for illustrative purposes and shall not create an express warranty that the goods purchased will conform to any such sample or model." This statement protects the seller from any warranty claim when your tub turns out to be two shades darker than the floor model.

> **Legalese**
> A seller or manufacturer **disclaims** a warranty when it specifically says that no warranty coverage exists, regardless of what else may have previously been said or implied about the product.

Many sales contracts also disclaim any verbal express warranties made by salespeople and limit warranty coverage to the express statements contained in the contract. The lesson is simple: Always read warranty information, no matter what the salesperson tells you about the product.

Implied warranties can be disclaimed as well. To be effective, a written disclaimer of the warranty of merchantability must be conspicuous (underlined, in bold print, or in different colored letters, for example), and it must specifically use the word "merchantability." To disclaim the implied warranty of fitness, the disclaimer must be in writing and must be conspicuous.

> **Legal Pitfalls**
> The trump card of all disclaimers is the phrase "as is." These two little words effectively disclaim all warranties, express and implied. Under the UCC, other phrases with the same meaning can also be used as a complete disclaimer—for example, the phrase "with all faults" is generally held to mean the same thing as "as is."

So What Does All This Get You?

Whether you're talking about implied or express warranties or differences between the coverage under the UCC or Magnuson-Moss, the bottom-line question is always "What do you do when the [fill in your favorite product] you just bought breaks the first time you use it?

Begin by reading your warranty material if there is any. See what's covered and what you have to do to exercise your rights under the warranty. Follow the warranty instructions and make your claim. If your claim is rejected, ask for an explanation. Remember that there are many reasons the product may not be covered: The warranty was effectively disclaimed, you didn't comply with the warranty's terms, or you used the product in an improper way, to name a few.

If your claim under a warranty was unfairly denied, you can try writing to the president of the company involved. If that doesn't get you anywhere, you can contact an attorney to discuss filing suit for the company's breach of warranty. Under certain circumstances, you might even find out that you're eligible to become part of a class-action suit.

If filing suit doesn't make economic sense—if you just can't justify spending money, time, and effort on litigation—you can file a complaint with the consumer-affairs division of your state's attorney general's office or contact the Better Business Bureau office in your area for other suggestions.

The Least You Need To Know

➤ Warranties can be expressly made by a seller or manufacturer, or they can be implied by law under the Uniform Commercial Code.

➤ Federal law (the Magnuson-Moss Act) requires that a company giving a warranty provide consumers with certain disclosures explaining the warranty coverage.

➤ Any warranty can be disclaimed, but the UCC sets up certain requirements for the form of the disclaimer.

➤ The phrase "as is" effectively disclaims all warranty coverage, express and implied.

Chapter 29

Born in the U.S.A.

In This Chapter

➤ Basic rights you have under the Bill of Rights

➤ When the government can interfere with your basic rights

➤ Common duties you have as a citizen

We enjoy a tremendous amount of personal freedom in the United States of America, and this freedom is guaranteed by the Constitution and the Bill of Rights. Of course, no society can ever be completely free; if everyone could do whatever they wanted, if there were no limits on what each of us could do, complete chaos would rule.

The state (I'm really referring to government in general) often has a need to limit our rights. Balancing an individual's rights against the interests of the state is not always an easy task. This chapter looks at some areas in which our constitutional rights can run up against the government's interest and how these cases are decided.

Speaking Your Mind

"Congress shall make no law…abridging the freedom of speech, or of the press…"

This statement, taken from the First Amendment to the Constitution, provides us with a fundamental freedom to express ourselves. This freedom exists without regard to the subject matter, ideas, or opinions we express. Each person's right to free speech is not absolute, however, and in certain situations speech can be regulated. For example, speech can be regulated in the following situations:

➤ The speech presents a clear and present danger of inciting a riot or other violent public disturbance. "Fighting words," as they're often referred to in court opinions, can be regulated because they invite immediate retaliation and can create a real threat to public safety. But the line between "fighting words" and free speech is a thin one: "Political speech" during a KKK rally, for example, is generally protected under the First Amendment unless it turns into a deliberate attempt to incite violence.

➤ The words are meant to (or could reasonably be interpreted as likely to) cause a public panic. As you might expect, I'm not protected under the First Amendment if I get on the 5:15 flight from Chicago to Denver and decide that it would be fun to yell, "There's a bomb on the plane!" at the top of my lungs while we're taking off.

➤ The speech is meant to advertise something or is otherwise commercial in nature. For example, state laws regulating the way medicines and other health treatments are advertised usually aren't considered unconstitutional because the state has a compelling interest in protecting the public from "quacks."

➤ The speech or expression is designed to interfere with judicial proceedings. Someone abusing the right of free speech in this way hurts the rights of the people before the court—the outbursts and disruption threatens their ability to receive a fair trial. If someone is so disruptive that the ability to conduct a fair trial is jeopardized, that person can be found in contempt of court and punished.

➤ The material is defamatory. Defamation is the act of making false statements about someone in a deliberate or reckless effort to injure her reputation. If I sue you for making intentional, false statements about me, you probably can't use the First Amendment as a defense for your actions.

➤ The material is obscene as defined by law. Of course, deciding what qualifies as "obscene" is the tricky part. Material is legally obscene when an average person, applying current community standards, would find that the material depicts or describes sexual conduct in a particularly lewd or offensive way and that the material has no serious artistic, literary, or scientific value. Not exactly a clear-cut definition, is it? You can see why courts often have a difficult time deciding these kinds of cases.

Just Saying "No:" The Freedom To Protest

Protests and similar demonstrations are also protected under the First Amendment. The same rules generally apply to demonstrations that apply to speech and other forms of expression. You have the right to voice your opinions and deliver your message, and you can't be punished for your views, even if they are completely off the wall. The state does have the ability to regulate how you deliver your message, and as with free speech, it requires a balancing of the state's interests with your personal freedoms.

The state's right to regulate how demonstrations are conducted stems from a need to protect public safety. As long as the regulations concern time, manner, and place and do not discriminate against a certain speaker or group, laws governing the time, place, and manner in which protests are conducted and laws requiring groups to obtain a city permit are not unconstitutional.

Suppose that the city of Anytown requires any group that wants to demonstrate or conduct a protest march to obtain a city permit, to schedule the demonstration between the hours of 10:00 A.M. and 2:00 P.M., and to hold the demonstration at one of the city's public parks. If challenged, this law would probably be constitutional. On the other hand, if the city ordinance states that those requirements apply only to "the Ku Klux Klan, Nazis, and other known hate groups," the ordinance would violate the First Amendment.

Pick a Church, Any Church: Freedom of Religion

The First Amendment also prohibits the government from making any laws "respecting an establishment of religion"—you're free to believe (or not to believe) whatever you want. The idea of preventing the "establishment" of a religion requires a state to keep itself separate from churches and other religious groups. For example, state governments and agencies are generally prohibited from displaying any religious signs or symbols to ensure that no religion or denomination is seen as getting preferential treatment.

This separation of church and state involves more than just symbols and displays. As you learned back in Chapter 8, for example, a court does not recognize a religious annulment as legally binding, and a church may not recognize an annulment issued by a court. Similarly, you can get married in a church, but you still have to get your marriage license from the state.

Your freedom to believe what you will is absolute, but the way you exercise your religious beliefs can be regulated under certain circumstances. Even if your particular "religion" calls for you to eat illegal, hallucinogenic mushrooms during certain rites, state drug laws still apply, and you can be prosecuted. And the fact that you were trying to revive an ancient religion that happens to require animal sacrifice doesn't mean that you'll have a defense at your state criminal prosecution. Generally speaking, a law won't be overturned on the grounds of freedom of religion unless it can be shown that the law in question was clearly aimed at interfering with the practices of a specific religious group. So if a particular law had one standard for Christians and another standard for Jews, it would be unconstitutional.

The Right to Privacy: More Than Closing the Bathroom Door

In recent years, courts have increasingly found that we all have certain privacy rights even though such rights aren't mentioned in the Constitution. Needless to say, some judges and legal scholars oppose reading things into the Constitution, and others say that constitutional interpretation should be broad enough and fluid enough to change as society changes.

Philosophical arguments aside, privacy rights usually involve highly personal matters, such as abortion, contraception, and, in some cases, even certain personal communications. Many cases turn on a person's reasonable expectation of privacy—you have a strong expectation, for example, that your home phone is not bugged. Eavesdropping, unless it's part of a criminal investigation authorized by court order, is an invasion of your privacy. Investigators must get a court order permitting them to use a wiretap during a criminal investigation, and the order generally expires after ten days. At that point, they have to either return to court and ask for a new order or end the surveillance.

But courts have recently held that the expectation of privacy is lower when you make a call from your cellular phone. Because it is common knowledge that scanners and other devices can easily pick up cellular-telephone frequencies, you should not expect this type of call to be as private as a call you make from home. Consequently, the cellular call does not receive as much legal protection as the call from home.

Privacy, at least as a constitutional issue, is a rapidly changing and developing area, and it's difficult to predict how far the courts will go as they continue to define this right. New technology develops far more quickly than new law does, and issues of privacy in relation to such things as computers, e-mail, and various Internet services will have to be decided in the years to come. Although few cases have been decided on these issues, you can expect that, in the future, they'll revolve around the idea of an expectation of privacy.

More Rights You Have as a Citizen

This chapter has only touched on a few of the rights discussed in the Bill of Rights (the first ten amendments to the Constitution), but you can see that there's always a struggle between the individual freedoms described in the Constitution and in the Bill of Rights and the government's interest in limiting those freedoms. There's also often a struggle about how to interpret the Constitution's language.

The Second Amendment, of course, is a classic example. Although the amendment does include the phrase "the right of the people to keep and bear arms," it is generally accepted that this wording was a reference to the states' right to maintain their own militias, not to every citizen's right to own a gun. Remember that when this phrase was written, the original 13 states had just finished fighting the British, and there were still other military threats to think about. Regardless of how you interpret the wording, though, you can see that another issue comes up: The government has a strong interest in putting certain restrictions on gun ownership in order to protect the public good.

This list shows some other important rights described in the Bill of Rights:

➤ The right to be free from unreasonable search and seizures.

➤ The right to remain silent and the right to be tried only once if accused of a crime.

➤ The right to a speedy and public trial in criminal cases.

➤ The right to not be subject to cruel or unusual punishment if convicted of a crime.

➤ The right to confront and cross-examine witnesses and to have the help of an attorney if accused of a crime.

➤ The right to a jury trial in civil cases.

➤ The right to hold private property without the threat of the government taking it for public use and not paying for it (a process called *condemnation*).

Your Responsibilities as a Citizen

Considering the amount of freedom we enjoy in this country, our government doesn't really demand all that much from us as citizens. Two of the common obligations you may encounter are registering with the Selective Service System and serving on a jury.

Is It Drafty in Here?

If you're just turning 18, you can breathe a qualified sigh of relief—our country does not currently have a draft. You are required, however, to register with the Selective Service System. This federal agency is the one that will contact you in case the draft is brought back into existence.

The registration requirement applies to all males, whether they're U.S. citizens or resident aliens, between the ages of 18 and 26. Registration is a simple process and only involves filling out a form at your local post office. It's a federal crime not to register, and you're likely to run into problems if you try to get student financial aid, apply for a government job, or take advantage of certain government benefits.

It Could Be Worse—You Could've Been Selected for O.J.'s Jury

Although it may be inconvenient, jury duty is a responsibility we all have as United States citizens. If you're over age 18 and a citizen, you may well open your mail one day and find that you've received a jury *summons,* which is the formal document requiring you to appear for jury duty. The county you live in usually picks up your name from driver's license and state identification-card records or from lists of registered voters.

Just because you're summoned doesn't mean that you'll serve on the jury. When a case goes to trial, the attorneys for the parties select a jury through a process called voir dire. *Voir dire* is an examination of a prospective juror to determine whether he can render a fair verdict. During voir dire, the lawyers or the judge or both can question you concerning your biases, prejudices, competency, and other relevant matters.

Each area has its own rules concerning what you must do if you're unable to serve on jury duty, and some larger metropolitan areas allow people to postpone their service. Contact the clerk of the circuit court that issues the jury summons to find out what the rules are in your area. Don't just ignore the summons—it's a court order for you to appear. If you don't, you can be fined for contempt of court.

The Least You Need To Know

➤ The rights described in the Bill of Rights are not absolute, and individual rights may need to be balanced against compelling state interests, such as protecting the public from harm.

➤ The right to privacy is not mentioned in the Constitution, but courts have inferred that such a right exists.

➤ You may have a duty to register with the Selective Service System, and every person has a duty to serve on a jury if summoned.

Legalese Glossary

IV-D ("4-D") agency   A federally funded state agency that provides parents with assistance in obtaining and enforcing child-support orders.

administrator   Someone appointed by a probate court to handle the distribution of the estate of a person who has died without a will (intestate).

agency adoption   An adoption in which a state-licensed adoption agency is involved in placing the child with his adoptive parents.

agent   A person legally authorized to act on someone else's behalf.

alimony   *See* maintenance.

annulment   A court order stating that a marriage was never legally valid because of certain circumstances that existed when it took place.

answer   Pleadings filed by a defendant that respond to the allegations in a plaintiff's complaint.

appellate court   A court that has jurisdiction over appeals and that has the power to review the rulings of trial courts.

arbitration   An alternative method of dispute resolution in which the parties present the facts of their case to an arbitrator (or a panel of arbitrators) who renders a decision.

"as is"   A phrase that effectively disclaims all warranties, express and implied.

attractive nuisance   An object or condition normally considered dangerous to children but that attracts them anyway.

audit   The process of reviewing and verifying all, or just a portion of, the information contained in a tax return.

automatic stay   In bankruptcy, a court order that puts a debtor's property under the protection of the court and that prohibits anyone from beginning or continuing any legal action against the debtor.

bankruptcy   A legal process designed to free a person from debt in order to start over financially and to make a fair distribution of his assets among his creditors.

bench trial   A trial conducted before a judge, without a jury.

breach of contract   A failure to perform the legal obligations under a contract.

codicil   A written amendment to an existing will.

community-property states   States that attempt, during a divorce, to split on a 50-50 basis everything that was acquired during a marriage.

compensatory damages   An award of money to compensate a person for her actual losses.

complaint   Pleadings filed by a plaintiff that serve as the basis of his lawsuit.

consideration   A contractual requirement that each party must have some obligation under the agreement.

contempt of court   1. Any act that interrupts court proceedings or impairs the court's ability to function. 2. Intentionally disobeying a court order.

contingent fee   A fee agreement between an attorney and a client, usually used in litigation cases, which says that the attorney will be paid based on a portion of the total amount recovered in the lawsuit.

contract   An agreement between two or more parties that creates a binding legal obligation to do (or *not* to do) something.

credit report   A written summary of a person's credit history, prepared by a private agency that gathers information from current and past creditors as well as from public records.

custody   The right, and the responsibility, of making all decisions concerning a child.

defamation   The act of making false statements about someone in a deliberate effort to injure her reputation.

default   Failure to comply with the terms of an agreement; the same as *breach*.

default judgment   A judgment entered against a defendant because he failed to answer the complaint or otherwise appear before the court.

defendant   The person being sued in a lawsuit; in a criminal case, the person charged with a crime.

defined-benefit plan   A retirement plan under which the employer pays out benefits based on a set formula that factors in the years the employee spent with the company and the employee's salary.

defined-contribution plan   A retirement plan under which the employer contributes a certain amount of money each year into the employee's individual account and then invests the money; the amount the employee gets at retirement is determined by the amount of the contributions and by how well the investments perform.

deposition   A person's sworn testimony, taken outside court but still under oath and documented by a court reporter.

direct adoption   A process in which a child's natural parents place him with the adoptive parents and no adoption service or agency is involved.

discovery   The general process of fact-gathering that parties to a lawsuit participate in before trial; tools that can be used in the process include depositions, physical inspections, and examinations.

district court   A federal trial court.

diversity suit   A lawsuit involving parties from different states; if a case involves $50,000 or more, it can be heard by a federal court.

divorce   A legal action to completely dissolve a marriage.

easement   A right to enter onto someone's property and use it for a limited purpose (to maintain utility lines, for example).

Employee Retirement Income Security Act (ERISA)   A federal statute that sets various rules for employers about how they administer retirement plans and requires that various disclosure statements be given to employees.

employment at will   An employment relationship that exists without a formal contract and that continues for an unspecified length of time; an employer can fire an employee at will for almost any nondiscriminatory reason and generally without notice.

encroach   To violate an easement, lot line, building line, or other similar boundary line.

encumbrance   Any matter that affects title to real estate, including such things as liens, easements, and homeowners' association regulations.

Equal Credit Opportunity Act (ECOA)   A federal statute aimed at stopping discrimination by lenders when they extend credit.

Equal Employment Opportunity Act (EEOA)   A federal statute designed to stop discrimination in hiring, firing, and other areas of employment.

Equal Employment Opportunity Commission (EEOC)   A federal agency that handles violations of the Equal Employment Opportunity Act.

equitable-distribution states   States which follow the rule that in a divorce a court should consider a wide range of relevant factors and try to make a fair property division between divorcing parties, not necessarily based on an automatic 50-50 split.

escheat   The process in which a person's estate passes to the state in the event that he leaves no will and has no heirs at the time of his death.

eviction   A legal process in which a landlord tries to take back possession of the leased premises and recover past-due rent.

executor   Someone who handles the distribution of the estate of a person who dies with a will.

express warranty   A representation about a product made by the seller or manufacturer; the representation can be made orally, in writing, or, in some cases, through the use of samples, models, or designs.

Fair Credit Reporting Act (FCRA)   A federal statute that regulates how credit bureaus prepare and distribute credit reports.

Fair Debt Collection Practices Act (FDCPA)   A federal statute designed to protect consumers when they deal with collection agencies.

guardian   A person, often named in a will, who is legally responsible for another person (usually a minor).

health-care power of attorney   A legal document that gives someone (the "agent") authority to make some or all medical decisions in the event that you cannot make them yourself.

holographic will   A will that is handwritten and not witnessed.

homeowner's insurance policy   A standard policy for property owners that provides both property damage and liability coverage.

implied warranty of fitness for a particular purpose   A warranty implied by law when a seller has reason to know that the buyer is buying an item for a specific purpose and that the buyer is relying on the seller's judgment, skill, or experience in her selection of the item.

implied warranty of merchantability   A warranty implied by law, made only by sellers who are considered merchants under the UCC, which says that an item must be reasonably fit for its normal, intended use.

independent administration   A simplified way to probate a small estate, involving much less court supervision than the normal probate process does.

intestate   Not having a valid will.

joint-custody agreement   An agreement between spouses, as part of a divorce, that gives them both the right to participate in decisions about their children.

judgment   A court's final and official decision about questions of both fact and law.

jurisdiction   The authority of a court to hear a specific kind of case.

legal separation   A legal action resulting in a court order that defines terms about how two spouses will live separately from each other without actually ending the marriage.

letters of office   Official notices issued by a probate court authorizing someone to handle all the financial matters of an estate.

liquidation   In bankruptcy, the court-ordered sale of assets in order to pay creditors.

litigation   A lawsuit.

living will   A document that indicates whether a person wants various life-support methods used in case she is in a permanent coma or has a terminal condition.

maintenance   The court-ordered payment of money by one spouse to help support the other after a divorce.

malpractice   An incident of professional misconduct or an unreasonable lack of skill or diligence that results in harm to a client or patient.

marital settlement agreement   An agreement attached to or part of a divorce decree, generally covering the division of property and assets, support for a spouse and the children, and child custody and visitation.

marketable title   In real estate, a title that's free from defects, liens, or other problems.

mediation   A process of dispute resolution that uses a neutral third person to assist the parties in communicating so that they can work out their own solution.

mortgage   A legal document that gives a lender a security interest in the real estate being purchased by a borrower.

motion   The way a party asks the court to do something during a pending lawsuit.

no-fault divorce   A divorce based not on traditional grounds of fault but rather on general irreconcilable differences.

nuisance   Any act or condition that seriously interferes with another person's right to use and enjoy her property.

offer   A proposal to do something or pay some amount according to certain terms and showing a willingness to enter into a contract.

partial performance   The completion of some but not all contractual obligations.

performance   The process of meeting one's contractual obligations.

plaintiff   The party who brings a lawsuit; in a criminal case, a state or the federal government charging someone with a crime.

pleadings   Court documents, such as a complaint and answer, that form the framework of a lawsuit and tell the court which issues are involved in the case.

prenuptial agreement   A contract between people who are planning to get married, usually describing how property and debts will be divided if they divorce or when one dies.

prequalification   A process similar to applying for a mortgage in which the lender issues a statement explaining what kinds of loan programs a borrower can qualify for and the amount of financing he can receive.

privileged communication   Information or communications that are confidential (between an attorney and a client, for example) and that cannot be disclosed to anyone else.

probate   A court proceeding designed to determine the validity of a will and oversee the administration of an estate.

punitive damages   Amounts awarded to a plaintiff by a court solely to punish the defendant (as opposed to compensating the plaintiff for her actual losses).

reaffirmation agreement   In bankruptcy, a new contract between a person and a creditor that is used to remove a particular transaction from the bankruptcy proceedings.

Real Estate Settlement and Procedures Act (RESPA)   A federal statute giving borrowers certain rights and protections when they apply for and obtain mortgage financing.

renter's insurance   Insurance that gives a tenant protection similar to a standard homeowner's policy, providing both property damage and liability coverage.

replacement-cost coverage   Coverage requiring an insurance company to pay a claim based on the current cost of replacing a damaged item.

retainer A deposit toward an attorney's total fees, usually payable before any work begins.

service of process A formal way of giving someone notice that you're suing him.

sexual harassment Improper sexual advances (verbal or physical) made in the workplace that interfere with an employee's work or that create an offensive or hostile work environment for an employee.

statute of limitations A time limit set by state law regarding how long you can wait before bringing a certain type of legal action.

subletting Leasing of property to another person for part of your original lease term.

summons A document which officially notifies a person that she's being sued and describes how she can appear before the court and answer the complaint.

testate Having a valid will.

title report A document identifying the current owner of a piece of real estate and providing a legal description for the property in addition to other general information about it.

tort A civil wrong or injury, other than a breach of contract, for which a court awards damages.

trust An agreement under which one person (the trustee) holds property for the benefit of another person (the beneficiary).

trustee Someone who administers a trust; in bankruptcy, the individual who conducts creditors' meetings and liquidates the assets of a debtor.

Truth In Lending Act (TILA) A federal statute requiring a lender to provide you with an accurate and meaningful disclosure about the terms of your credit.

unconscionable A term used to describe an agreement (or part of an agreement) so grossly unfair that a court will not enforce it.

Uniform Interstate Family Support Act (UIFSA) The more recent, and broader, of two statutes in use that enables a person to enforce a child-support order against someone in another state.

Uniform Reciprocal Enforcement of Support Act (URESA)   One of two statutes in use that enables a person to enforce a child-support order against someone in another state.

vest   To become permanent; a retirement or other benefit vests when your right to receive it cannot be lost if you leave the employer.

voir dire   An examination of a prospective juror to determine whether she is free from bias and able to render a fair verdict.

wage garnishment   A court order to an employer requiring him to withhold a specified amount from an employee's wages and to pay it to the employee's creditor.

warranty   A promise by a seller or manufacturer that certain things about a product are true.

writ of certiorari   An order from the U.S. Supreme Court requiring a lower court to produce the records of a case so that an appeal can be heard.

Sample Legal Documents

This appendix contains some sample legal forms for you to review as you go through this book. Keep in mind that they're only samples and that the forms used in your area may be different. Even in the case of something as "standard" as a will, different states have different requirements about how the will must be signed and witnessed. It's important that your documents and forms comply with your state's requirements.

Bankruptcy Court Notice to Debtor

B 201
(Rev. 11/93)

United States Bankruptcy Court

NOTICE TO INDIVIDUAL CONSUMER DEBTOR

The purpose of this notice is to acquaint you with the four chapters of the federal Bankruptcy Code under which you may file a bankruptcy petition. The bankruptcy law is complicated and not easily described. Therefore, you should seek the advice of an attorney to learn of your rights and responsibilities under the law should you decide to file a petition with the court. Neither the judge nor the court's employees may provide you with legal advice.

Chapter 7: Liquidation ($130 filing fee plus $30 administrative fee)

1. Chapter 7 is designed for debtors in financial difficulty who do not have the ability to pay their existing debts.

2. Under chapter 7 a trustee takes possession of all your property. You may claim certain of your property as exempt under governing law. The trustee then liquidates the property and uses the proceeds to pay your creditors according to priorities of the Bankruptcy Code.

3. The purpose of filing a chapter 7 case is to obtain a discharge of your existing debts. If, however, you are found to have committed certain kinds of improper conduct described in the Bankruptcy Code, your discharge may be denied by the court, and the purpose for which you filed the bankruptcy petition will be defeated.

4. Even if you receive a discharge, there are some debts that are not discharged under the law. Therefore, you may still be responsible for such debts as certain taxes and student loans, alimony and support payments, criminal restitution, and debts for death or personal injury caused by driving while intoxicated from alcohol or drugs.

5. Under certain circumstances you may keep property that you have purchased subject to a valid security interest. Your attorney can explain the options that are available to you.

Chapter 13: Repayment of All or Part of the Debts of an Individual with Regular Income ($130 filing fee plus $30 administrative fee)

1. Chapter 13 is designed for individuals with regular income who are temporarily unable to pay their debts but would like to pay them in installments over a period of time. You are only eligible for chapter 13 if your debts do not exceed certain dollar amounts set forth in the Bankruptcy Code.

2. Under chapter 13 you must file a plan with the court to repay your creditors all or part of the money that you owe them, using your future earnings. Usually, the period allowed by the court to repay your debts is three years, but not more than five years. Your plan must be approved by the court before it can take effect.

3. Under chapter 13, unlike chapter 7, you may keep all your property, both exempt and non-exempt, as long as you continue to make payments under the plan.

4. After completion of payments under your plan, your debts are discharged except alimony and support payments, student loans, certain other debts including criminal restitution and debts for death or personal injury caused by driving while intoxicated from alcohol or drugs, and long term secured obligations.

Chapter 11: Reorganization ($800 filing fee)

Chapter 11 is designed primarily for the reorganization of a business but is also available to consumer debtors. Its provisions are quite complicated, and any decision by an individual to file a chapter 11 petition should be reviewed with an attorney.

Chapter 12: Family Farmer ($200 filing fee)

Chapter 12 is designed to permit family farmers to repay their debts over a period of time from future earnings and is in many ways similar to a chapter 13. The eligibility requirements are restrictive, limiting its use to those whose income arises primarily from a family-owned farm.

I, the debtor, affirm that I have read this notice.

_____   _____   _____
            Date   Signature of Debtor   Case Number

WHITE—DEBTOR COPY   PINK—COURT COPY

Contingent Fee Agreement

CONTINGENT FEE AGREEMENT

PAULA PLAINTIFF ("Client") hereby retains ALLAN ATTORNEY, ("Attorney") to assist her in the prosecution of a breach of contract claim against HARRY'S USED CARS, INC., and to represent her in any litigation based on this claim.

In consideration of the services rendered and to be rendered by Attorney, Client agrees that the fee for such services, whether the matter be settled prior to trial or not, shall be thirty percent (30%) of any amounts actually recovered. By signing this Agreement, Client assigns and conveys to Attorney such percentage interest in the above mentioned claim.

It is further agreed that Client will pay $750.00 to Attorney as a nonrefundable retainer. The parties agree that this amount shall be credited to Client against the final fee amount billed.

Client agrees to pay all costs and expenses incurred during litigation of her claim, including but not limited to court costs, witness fees, and deposition costs. Any amounts forwarded to Attorney by Client for payment of future expenses will be held by Attorney in a trust account. If any costs or expenses are advanced by Attorney, Client agrees to promptly reimburse Attorney for said advances.

No suits will be instituted, settled or dismissed without prior approval from Client.

Attorney hereby agrees to provide Client with regular, periodic reports on the progress of her case, as well as with periodic statements of account regarding Client's expenses and fees.

By signing this Agreement, Client appoints ALLAN ATTORNEY her attorney in fact, with power and authority to do any and all things in connection with the above action that Client could personally do, except that Client shall retain sole authority to authorize settlement of a claim.

Dated April 7th, 1995

_____   _____
ALLAN ATTORNEY   PAULA PLAINTIFF

Eviction Complaint

```
0005
0006
```

COMPLAINT IN FORCIBLE DETAINER AND RENT OR DAMAGE CLAIMS   (2-81) CCMD-20A

IN THE CIRCUIT COURT OF COOK COUNTY, ILLINOIS.,. . . . . DISTRICT

plaintiff. . .

No. . . . .

v.

Rent or damage claimed $. . . . .

Return date . . . .

defendant. . .

COMPLAINT

The plaintiff . . . . claim. . . . as follows:

1. The plaintiff . . . . . . entitled to the possession of the following described premises in the City or Village of. . . . .

. . . .

. . . .

. . . .

. . . .

2. The defendant . . . . . . .unlawfully withhold . . . . possession thereof from the plaintiff . . . .

3. There is due to plaintiff . . . . from the defendant . . . . for rent of or for damages for withholding possession of said premises from . . . . , 19. . . ., to . . . . , 19. . . ., after allowing the defendant. . . . all just credits, deductions and set-offs, the sum of $ . . . .

The plaintiff. . . . claim . . . . possession of the property and $ . . . . as rent or damages.

Name
Attorney for
Address
City
Telephone
Atty No.

. . . .
Attorney. . . .for plaintiff. . . .

I. . . . ., on oath state that I am the

. . . . .plaintiff in the above entitled action. The allegations in this complaint are true.

. . . .

Signed and sworn to before me . . . . , 19. . . .

. . . .
Notary public

Natural Parent's Consent to Adoption

```
              IN THE CIRCUIT COURT OF JACKSON COUNTY
                       FAMILY LAW DIVISION

In the Matter of the Petition of  )
                                  )
_____,  )
                                  )
              Husband and Wife,   )  No. 95 A 387
                                  )
TO ADOPT                          )
                                  )
_____,  )
                                  )
              a Minor.            )


              FINAL AND IRREVOCABLE CONSENT TO ADOPTION


I, _____, the (mother/father) of _____
_____, a (male/female) child, state on oath as follows:

1.  This child was born on _____, at _____,
County of _____, State of _____.

2.  I reside at _____, County of _____,
State of _____, and I am _____ years old.

3.  I have entered my Appearance in this matter and have waived
service of summons.

4.  I hereby agree and consent to the adoption of this child by
Petitioners.

5.  I want to, and understand that by signing this consent form I
do, permanently and irrevocably give up all custody and other
parental rights I have to this child.

6.  I fully understand that this child will be placed for adoption
and that under no circumstances will I be able to change my mind,
or revoke or cancel this consent form once I have signed it.  I
understand that once my custody and other parental rights to this
child have been terminated, I will be unable to reinstate or
recover them.

7.  I am signing this consent form as my free and voluntary act.


Dated: _____


_____
```

Order for Withholding Child Support

**IN THE CIRCUIT COURT FOR THE SIXTEENTH JUDICIAL CIRCUIT
KANE COUNTY, ILLINOIS**

_____)
)
            vs.   )   NO. _____
_____)
)
_____)   IV-D NO. _____
)

ORDER FOR WITHHOLDING

This cause coming on to be heard on the matter of the withholding of income to secure payment of support and/or maintenance (hereinafter support), due notice having been given, the _____ not appearing in person (and/or by counsel) in open court, and the Court having jurisdiction of the parties and subject matter, having heard all the evidence and being fully advised in the premises,

THE COURT FINDS:
1. That an order for Support was entered in the above case on _____ 19 _____ .
2. That the court is required to enter an Order for Withholding pursuant to the provisions of IL. Rev. Stat. 19 _____ . Ch. _____ , Par. _____ .

WHEREFORE IT IS ORDERED:
1. That this Order may be served upon any Payor of _____ , Social Security Number _____ , the Obligor herein:
    ( ) Only under the conditions stated on page 2 of this Order.
    ( ) Immediately. The conditions stated on page 2 of this Order may be satisfied prior to first service and shall be satisfied prior to any subsequent service.
2. That any Payor who shall have been served with a specially certified copy of this Order shall withhold from the income of the obligor:
    ( ) $ _____ per _____ for current support; and
    ( ) $ _____ per _____ on an arrearage of $ _____ owed _____ and $ _____ owed the Public Office until such arrearage is paid in full; and
    ( ) _____ ; and
    (X) $ _____ per _____ on the delinquency stated in any Notice of Delinquency served with this Order until paid in full; and
    (X) pay over each amount withheld promptly to:
        ( ) The Clerk of the Circuit for Kane County, P.O. Box 430, Batavia, Illinois 60510
        ( ) _____ until notified otherwise by the Obligee/Public Office. All payments require the payor name and case number.
3. That the conditions for service, the rights, remedies and duties of the Obligor and the duties of the Payor appearing on page 2 of this Order are incorporated herein.

DATE: _____ 19 _____   ENTER: _____
                                                        Judge

PAYOR: EXECUTE AGAINST INCOME ONLY WHEN CERTIFIED BELOW.
CLERK: CERTIFY BELOW ONLY IN ACCORDANCE WITH PAR. (B) (1) OR (E) (2) OF THE ABOVE STATUTE.

                                I HEREBY CERTIFY THE ABOVE TO BE

    (Seal of Clerk
    of Circuit Court)   _____
                            Clerk of the Circuit Court of Kane County, Illinois

    Date: _____ 19 _____   THIS ORDER IS THE COMMAND OF THE CIRCUIT COURT AND
                                            VIOLATION THEREOF IS SUBJECT TO THE PENALTY OF LAW.

DPA 2579 (1/94)   Part 1 of 2

288

ORDER FOR WITHHOLDING _____ vs. _____ NO. _____

4. That the conditions for service referred to in Paragraph 1 of this Order are:
   a. The Obligor becomes delinquent in payment of an amount equal to at least on month's support obligation pursuant to the Order for Support.
   b. The Public Office or Obligee serves a Notice of Delinquency on the Obligor reciting the terms of the Order for Support and containing a computation of the period and total amount of the delinquency as of the date of the Notice.
   c. The Obligor fails to pay the total amount stated in the Notice of Delinquency and fails to file a Petition to Stay Service with the Clerk of the Circuit Court, each within 20 days after service of the Notice of Delinquency.

5. That the rights, remedies and duties of the Obligor are:
   a. The right to be served with a Notice of Delinquency advising of the amount of any claimed delinquency and of intended income withholding action.
   b. The right to avoid income withholding action by taking the following action within 20 days of the date of service of the Notice of Delinquency:
      1) Payment of the full amount stated in the Notice.
      2) Filing a Petition to Stay Service with the Clerk of the Circuit Court for the following reasons:
         a) A dispute concerning the existence or amount of delinquency, or
         b) A substantial change in circumstances beyond his/her control.
   c. The right to file a petititon with the Clerk of the Circuit Court to:
      1) Modify, suspend or terminate the Order for Withholding because:
         a) The underlying Order for Support has been modified, suspended or terminated.
         b) The delinquency stated in the Notice of Delinquency has been paid in full.
         c) Payments cannot be delivered because of the Obligee's failure to provide a mailing address or other means of delivery.
         d) The duty to notify the Clerk of Court of any new Payor, within 7 days, when he/she is having income withheld or has been served with a Notice of Delinquency.

6. That the duties of the Payor are:
   a. To begin withholding from the income of the Obligor the amount specified in this Order, supplemented by any attached Notice of Delinquency, beginning with the next payment of income due after 5 days following service of a specially certified copy of this Order and continuing until served with further order of this Court.
   b. To identify each payment by providing the names of the parties and court file number shown on this Order.
   c. To take into account any other support payment made, including but not limited to, a set-off under federal and State law or partial payment of delinquency, when notified thereof by the Obligee or Public Office.

7. That any Obligee, Public Office or Obligor who willfully initiates a false proceeding under a statute for income withholding or who willfully fails to comply with the requirements thereof shall be punished as in cases of contempt of court.

PAYOR: EXECUTE AGAINST INCOME WHEN CERTIFIED BELOW.
CLERK: CERTIFY BELOW ONLY IN ACCORDANCE WITH PAR. (B) (1) or (E) (2) OF THE ABOVE STATUTE.

(Seal of Clerk
of Circuit Court)

I HEREBY CERTIFY THE ABOVE TO BE CORRECT

_____
Clerk of the Circuit Court of Kane County, Illinois

Date:_____ 19 _____

THIS ORDER IS THE COMMAND OF THE CIRCUIT COURT AND
VIOLATION THEREOF IS SUBJECT TO THE PENALTY OF LAW.

DPA 2579 (1/94)

Part 2 of 2

289

RESPA Closing Statement

A.		B. TYPE OF LOAN		
U.S. DEPARTMENT OF HOUSING AND URBAN DEVELOPMENT **SETTLEMENT STATEMENT**	1. ☐ FHA 2. ☐ FmHA 3. ☒ CONV. UNINS. 4. ☐ VA 5. ☐ CONV. INS.			
	6. File Number: SD-477	7. Loan Number: 23LC8762		
	8. Mortgage Insurance Case Number:			

C. NOTE: *This form is furnished to give you a statement of actual settlement costs. Amounts paid to and by the settlement agent are shown. Items marked "(p.o.c.)" were paid outside the closing; they are shown here for informational purposes and are not included in the totals.*

D. NAME OF BORROWER:	E. NAME OF SELLER:	F. NAME OF LENDER:
John A. Buyer 1234 Main Street Anytown, OH	Mary T. Seller 65237 Grove Avenue Somewhere, PA	A-1 Mortgage Company 267 Park Blvd. Wherever, CA

G. PROPERTY LOCATION:	H. SETTLEMENT AGENT:	I. SETTLEMENT DATE:
65237 Grove Avenue Somewhere, PA	Best Title & Escrow Services	06-30-95
	PLACE OF SETTLEMENT: 82 S. Oak Street, Somewhere, PA	

J. SUMMARY OF BORROWER'S TRANSACTION		K. SUMMARY OF SELLER'S TRANSACTION	
100. GROSS AMOUNT DUE FROM BORROWER:		**400. GROSS AMOUNT DUE TO SELLER:**	
101. Contract sales price	130,000.00	401. Contract sales price	130,000.00
102. Personal property		402. Personal property	
103. Settlement charges to borrower (line 1400)	1,871.00	403.	
104.		404.	
105.		405.	
Adjustments for items paid by seller in advance		*Adjustments for items paid by seller in advance*	
106. City/town taxes to		406. City/town taxes to	
107. County taxes to		407. County taxes to	
108. Assessments to		408. Assessments to	
109.		409.	
110.		410.	
111.		411.	
112.		412.	
120. GROSS AMOUNT DUE FROM BORROWER	131,871.00	**420. GROSS AMOUNT DUE TO SELLER**	130,000.00
200. AMOUNTS PAID BY OR IN BEHALF OF BORROWER:		**500. REDUCTIONS IN AMOUNT DUE TO SELLER:**	
201. Deposit or earnest money	2,000.00	501. Excess deposit (see instructions)	
202. Principal amount of new loan(s)	110,000.00	502. Settlement charges to seller (line 1400)	6,405.00
203. Existing loan(s) taken subject to		503. Existing loan(s) taken subject to	
204.		504. Payoff of first mortgage loan	78,635.00
205.		505. Payoff of second mortgage loan	
206.		506.	
207.		507.	
208.		508.	
209.		509.	
Adjustments for items unpaid by seller		*Adjustments for items unpaid by seller*	
210. City/town taxes to		510. City/town taxes to	
211. County taxes to	1,365.00	511. County taxes to	1,365.00
212. Assessments to		512. Assessments to	
213.		513.	
214.		514.	
215.		515.	
216.		516.	
217.		517.	
218.		518.	
219.		519.	
220. TOTAL PAID BY/FOR BORROWER	113,365.00	**520. TOTAL REDUCTION AMOUNT DUE SELLER**	86,405.00
300. CASH AT SETTLEMENT FROM/TO BORROWER		**600. CASH AT SETTLEMENT TO/FROM SELLER**	
301. Gross amount due from borrower (line 120)	131,871.00	601. Gross amount due to seller (line 420)	130,000.00
302. Less amounts paid by/for borrower (line 220)	(113,365.00)	602. Less reductions in amount due to seller (line 520)	(86,405.00)
303. CASH (☒☒ FROM) (☐ TO) BORROWER	18,506.00	**603. CASH (☒ TO) (☐ FROM) SELLER**	43,595.00

Seller	Buyer
Seller	Buyer

HUD 1-886 2MGG

-2-

L. SETTLEMENT CHARGES		
700. TOTAL SALES/BROKER'S COMMISSION based on price $ 130,000 @ 6 % = 7,800.00	PAID FROM BORROWER'S FUNDS AT SETTLEMENT	PAID FROM SELLER'S FUNDS AT SETTLEMENT
Division of Commission (line 700) as follows:		
701. $ 7,800.00 to Star Real Estate Brokers, Inc.		
702. $ to		
703. Commission paid at Settlement	.	5,800.00
704.		
800. ITEMS PAYABLE IN CONNECTION WITH LOAN		
801. Loan Origination Fee 1 %	1,100.00	
802. Loan Discount %		
803. Appraisal Fee to We-Tell-All Appraisal	125.00	
804. Credit Report to		
805. Lender's Inspection Fee		
806. Mortgage Insurance Application Fee to		
807. Assumption Fee		
808.		
809.		
810.		
811.		
900. ITEMS REQUIRED BY LENDER TO BE PAID IN ADVANCE		
901. Interest from to @ $ /day		
902. Mortgage Insurance Premium for months to		
903. Hazard Insurance Premium for 1 years to Protect 'Em Insurance	300.00	
904. years to		
905.		
1000. RESERVES DEPOSITED WITH LENDER		
1001. Hazard insurance 2 months @ $ 25.00 per month	50.00	
1002. Mortgage insurance months @ $ per month		
1003. City property taxes months @ $ per month		
1004. County property taxes months @ $ per month		
1005. Annual assessments months @ $ per month		
1006. months @ $ per month		
1007. months @ $ per month		
1008. months @ $ per month		
1100. TITLE CHARGES		
1101. Settlement or closing fee to Best Title & Escrow	115.00	
1102. Abstract or title search to		
1103. Title examination to		
1104. Title insurance binder to		
1105. Document preparation to		
1106. Notary fees to		
1107. Attorney's fees to		
(includes above items numbers:)		
1108. Title insurance to Best Title & Escrow	120.00	418.00
(includes above items numbers:)		
1109. Lender's coverage $		
1110. Owner's coverage $		
1111.		
1112.		
1113.		
1200. GOVERNMENT RECORDING AND TRANSFER CHARGES		
1201. Recording fees: Deed $ 12.00 ; Mortgage $ 24.00 ; Releases $ 12.00	36.00	12.00
1202. City/county tax/stamps: Deed $; Mortgage $		
1203. State tax/stamps: Deed $; Mortgage $		
1204.		
1205.		
1300. ADDITIONAL SETTLEMENT CHARGES		
1301. Survey to Ted's Survey Shop		175.00
1302. Pest inspection to Termite Finders, Inc.	25.00	
1303.		
1304.		
1305.		
1400. TOTAL SETTLEMENT CHARGES (enter on lines 103, Section J and 502, Section K)	1,871.00	6,405.00

HUD 1-879 4MAG

Small-Claims Complaint

CIRCUIT COURT FOR THE 16TH JUDICIAL CIRCUIT
KANE COUNTY, ILLINOIS

Case Number_____

Amount Claimed $_____ Plus Costs

VS.

PLAINTIFF(S) | DEFENDANT(S)

SMALL CLAIMS COMPLAINT

I, the undersigned, claim that the defendant is indebted to the plaintiff in the sum of $ _____

for (The Nature of the Plaintiff's Claim, Giving Dates and other relevant information): _____

_____

_____

_____

_____

_____

_____

_____

and that the plaintiff has demanded payment of said sum; that the defendant refused to pay the same and no part thereof has been paid.

Plaintiff Resides At:	Defendant Resides At:
	(Give residence address — not service instructions)
Name_____	Name_____
Address_____	Address_____
City_____	City_____
State_____ Zip____	State_____ Zip____
Phone_____	Phone_____

Date _____ _____
  (Month - Day - Year)   (Signature of Plaintiff)

WHITE — Court Copy   PINK — Defendant's Copy   CANARY — Plaintiff's Copy

P2-SC-002

292

Summons

2120 - Served	2121 - Served	
2220 - Not Served	2221 - Not Served	
2320 - Served By Mail	2321 - Served By Mail	
2420 - Served By Publication	2421 - Served By Publication	
SUMMONS	**ALIAS - SUMMONS**	(2-81) CCG-1

IN THE CIRCUIT COURT OF COOK COUNTY, ILLINOIS
COUNTY DEPARTMENT,   DIVISION

(Name all parties)

V.   No. ....

SUMMONS

To each defendant:

YOU ARE SUMMONED and required to file an answer in this case, or otherwise file your appearance in the office of the clerk of this court (located in the Richard J. Daley Center, Room *
Chicago, Illinois 60602), within 30 days after service of this summons, not counting the day of service. IF YOU FAIL TO DO SO, A JUDGMENT BY DEFAULT MAY BE TAKEN AGAINST YOU FOR THE RELIEF ASKED IN THE COMPLAINT, A COPY OF WHICH IS HERETO ATTACHED.

To the officer.

This summons must be returned by the officer or other person to whom it was given for service, with indorsement of service and fees, if any, immediately after service. If service cannot be made, this summons shall be returned so indorsed. This summons may not be served later than 30 days after its date.

WITNESS, ..., 19....

....
Clerk of court

Atty No.

Name
Attorney for
Address
City
Telephone

Date of service:........................., 19....
(To be inserted by officer on copy left with
defendant or other person)

MORGAN M. FINLEY, CLERK OF THE CIRCUIT COURT OF COOK COUNTY

*Law Division Room 801
 Chancery-Divorce Division Room 802
 County Division Room 801
 Probate Division Room 1202

Will

LAST WILL AND TESTAMENT

I, JOHN WILSON, a resident of Chicago, Illinois, hereby revoke all prior wills and codicils and declare this to be my Last Will and Testament.

ARTICLE ONE

1.01   I direct my executor to pay as part of the expense of administering my estate:

(a) All expenses of my last illness and my funeral as soon as may be practicable after my death.

(b) All costs of the administration of my estate.

(c) All indebtedness owed by me at the time of my death, except such indebtedness as then is secured by a mortgage of real estate.

(d) All valid inheritance, estate, transfer and succession taxes which are payable because of my death, including interest and penalties thereon, in the discretion of my executor.

ARTICLE TWO

2.01 I was divorced from my wife, KAREN JAMES, in October of 1994. I have one child now living, namely:

MARTIN WILSON, born June 19, 1981

ARTICLE THREE

3.01   I give and bequeath to my son all of the household furniture, furnishings and equipment, automobiles, jewelry, silverware, books, paintings and in general, all of the tangible personal property which I may own at the date of my death. If my son does not survive me, I give and bequeath such chattel property to my father, THOMAS WILSON, and my mother, SUSAN WILSON, to be equally divided among them by agreement, or, if they cannot agree within six (6) months after my death, as my executor shall determine.

ARTICLE FOUR

4.01   I give, devise and bequeath all the rest, residue and remainder of my estate, of every kind wherever situated, which I may own at the time of my death or to which I may be entitled at my death, including all bequests and devises to any person who may predecease me or which for any reason may lapse or fail, except as

---

otherwise in this Will specifically provided and excepting any property over which I may have power of appointment, as follows:

(a)   To THOMAS WILSON, as Trustee, to have and to hold, in Trust, for the use and benefit of my son if he survives me, until he attains the age of twenty-one (21) years, at which time the Trust shall be distributed to him, per stirpes, on the terms and conditions of the following described Trust.

(b)   If my son does not survive me, to my father, THOMAS WILSON, and my mother, SUSAN WILSON, in equal shares, per capita.

4.02   The Trustee named in Section 4.01(a) shall have full power and authority to manage and control the Trust and to sell, exchange, lease for terms which may extend beyond the termination of said Trust, rent, assign, transfer or otherwise dispose of all or any part thereof, including real property, upon such terms and conditions as he may, in his discretion, deem proper.   He may invest and reinvest all or any part of the Trust in such common and preferred stocks, bonds, debentures, mortgages, deeds of trust, notes, or other securities, investments or property which the Trustee, in his absolute discretion, may select or determine, it being my express desire and intention that the Trustee shall have full power to control the Trust as I might do if living, without being restricted to forms of investment and without regard to the extent of diversification of the Trust.   The Trustee may register securities or other property, real or personal, in the name of a nominee and the Trustee may continue to hold, in the form in which received, any securities or other property, including real property, which I may own at the time of my death or which the Trust may at any time acquire hereunder.   The Trustee may also invest any part of the Trust in property located outside the State of Illinois.

4.03   The Trustee may, if he desires, apply to a court of competent jurisdiction, for reasonable fees, determined by said court, for the administration of said Trust.

4.04   Until the termination of the Trust, the Trustee shall pay on behalf of the child so much or all of the net income and principal thereof as the Trustee determines from time to time to be necessary for the child's health, support and education, after considering the child's other resources known to the Trustee.   Any undistributed income shall be added to principal.

4.05   Payments for the general support and day to day living expenses of the child may be made to a guardian or to any other person to then be applied to the care of the child by that person. Until the termination of the Trust, the Trustee will make all other payments directly to the provider of the services.

2

4.06 At such time there is no living child of mine under the age of twenty-one (21) years, the trustee shall distribute the principal, as then constituted, and any undistributed income in accord with 4.01(b).

4.07 If for any reason THOMAS WILSON fails or refuses to act as Trustee, SUSAN WILSON shall become Trustee in his place.

ARTICLE FIVE

5.01 I hereby nominate and appoint my father, THOMAS WILSON of Rome, Wisconsin, as Executor of this, my Last Will and Testament. If for any reason my father fails to become or ceases to act as Executor, I appoint my mother, SUSAN WILSON, to act as Executor. I direct that no surety on the executor's bond be required of either my father or my mother. Should administration or ancillary administration of my estate be required in any jurisdiction in which said executor shall be unauthorized or unable to act, then I name as administrator or ancillary administrator with will annexed of my estate, such person or corporation as may be appointed by my executor. In addition to any authority conferred by law upon my legal representative, I specifically give to such representative the following powers and discretions, in each case to be exercisable without order of court:

(a) To pay, settle, compromise or contest any and all rights, debts, demands or claims, either in favor of or against my estate, upon such terms as such representative deems proper, and to give or receive full receipts and discharges;

(b) To sell, lease, mortgage, or pledge the whole or any part of my estate, real or personal, for such prices, on such terms, and to such parties as such representative deems proper. No purchaser dealing with such representative shall be obliged to inquire as to its powers or to see to the application of any money or property paid or delivered and no bond shall be required of such representative upon the sale of any property;

(c) To satisfy general and residuary bequests in cash, kind, or both upon the basis of fair market values at the time of such distribution and to determine the market value of any assets for such purpose on the basis of such quotations, data or other information as such representative deems pertinent and reliable; to make partial distributions prior to final determination of Federal estate tax values on the basis of reasonable estates and to make adjustment upon final settlement. The decision of such representative shall be binding and conclusive upon all persons;

(d)   To litigate, compound or settle inheritance, estate, transfer or succession taxes assessed by reason of my death, and gift, income or other taxes assessed against me or my estate; to make deposits to secure the payment of any inheritance tax, which deposits shall be conclusive on all persons;

(e)   To continue to hold any assets or any increase thereof received as part of my estate; to invest funds available for investment in stocks, bonds, notes or other property as my executor deems prudent, without being limited by any statute governing investments by executors;

(f)   To cause any of the assets delivered to or acquired by such representative to be registered in my executor's name or in the name of a nominee; any corporation or its transfer agent may presume conclusively that such nominee is the actual owner of any assets submitted by it for transfer;

(g)   To claim administration expenses as either estate or income tax deductions when an election is permitted by law and in my representative's sole judgment such action will reduce the total estate and income taxes payable. No compensating adjustments shall be made between income and principal or with respect to any bequest or devise hereunder on account of such election;

(h)   To delegate discretionary or other powers for any purpose to one or more nominees or proxies with or without power of substitution; to consent to and to take any action to obtain the benefit of the reorganization, consolidation, or readjustment of the financial structure or sale of the assets of any corporation or other organization and to accept and retain the property resulting therefrom as a part of my estate;

(i)   To distribute directly to any beneficiary such portion or all of any trust mentioned herein which would be immediately distributable to such beneficiary upon receipt by the trustee under the provisions of such trust;

(j)   To file joint income or gift tax returns with my spouse for periods prior to my death; and, in its discretion, to pay any part or all of the taxes, interest or penalties in connection with any joint returns of my spouse and myself. The decision of my representative shall be binding and conclusive on all persons;

(k)   To exercise any stock option which I may have at the time of my death, to borrow money from any bank or trust company, including my executor, upon such terms and in such manner as

4

shall seem advisable, for the purpose of exercising any such options, and to pledge or mortgage the assets of my estate as collateral for said loan. I further give my said executors complete power in their discretion to retain the stock so purchased for as long a time as said executors deem desirable.

ARTICLE SIX

6.01 If my former wife, KAREN JAMES, does not survive me, or dies after my death without making provision for the care and custody of the person of my child, I nominate THOMAS WILSON as guardian of the person and as guardian of the estate of my minor child. If THOMAS WILSON is unable or unwilling to act as guardian, I nominate SUSAN WILSON To act as guardian of the person and as guardian of the estate of my minor child. I direct that no surety be required on the guardian's bond of either THOMAS WILSON or SUSAN WILSON.

ARTICLE SEVEN

7.01 No person named in the Will shall be deemed to have survived me unless he or she is living on the 30th day succeeding the day of my death.

7.02 If any beneficiary of mine has not attained legal age at the time any property becomes distributable to him or her, the executor or trustee may distribute any part or all of such property to a parent or adult relative of the beneficiary, as trustee, against such person's receipt and upon his written undertaking to deliver the property to the beneficiary at the time he or she attains legal age, and in the meantime, to hold it in trust and use it for the benefit of the beneficiary. Such receipt and written undertaking shall fully discharge the executor or trustee.

7.03 No interest shall accrue during the period of probate on unpaid general legacies hereunder whether payable outright or held in trust.

I have signed this Will consisting of _____ pages, this _____ day of May, 1995.

_____(SEAL)
JOHN WILSON

5

On the date it bears, the foregoing instrument was signed and declared by JOHN WILSON, in our presence as his Will and at his request, and in his presence, and in the presence of each other, we have signed our names as witnesses, believing him to be of sound mind at the time of so signing.

_____
WITNESS

_____
ADDRESS

_____
CITY AND STATE

_____
WITNESS

_____
ADDRESS

_____
CITY AND STATE

6

```
STATE OF ILLINOIS   )
                    ) SS.
COUNTY OF COOK      )


We, the attesting witnesses to the Will of JOHN WILSON, on oath
state that each of us was present and saw him sign the Will, of
which this affidavit is a part, in our presence; that the Will was
attested by each of us in his presence; and that each of us
believed him to be of sound mind and memory at the time of signing.


_____
WITNESS


_____
WITNESS




SUBSCRIBED and SWORN to before
me this _____ day of _____, 1995


_____
NOTARY PUBLIC
```

Index

305

W-Z

Everyone's talking about

"Thanks for helping me get started."
Jim Ellars, Greenfield, IN

"It is written in plain, old English and tells me what I need to know to do what I want to do."
Craig Connolly, Lincoln, NE

"I've made friends with my computer."
Marjorie Bock, Slidell, LA

"...quite helpful in gaining familiarity and confidence in various computer topics."
Martin Bondy, New York, NY

"...most of all, the books helped build a much-needed confidence."
Bill Shepson, Sacramento, CA

"I could hardly put it down—anxious to find out a little more and more."
June Littlejohn, Irving, TX

"...covered the basics of the entire program without getting too bogged down in details."
Robert Matson, New York, NY

"...one of the best introductory computer books that I have come across in the past few years. It's refreshing to have instructional material written at the level of the beginner and not making many assumptions regarding prior computer ability."
Daniel Green, Saratoga Springs, NY

"It teaches in such a simplified, straightforward manner."
Richard Boehringer, Miramar, FL

"This book taught me that I'm in control."
Greg Wright, Ashmore, Australia

"...simple, easy to read, and enjoyable. I felt like someone was talking to me."
Jon Marshall, Dover, OH

"The best thing about the book is the readability."
Gerard van Os, The Netherlands

"I appreciate material that assumes me to be lacking in information rather than lacking in intelligence."
Holly Waldrop, Nashville, TN

"I have to say that this is THE book for teaching in this area."
Richard Caladine, University of Wollongong, Australia

"After really close review, I have found it to be superb. The concepts are as clear as I have seen."
Barry Owen, San Juan, CO

"Lest I forget, your bright orange cover and cheat sheet proved to be invaluable amongst a cluttered desk."
Darryl Pang, Honolulu, HI

The Complete Idiot's Guides—For People With Better Things To Do

Don't Let Everyday Life Make You Feel Like An Idiot!

Whatever the topic, there's a Complete Idiot's Guide ready and waiting to make your life easier!

The Complete Idiot's Guide to Getting into College
ISBN: 1-56761-508-2
$14.95 USA

The Complete Idiot's Guide to Buying & Selling a Home
ISBN: 1-56761-510-4
$16.95 USA

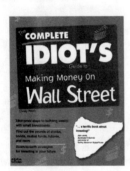

The Complete Idiot's Guide to Making Money on Wall Street
ISBN: 1-56761-509-0
$16.95 USA

Also Available!

The Complete Idiot's Guide to Managing Your Money
ISBN: 1-56761-530-9, $16.99 USA

The Complete Idiot's Guide to Starting Your Own Business
ISBN: 1-56761-529-5, $16.99 USA

The Complete Idiot's Guide to Cooking Basics
ISBN: 1-56761-523-6, $16.99 USA

The Complete Idiot's Guide to the Perfect Wedding
ISBN: 1-56761-532-5, $16.99 USA

The Complete Idiot's Guide to VCRs
ISBN: 1-56761-294-6, $9.95 USA

Look for these books at your favorite bookstore, or call 1-800-428-5331 for more information!

Down-to-earth answers to complex questions!